Exploring the Edges of the

INFORMATION AGE

MJ D'Elia

Kendall Hunt
publishing company

Kendall Hunt
publishing company

www.kendallhunt.com
Send all inquiries to:
4050 Westmark Drive
Dubuque, IA 52004-1840

For my girls: Jen, Mirella & Charlotte

The world isn't run by weapons any more, or energy, or money. It's run by little ones and zeroes, little bits of data. It's all just electrons.

There's a war out there, old friend—a world war. And it's not about who's got the most bullets, it's about who controls the information. What we see and hear. How we work, what we think. It's all about the information.

—COSMO, *SNEAKERS* (1992)

Contents

3 The Information Environment

4 Information Fluencies

5 The Information Paradigm

12 **Participation** 231

Apology to the Reader

This is not a textbook

I feel like I must begin with a bit of an apology (unorthodox, I know). This is not a textbook. You may have purchased it at your campus bookstore and your instructor may have required you to buy it (for reasons that remain unclear to you). But—I can assure you—this is not a textbook. Well, it's not a textbook in any traditional sense of the term. What you hold in your hands is more like an experiment—an ongoing investigation of the Information Age. What it means to people. What it means to society. What it means to business. And more directly: what it means to you.

This book does not pretend to have all the answers; in fact, on it's own—without reader engagement—this book may have no answers at all (but I'm getting ahead of myself). While I have attempted to organize the information in this book according to a logical scheme, the reality is that information doesn't fit into neat little categories with standard definitions. If anything, information defies our attempts at organization (more on that later). Suffice it to say that language shifts, technology advances, and information continues to evolve. As a result, attempting to write a traditional textbook at the intersection of information, technology and business is like attempting to hit a moving target.

Instead, this project represents my attempt to fill a gap—a gap where people can truly engage with the issues of the Information Age. Textbooks do an incredible job of delivering large amounts of content, usually by presenting the material in a fairly standard (almost sterile) manner. While this simple, fact-based approach is a tried and true method in education, I think we can do better.

Ultimately, what is missing from your average textbook is an acknowledgement of perspective—even bias. What's missing is a point of view. What's missing is the story. What's missing is the *why*: Why does this matter? Why should you care? Why are things the way they are? And why do we accept things the way they are? This book is designed to get you thinking about the "whys" of the Information Age (note: I didn't say that this book is designed to answer those "whys").

For some of you, this book will be entirely too conversational. It won't have the look and feel of a traditional textbook, which will make you wonder whether you're learning anything at all. I sympathize with you. I do. But to you I say: give this a chance—you may be surprised.

For others, the technology in this book will be intimidating. Don't worry, you haven't picked up a computer science textbook, but dissecting technology is unavoidable when it comes to discussing issues of the Information Age. Here's my advice to you: don't let the "geek-speak" or technology talk obscure the real issues behind the text and stop you from engaging.

Lastly, there may be a few of you who will be frustrated by this book's lack of answers. In these pages, you will find few definitive rules. This distinct lack of "black and white" answers may leave you unsettled and uneasy. I know that ambiguity can be maddening when you're trying to learn, but I would argue that sorting your way through such confusion is the first step toward true knowledge anyway. Besides, the "real world" (whatever that means) is full of ambiguity and apparent contradictions—trust me, you can handle it.

Let me be absolutely clear: I am not an expert. I am an interested observer. It is my plan to show you what I think is so interesting about business, information, technology and society at this particular time in history. For the reasons you've just read, and many more that you'll discover, please remember this is not a textbook. Hopefully, you'll find that it's something more, something intriguing—an experiment that you actually enjoy. Now let's get started. …

A Note for Instructors

From instructor to facilitator

As instructors, we are tempted to look at the content of our courses as something that simply needs to be delivered. Often there is too much material for us to cover in class, so we rely on the textbook to be an authority in our absence. But if teaching and learning are about relationships (teacher-to-student, student-to-student, student-to-teacher), then the textbook is a poor substitute for the learning process.

The reality is that this approach to teaching (and the requisite assessment methods) heavily favors memorization and not application. Why do we assess our students' ability to memorize content when nearly every fact, definition, or concept can be located with exceeding speed and accuracy? (It's called the Internet). Quite frankly, we're sticking with the status quo because it's the easiest way *for us* to upload content to young minds. This is the age of the Internet, there has to be a better way than memorization.

Courses about information and technology (in business, computer science, media studies, and other disciplines) provide us with an incredible opportunity to experiment. Indeed, if true information management is about using technology to deliver better and timelier information to people, then surely the traditional textbook approach cannot be our best "technology" for educating students on the issues of the current age.

Students do not come to us with empty minds that need to be filled; they bring their own perspectives and experiences to the classroom. It is our responsibility to extract those views, challenge perspectives, encourage discussion, guide the learning process, and help the students construct their own meaning. This book was designed with a specific intent: to encourage instructors to become facilitators. Don't misunderstand me, I'm not suggesting that we should stop lecturing, and I certainly don't think we should abandon our authority or expertise. I'm only suggesting that we adopt an "issues-based" approach—as opposed to the traditional "answers-based" one. As Marc Prensky says, we need to "practice putting engagement before content when teaching."[i] It's not that the content is secondary, just that for students to recognize the importance of the content, they need to be interested.

This generation of students literally inhabits the Information Age. Their habits are second nature to the point that they rarely stop to reflect on the key issues.[ii] That's where we, the experienced facilitators, come in. We are the ones who can encourage them to think more broadly and more deeply than their individual experience has taught them so far. By choosing to ignore the students' voices, we do disservice to them and to ourselves. We need to focus on teaching students *how* to think—not *what* to think. The world is changing too fast to focus on memorizing content. We need to teach them to engage, to experiment, and to use the information they encounter to make effective decisions. Who knows? We might even learn something from them in the process.

Perhaps some of you are hesitant to incorporate more facilitation in the classroom. You feel the pressure to provide the hard facts to students. After all, business works on certainties, not airy notions of the Information Society. In response, I would argue that organizations do not operate in a vacuum, nor do the individuals that comprise an organization. To ignore the social aspects of technology or the impact of information in society is to misunderstand business, consumers, and the Information Age.

Exploring the Edges of the Information Age is an attempt to take our hands off the keyboard, to step away from the glow of our monitors and actually reflect on the issues at hand. The discussions you find in the book are designed to get students thinking. They might be used as an introduction to a lecture, or as a centerpiece for an assignment, or class discussion.

You are free to follow my order of topics, or you can pick and choose at will. After all, the true nature of knowledge lies in its tangled mess of connections, not in artificial linear progression. You're only limited by your creativity. Let your imagination run wild. Dare to ask what your students think of these issues. And, of course, if you have any questions, comments or suggestions, you can always contact me. I'd be happy to hear from you.

M.J. D'Elia
mdelia@uoguelph.ca
University of Guelph

Read, think, discuss

Well, this is a book, so the instructions for use are pretty straightforward: Read. Think. Discuss. Simply put, *Exploring the Edges of the Information Age* should be used as a tool, a jumping off point, a discussion starter. It does not pretend to be an authority like a dictionary, encyclopedia, or even a textbook. Perhaps, this book is more like a collection of short stories—where each story adds a new perspective to the Information Age. To use it as an ultimate reference or final word is to misunderstand its purpose (and to misunderstand the changing nature of information).

Take a moment to flip through the pages of this book. Seriously, go ahead. Do you notice anything unusual? At first glance it seems like there are a lot of things missing from this book (I told you this wasn't a textbook). For example, you won't find detailed learning objectives, multiple sidebars, colorful graphics, a glossary of terms, or bolded keywords. These choices have been made purposely. I have made a deliberate attempt to reduce "feature-bloat" so that we can start with a simple introduction to issues presented by information and information technology.

Many of the issues contained in these chapters do not have simple answers. It will be up to you to draw your own conclusions. You have my full permission (and encouragement) to write, or doodle in the margins, to highlight sections of text, or to scratch them out. Feel free to use whatever strategies work for you, as you attempt to figure this stuff out. The ultimate goal of this book is to drive you beyond these pages and into the world of information and technology.

In my opinion, the best way to learn this stuff is to interact with the material. Get involved in the discussion and try to apply what you're learning. Sometimes you just need to get your hands dirty. To that end, you will find experiments designed to encourage you to delve into the online world. For example, in Section 10.6 you will explore the weird and wonderful world of patents. Each chapter also directs you to articles and resources that are beyond the scope of this book (I can only cover so much). The point of these readings is to recognize the issues of the Information Age and get you to discuss them with your colleagues. For example, in Section 11.8 you will read an article about censorship and the Great

Firewall of China. Lastly, this book includes a number of hypothetical scenarios. Your task is to read the scenario, evaluate each potential option, and then defend an appropriate course of action. For example, in Section 7.9 you will help Naomi decide what to do with her competitor's confidential information.

Remember: these activities are not designed to give you "extra" work; they're designed to get you to think more deeply. They're designed to get you reading, thinking and discussing. Good luck!

Your own personal guidebook

Perhaps it would be helpful to look at this book as your own personal guidebook to the Information Age. A typical guidebook features places to eat, sights to see, and things to do for travelers who find themselves in unfamiliar environs. These guides are full of maps, reviews, and points of interest, featuring key pieces of information from people who have been there before. *Exploring the Edges of the Information Age* is designed with a similar intent. I selected this collection of issues because I feel that they're relevant, or interesting, or just odd enough to deserve a second look.

I know what you're thinking. You're thinking that this approach to information management is a little too biased. Exactly. Information is always biased (which in its broadest sense simply means that it comes from a particular perspective). However, if you treat this book as a guidebook, then you're free to disagree with the issues that I've raised, the activities that I've designed, and the points of view that I've presented. Remember, the great thing about guidebooks is that they simply provide a smorgasbord of options. Each traveler chooses different paths to explore. Which ones will you choose?

Epigraph
Phil Alden Robinson, Lawrence Lasker, and Walter F. Parkes, *Sneakers,* DVD, directed by Phil Alden Robinson (Universal City, CA: Universal Studios, 1992).

Frontmatter Notes
[1] Marc Prensky, "Listen to the Natives," *Educational Leadership* 63, no. 4 (2005/2006): 9.
[2] Marc Prensky, "Digital Natives, Digital Immigrants Part 1," *On the Horizon* 9, no. 5 (2001): 1, 3-6. Prensky first coined the term "digital natives" to describe the unique characteristics of the current generation. This theme has been further developed in John Palfrey and Urs Gasser's *Born Digital* (New York: Basic Books, 2008), and Don Tapscott's *Grown Up Digital* (New York: McGraw-Hill, 2009). Although Clay Shirky doesn't use the term digital native, his book *Here Comes Everybody* (New York: Penguin Press, 2008), discusses a significant shift in technology that younger generations intuitively grasp.

Chapter 1

The Information Age

1.1 Welcome

Here be monsters

In the sixteenth century the world was a very different place. In fact, entire sections of the globe were undiscovered (at least by Western eyes). As explorers like Jacques Cartier, John Cabot and Samuel de Champlain traversed the seas looking for new lands and new riches, they drew maps. On a basic level, these maps were an attempt to produce scale representations of the land and seas to benefit future explorations. However, these maps also represented a new kind of knowledge, a knowledge that meant power.

Portugal and Spain, for example, were two of the first nations to set up bureaucracies devoted to collecting geographic information. Clearly, they recognized how important charting the seas was to their expanding empires. In fact, these bureaucracies were responsible for more than simply accumulating information. They were charged with reducing inconsistencies and inaccuracies in the information (quality control), and instructed to keep the knowledge of new discoveries secure (state control).[1]

Much has been written about the early explorers and their discovery of new lands, but we're actually more interested in their mapping of the seas. For centuries huge swaths of ocean remained largely unmapped, but these early mapmakers chose not to leave the unknown areas blank or incomplete. Instead, they filled the uncharted territories with detailed depictions of sea creatures. In some cases, they even included an accompanying warning: "Here be monsters."

Of course, these illustrations did not represent actual encounters between European explorers and creatures of the deep, but they weren't just doodles in the margins either. The monsters were intended to be messages. In other words, some information—even if it was misinformation—was preferable to no information when sailing the stormy seas.[2] We might speculate a little on the appearance of these sea serpents and their curious set of messages:

- *"Here be monsters" was an admission of fear.* To us, this seems strange, but early mariners believed that these creatures swam the depths of the world's oceans and it was best to steer clear of them.[3] The appearance of a monster meant: "We're afraid of this area—and you should be too."

- *"Here be monsters" was an acknowledgement of ignorance.* These sections of the map were unknown.[4] Perhaps the explorers hadn't traveled through that area, or perhaps they were simply unable to reliably map the territory. The appearance of a monster simply meant: "We don't know what's here. We're missing information."

■ *"Here be monsters" may have also served as a warning to future travelers.* Perhaps the territory remained uncharted because it was too dangerous to map. Maybe the seas were too treacherous, or the rocks too jagged, or the fog too thick, but the appearance of a monster meant: "We've seen some of what's here, and you're not going to like the information we have. You should take the path most traveled."

Today, there are few unknowns in our physical environment. Orbiting satellites have enabled us to map nearly every square inch of this planet. But we haven't stopped there. Thanks to Global Positioning Systems (GPS), Wi-Fi frequencies, and even cell phone signals, we are able to triangulate and track people (and objects) as they travel across the globe. We can track them in real time and often within meters of their precise locations. In essence, we can create dynamic real-time maps of *moving* things—a far cry from the trial and error approach of the sixteenth century.

While the tangible world poses little mystery to us in the twenty-first century, the digital world remains largely uncharted, unmapped and unwritten. We're still finding our way. Don't believe me? Here are just a few recent examples from the open seas of the Information Age:

■ A commuter train collided with a freight train in Los Angeles killing 25 and injuring more than 130. Why is this significant? Investigators revealed that the engineer was sending text messages and missed the signal to stop.[5]

■ A British woman divorced her husband after she found him having an affair with a prostitute. Why is this significant? The events occurred in *Second Life,* a popular online world. The husband, wife, prostitute and even the private investigator she hired to catch him were virtual characters called avatars.[6]

■ A teen in Florida committed suicide by taking a deadly mixture of prescription drugs. Why is this significant? He broadcast the event live online while others watched (and possibly encouraged) him.[7]

■ United Airlines lost $1 billion in value on the stock market in less than an hour. Why is this significant? Somehow an old story about United Airlines filing bankruptcy in 2002 was republished online and picked up by Bloomberg News, causing investors to dump stock.[8]

Perhaps we would do well to remember those early mariners as we explore the Information Age. There may be times when we need to admit our fears, acknowledge our ignorance, and warn our fellow digital citizens. Fortunately, as the unknown became known, those monsters on the margins of early maps disappeared. Monsters don't stop true explorers. A few uncertainties in the digital world aren't going to stop us either, but consider yourself warned: "Here be monsters."

1.2 Information as Commodity

It's all good(s)

It is often said that we live in the Information Economy,[9] but what does that mean? Hasn't information always been at the heart of commerce? After all, to exchange goods or services, manufacturers distribute information to retailers, retailers share information with customers, and customers provide personal information in return. Nearly every organization collects information to better understand their markets, to improve their goods and services, and to make quality decisions.

However, information does more than just facilitate transactions, or assist in understanding the market. It is becoming increasingly valuable as a good or service in its own right. Note the subtle shift: information doesn't just help exchange commodities, it *is* a commodity—a product that can be bought or bartered. The rules are changing.[10] Customer information, for example, traditionally provided value to an organization as an internal asset, lending insight into customer behavior. In the Information Economy that information also becomes an attractive commodity to be sold to the highest bidder. As long as the information is good, advertisers are more than willing to pay top dollar for lists of potential customers and qualified leads. Financial institutions, Internet service providers, mobile phone companies, and many other organizations are continually looking for ways to monetize the information they collect.

To take the example one step further, companies like ChoicePoint and Acxiom have structured their very business models around selling personal information about individual citizens in a practice known as data brokering.[11] Clearly, information presents a new value proposition for its owner. In the Information Economy, organizations expect information to contribute value to their bottom lines in the same way that real property does. But is such an expectation realistic? Can information really be considered a commodity?

At its basic level, a commodity is an article of trade or commerce; most often, the term is used to describe a tangible product rather than a service. For example, today we have commodities markets like the Chicago Mercantile Exchange, or the London Metal Exchange, where agricultural products (wheat, corn, cattle), energy materials (natural gas, crude, propane), metals (gold, copper, zinc), and other raw materials are exchanged.

At first glance, information does indeed behave like commodity. When raw materials like wheat are mixed with other ingredients and baked according to a recipe, we get a tasty finished product (e.g. warm fresh bread). Similarly, information can be collected, analyzed, and combined into an advantageous end product (e.g. more information). Adding a little bit of labor can turn previously useless data and information into new products for the market. The similarities don't stop there. Like physical assets or property, information faces quality control inspection before it is distributed and it can depreciate (lose its value) over time.[12]

Upon closer investigation, however, the claim that information is a commodity begins to break down. Commodities are things (products of manufacturing), meaning they can be measured and priced according to the rules of supply and demand. But information is not tangible, nor is it limited in quantity, nor is it manufactured (at least in the traditional sense). For commodities, the specifications are clear: a diamond is a diamond whether it was mined in Brazil, or in Canada. In contrast, each piece of information is different. And each piece is consumed (and regurgitated) multiple times by multiple parties, making information more uncooperative as a commodity.[13] For our purposes however, it is precisely this mutability that makes information exceedingly interesting.

There is an older definition for commodity that is also worth introducing to our discussion. Historically, the term was used to describe a situation of personal advantage, benefit, or opportunity; in particular, an opportunity for private profit or selfish interest.[14] While this usage of the term is now obsolete, it illuminates one of our key assumptions about information; namely, that information is a differentiator. Or to put it in business terms, information creates competitive advantage (section 3.4). We believe that organizations or individuals who acquire, analyze, and act on available information generate more advantageous opportunities for themselves than their competitors (or colleagues). Rightly or wrongly, this is one of the fundamental maxims of the Information Economy (and whether you realize it or not, you probably operate under this assumption as well).

 ## 1.3 Information Overload

Everything about everything

Living in the Information Age means that we have access to an unprecedented amount of information. For instance, Google recently announced that its index now includes over one trillion unique URLs (web pages)—or, approximately

150 pages for every person living in the world today—and they estimate that the web is still growing by billions of pages everyday.[15] Indeed, the Internet makes it possible to find something about everything (or, in some cases, everything about something). Need to know when the computer mouse was invented? (1964, by Douglas Engelbart). Or, who sings the geeky song "Computer Friends?" (Sniper Twins). In a matter of seconds these answers flash across our browsers and we rarely give it a second thought.

However, as our information needs increase in complexity, we begin to run into trouble. We start to have second thoughts about our assumption that information is inherently good (and that *more* information is inherently better). Truth be told, having access to this much information can be detrimental to our ability to set priorities, to manage time, and to make decisions. More information might actually mean more confusion.

Information overload is the general description we give to this dilemma, but there are many other terms that point to our love-hate relationship with information.[16] For example, literature in management and psychology is full of references to cognitive overload, information fatigue syndrome, data smog, analysis paralysis, sensory overload, information pollution, or, my personal favorite, document tsunami.[17] In its broadest sense, information overload describes two conditions: 1) having too much information to make a quality decision; 2) receiving too much information to be informed about a topic. And each of these conditions adds to our mental stress.[18] Essentially, the sheer volume of information available to us obscures the few meaningful pieces we're looking for.

It is difficult to define a cause for information overload, but it is clear that phenomenon results from a mixture of factors related to information, technology and people. It's not just the quantity of information produced that leads to increased stress levels; it's the type of information too. Different formats (audio, video, text, illustrations, photographs, etc.), different granularities (levels of detail), and different sources increase the amount of time it takes to find relevant, meaningful information.

Technology also makes it possible to transmit or send data much easier, so we are bombarded regularly with messages—some legitimate, others not so much (e.g. spam). We are exposed to an increasing number of channels or modes of communication (email, telephone, podcasts, blogs, instant messaging, etc.), which duplicate or repeat information, leading to redundancies and inefficiencies. While the feelings associated with information overload are not unique to the current age,[19] the rapid developments in communication technology have certainly intensified our experience with information overload and contributed to our techno-stress.

The problem of information overload has a human factor as well. We have moved to the "always-on" world because we fear that we might miss something. Unfortunately, this mentality further perpetuates the overload cycle (more on that later). We attempt to multitask so we can get more done, but we end up diffusing our focus and spreading ourselves too thin. Inevitably, we experience an inability to make clear and accurate decisions, we have increased stress, and we lose the ability to concentrate due to interruptions.

In an attempt to cope with information overload, we develop new habits to seek, find and evaluate information. Unfortunately, not all of these habits are good. Research shows that as we become overwhelmed with information we develop a lack of desire to learn (we feel we don't have the time); we have a greater tolerance for error (we feel that our work is simply good enough); we create poor search strategies (we use whatever is easiest); we contribute superficial analysis (we believe everything we read); and, we are unable to differentiate between details and the big picture. Here's the crazy part: despite our poor decision-making and sloppy information habits we still develop overconfidence in our own abilities. We believe we're better at handling information than we really are.[20] That sounds like a recipe for trouble.

Fortunately, there are strategies and solutions for dealing with information overload. First, to reduce information overload we need to improve the overall quality of information. We need to set quality standards for the information we create, we need to add value to existing information, and reduce the duplication of information we retain. We also need to improve the way we aggregate, categorize and organize information. The solution to information overload is not less information; it is *better* information.

Second, we need to be aware of tools that will help us manage our information exposure. We might turn to customized desktops and intelligent interfaces, or set up filters to help us sort the messages we want to receive. News aggregators, social bookmarks, and RSS feeds, for example, might provide more efficient ways of staying informed. Technology contributes to the problem of information overload, but it also contributes potential solutions.

Improving information quality and using technology more efficiently will help, but we also need to improve the competence of individuals and their ability to deal with large amounts of diverse information. If we work to clearly define information needs from the beginning, we will find it much easier to distinguish the relevant pieces of information from the irrelevant. If we learn to evaluate and select appropriate sources of information, we will improve our decision-making. If we increase our willingness to share information, we will reduce the amount of duplicated effort. The choice is ours.

Even though we will never know everything about everything, it is up to us to refine our information management practices so that we will know when enough is enough. Fortunately, the purpose of this book is to help us to do just that.

1.4 The Attention Economy

Lend me your eyes

Information overload is a problem for individuals and for organizations, but some observers claim that the root of the problem is not that we have too much information; it is that we do not have enough attention. In other words, our ability to process information and make good decisions is limited by our short attention spans. We do not have the human bandwidth required to attend to everything that comes our way.[21]

We claim to live in the Information Economy, but the word "economy" poses a bit of a dilemma. Economics is usually about scarcity. It's about the choices we make to distribute our finite goods and services. However, as we've already discussed, information is not particularly scare in the Information Age—nor are we experiencing a shortage of ideas, capital, talent, or labor. So where is the scarcity? You guessed it: we have a scarcity of attention. The new currency of the Information Age is not information at all, but attention. Forget the information economy; we're living in the attention economy.[22]

Thomas Davenport and John Beck articulated this fundamental shift in their aptly titled book, *The Attention Economy*. For them, "Attention is focused mental engagement on a particular item of information. Items come into our awareness, we attend to a particular item, and then we decide whether to act."[23] Pay close attention: this definition suggests there is a causal chain from awareness to attention to action. This definition also implies that attention is about more than spending time on something, it is about spending *focused* time. As Davenport says, "attention is a combination of how much time you devote to something, as well as how many brain cells you devote to something."[24]

In the continual competition for our attention, it is inevitable that we will miss information. Given the time constraints and situational complexities, we simply cannot pay attention to everything we encounter. However, Howard Rheingold has suggested two guidelines that might help us find our way through the attention economy: "Rule number one is to pay attention. Rule number two might be: Attention is a limited resource, so pay attention to where you pay attention."[25] Acknowledging these two simple rules will go a long way towards helping individuals and organizations recognize and evaluate their priorities.

Organizations know that they can make more money if they can attract more eyeballs. In fact, this is one of the core principles of advertising. The more people who subscribe to your magazine, watch your television show, drive by your storefront, read your blog, or visit your website, the more money you can command for advertising rights. It is safe to say that the advertising industry is about getting noticed. In the online world, the examples are everywhere:

- In 1996, Hotmail was an innovative email operation offering free email accounts. Just two and a half years later, there were over 25 million active users. Attractive enough that Microsoft simply purchased the company for about $400 million to enter the email game.[26]

- In February 2005, YouTube launched as a fledgling video sharing service. Despite the fact that it hadn't made much money, Google purchased the service for 1.65 billion in Google stock in 2006. Google certainly didn't buy YouTube because of the quality of the amateur videos posted to the site— Google purchased it because that's where the eyeballs are.[27]

- In February 2004, Facebook launched as a small social network restricted to people affiliated with Harvard University. Two years later, Facebook was expanded to anyone with an email address. Now, worldwide users spend 2.6 billion minutes per day on the site.[28]

More people mean more advertising opportunities, and more advertising opportunities mean more revenue. Clearly, it's all about attracting (and keeping) attention. Without attention a project, service, or organization may be destined for obscurity. It's like the famous philosophical riddle about the tree falling in the forest. We might ask the question a little differently: if a service fails in the Information Age, does anyone pay attention? According to the attention economy argument, it might be more accurate to say that the service failed *because* no one paid attention.

1.5 Learning the (Digital) Language

Lost in translation

Young people are notorious early adopters of trends and technologies. The introduction of nearly every new technology (Internet, email, video games, cell phones, SMS, instant messaging, blogs, wikis, etc.) featured widespread adoption by young people well before the general population. Indeed, the current generation of youth (sometimes called millennials, Gen Y, or the Net Generation) is the first generation to be born surrounded by gadgets. This generation (which you belong to if you were born after 1980) practically lives on the Internet, making itself at home in the digital world. As such, today's youth are sometimes called digital natives,[29] but what exactly does that mean?

According to some observers, digital natives take control of their information consumption—both in what they consume and in how they consume it. For example, they like the content of traditional media (e.g. television), but dislike the restrictive formats (e.g. television's broadcast schedule). Instead, they use file-sharing networks, streaming Internet video, or personal video recorders (PVR) to time shift the content they want (and to skip advertising).

Digital natives also proactively manage tasks and technology. In a world of infinite choice, digital natives have developed strategies for multitasking. For example, they filter content from multiple services and use sophisticated search tools to find information. What's more, they expect the information they retrieve to be instantly relevant and applicable.[30]

As the theory goes, digital natives regularly share personal thoughts and contribute content. These natives create videos, share photos, recommend music, and comment on blogs all over the Internet. As a result, they lend more credence to similar content from other pseudo-anonymous contributors (e.g. Wikipedia).

Lastly, digital natives cultivate opportunities for community interaction. Community, for the native, is not limited by physical space. For them, the Internet is a platform for connection and personalization.[31] In essence, it is a place where they learn how to be a digital native from other digital natives, furthering their sense of community.

For digital natives, the rapid development and convergence of information and communication technologies is simply a fact of life; for others, call them digital immigrants, the Information Age feels familiar yet somewhat peculiar. For these people, operating in a techno-centric world is like learning a new language. There are new vocabularies to remember, new rules for usage, new social skills to develop, and new nuances to grasp—and some concepts simply don't translate well.

As these immigrants learn to adapt to their new environment, they retain some of their *accent;* some of their past habits in the process. For example, digital immigrants might print out and file important emails (instead of keeping them online), they might choose to edit documents on paper (instead of editing them directly with word processing software), or they might bring people to their computer to show a website (instead of simply emailing the link).[32] Think of your parents or grandparents for a moment, how are they coping in the Information Age? Are they like more like an immigrant or a native?

Of course, we should be careful about making sweeping generalizations. Not every young person is equally sophisticated with technology, nor is every person from previous generations struggling to cope with the digital world. However, these differences can help us understand potential areas of conflict between natives and immigrants. For example, digital natives tend to choose graphics and multimedia over text, like to parallel process (or multitask), and prefer random access to information. In contrast, digital immigrants favor text over multimedia, prefer single processes, seek linear and sequential routes to information, and believe that information should be learned 'just-in-case.'[33]

It is tempting to downplay the digital native-digital immigrant divide as simply generational conflict, but our shift into the Information Age is more complicated than that. Think about it, today's organizations typically reflect the mindset of the digital immigrant, featuring command and control management styles, levels of bureaucracy and structured authority. But most future employees are digital natives and as such they may not have the patience for these "restrictive" management practices. Instead, the typical digital native will expect fewer organizational boundaries, access to technologies for work and play, and multiple methods of communication.[34] Obviously, something has to give.

The ways in which this digital native-digital immigrant conflict is negotiated will vary by individual and by organization, but the key is to develop a shared understanding. Some people have suggested that it is only a matter of time before everyone joins the Information Age and the digital cultural migration will be complete (i.e. when the current cohort of digital immigrants quite literally "passes away"). At this time, they claim, we will be left with only digital natives;[35] however, this statement ignores the history of technology and culture. Younger generations will continue to instinctively grasp new technology, while previous generations will struggle to keep up. Today's native is tomorrow's immigrant.

1.6 Experiment

Take a break from information technology

We're living in a time when information and technology are converging to create new issues for business and society. Indeed, information flies around the globe at breakneck speeds and yet we rarely take time to stop and reflect. What do these changes mean? Are these advances in technology necessarily good? What impact do these changes have on our society? Is this the future we want?

In this experiment, your task is to take a 24-hour break from technology. Yes, you read that right. No technology for an entire day. More specifically, you need to take a break from information and communication technologies (ICTs). That means no surfing the Internet, no checking email, no Facebook, no cell phone calls, no texting or SMS messages, no television, no radio, no MP3 player, no cameras, no video games, no computers—you get the idea. Sometime in the next week choose one 24-hour period to go without these modern conveniences.

To be clear, the goal of this activity is not to encourage Luddism (opposition to technological innovation), or to romanticize an earlier era without technology. Instead, the goal is to recognize how prevalent information and communication technologies are in our daily lives. It may seem strange, but this experiment is not without precedent. Intel, for instance, has experimented with "zero-email Fridays," and IBM has implemented "Think Fridays" in an effort to help their workers limit the number of interruptions.[36]

Depending on your habits in the Information Age this could prove to be one of the hardest experiments in the book. This is your opportunity to hit the reset button. What should you do with all your free time? Well, you could read a book, you could go for a walk, you could play a sport, you could paint a picture, or you could just hang out with your friends. You're only limited by your imagination. Use the worksheet and questions on the following page to reflect on your experience.[37]

Worksheet

Name _____ Date _____

Part A

1. Do you think this experiment will be easy? Why or why not?

2. Which technology do you think you will miss most? Why?

3. When did you choose to take your break from information technology?

Start time (date, time): _____.

End time (date, time): _____.

Part B

1. Did you make it through the entire 24 hours without turning to information or communication technologies?

13

2. What did you miss the most?

3. What did you miss the least?

4. What was the hardest part?

5. What did you do instead?

6. What was the first piece of technology you turned to after your technology break?

7. Based on your experience, how important are information and communication technologies to your daily life?

8. Would you ever purposely choose to take a break from technology? Why or why not?

9. Provide any additional comments.

1.7 Reflect

The currency of attention

Goldhaber claims that we live in the attention economy, where the goal is to attract as many eyeballs as possible. Read his article (published over ten years ago now) and consider the questions below:

Goldhaber, Michael H. "Attention shoppers!" *Wired* 5, no. 12 (December 1997), http://www.wired.com/wired/archive/5.12/es_attention.html

---

QUESTIONS

1. Goldhaber suggests that one of the problems in the attention economy is "the possibility that increasing demand for our limited attention will keep us from reflecting, or thinking deeply (let alone enjoying leisure)." What do you think of this statement? Is he right? Why or why not? Is the abundance of information keeping us too distracted?

2. Goldhaber claims that the attention economy marks the end of money. He states, "in the future, ads will exist only to attract and direct attention, because money will be obsolete." What do you think of this statement? Does the advertising industry need to reinvent itself? Can you foresee a time when money will not exist, or is this suggestion too outlandish?

3. At the conclusion of his article, Goldhaber remarks, "To thrive in the coming century, you will have to look beyond money in any form and build a stock of attention for yourself as best you can." What do you think of this statement? Is he right? Why or why not? What evidence do you see for the "attention economy"?

1.8 Reflect

Identity + personal information

Andy Oram's short article focuses on the nature of personal information on the Internet (particularly information posted by digital natives). He suggests that we need a certain level of discernment when looking at other people's information. Read his thoughts (published online), and consider the questions below:

Oram, Andy. "Looking under what rises to the top: personal information in online searches." (December 10, 2008), http://www.praxagora.com/andyo/article/search_discernment.html

---

QUESTIONS

1. Oram suggests that we must use discernment when viewing others' personal information online. He claims that we have a responsibility "to empathize with the reasons people put information online, and then to adapt our ways of viewing it." What does he mean by this statement? Do you think empathy is important in the Information Age? Why?

2. As we struggle with what is and isn't appropriate personal information to post online, we have to face the fact that some of the information is beyond our control. As Oram says, "a lot of what goes online about you is posted by others." Are you concerned with what others post about you online? Are you worried it might negatively affect your reputation? Why or why not?

3. In judging others based on their portfolio of personal information posted online, Oram suggests four questions that might help us determine whether or not we are using the information responsibly. What do you think of his questions? Are they realistic, or idealistic? Why?

1.9 Decide

Professional life vs. personal life

Andrew runs a small lifestyle clothing company. His brand, Apex Eleven, is popular among outdoor lifestyle enthusiasts for its high quality and innovative designs. Five years ago, Andrew began selling Apex Eleven branded garments to extreme hikers via a small e-commerce storefront. Now Apex Eleven includes a handful of young designers and offers a variety of product lines, covering everyone from snowboarders to windsurfers.

While the Apex Eleven website remains the primary retail channel, Andrew has spent the past few months developing a regional network of sales representatives. His goal is to expand the Apex Eleven brand through specialty retail shops. He hopes these sales representatives will be able to represent the brand and maintain good relationships with potential retail partners.

To date, Andrew has hired five representatives and he has one key spot to fill before his network is complete. The search has come down to two candidates: Tim and Julia. Julia is quiet, but competent. She has little direct sales experience and would need some assistance, but Andrew believes she would be a quick study. Tim has more experience in the sporting goods and apparel industry. With his outgoing personality and his network of contacts, Andrew believes that Tim is probably the better person for the job.

Before making a final decision, Andrew decided to "Google" each candidate. He found Julia's profile on LinkedIn and a few references to her extracurricular activities at school, but nothing that surprised him. When he searched for Tim, he found numerous references to Tim's extreme party lifestyle. His Facebook and MySpace pages were littered with pictures, profanity and other incoherent ramblings.

Andrew knows Tim's personal life is separate from his professional life, but Andrew is worried that potential retail partners will associate this type of behavior with Apex Eleven. He was leaning toward offering Tim the job, but now he's not sure if that's the right decision.

What do you think Andrew should do? Four potential options are presented on the following page.

Name _____ Date _____

In the space provided, discuss the advantages and disadvantages of each option and make a final recommendation.

A) Andrew should bring Tim in for a second interview to ask more direct questions about Tim's party lifestyle.

B) Andrew should hire Tim without reservations.

C) Andrew should go with Julia; she's clearly the more reliable candidate.

D) Andrew should hire Tim, but keep a close eye on him.

So, what do you think Andrew should do? Why?

_____

_____

_____

_____

_____

_____

_____

_____

Information Concepts

2.1 What is Information?

Resolving uncertainty

The word information is thrown around without much discretion. It is used so ubiquitously that we barely give it a second thought (in fact, I used it repeatedly in the opening chapter without much of an explanation). Unfortunately, this widespread usage tends to dilute and diffuse its meaning. Most people assume that we mean the same thing when we say information, but in fact each of us might mean something quite different.

When you ask people to define information the answers vary considerably. How would you define information? Seriously, take a minute and jot down a few ideas.

What did you come up with? Did you take the business approach (information is a source of advantage)? Did you take the learning approach (information is the key to enlightenment)? Maybe you chose the relationship approach (information is shared between people)? Or, perhaps you liked the anarchist approach (information is a weapon)? All of these are right—and wrong—it just depends on the context.

If we're going to spend most of this book discussing information issues, then we should have a good grasp of what that term means—or, at least its range of definitions. Let's start with a simple perspective: "Information is data that have been organized and communicated."[1] What's clear from this definition is that data are not the same thing as information. Data are combinations of symbols arranged according to a set of rules or conventions.[2] For example, Samuel Morse used two symbols (a dot and a dash) to create his Morse code system. These dots and dashes were combined in various patterns to form letters of the alphabet (more *symbols*), and could eventually be combined to form words (part of the broader *system* of language). According to this definition, however, it's not enough to have symbols and systems. For data to be important it has to make the leap to information. How does it do this? By being organized. In other words, by its definition information is of a higher order than data.

The International Standards Organization defines information as: "The meaning that a human assigns to data by means of the human conventions used in their representation."[3] Again, we see that data are different than information. Not only are we (humans) responsible for attaching meaning, we are also responsible for defining the methods with which we will communicate that meaning (representation). The creation and communication of information through tangible form, then, might be considered a uniquely human behavior.

A third definition states: "Information denotes any stimulus that alters cognitive structure in the receiver."[4] We tend to think information is limited to text and images that we process consciously, but this definition suggests that anything we observe with our senses (any stimulus) can be information. Note that this definition also includes a qualification: information must alter or change the awareness (cognitive structure) of the person receiving it. Information has the power—no, responsibility—to influence. According to this approach, if the receiver already knows the information, then it isn't information. Translation: something that is information to me is not necessarily information to you.

Perhaps these definitions are too restrictive. After all, they focus almost exclusively on how humans relate to information. They don't consider how the word is used in computer science (e.g. technical aspects of storage), chemistry (e.g. information exchange in chemical reactions), psychology (e.g. cognitive functions), or other disciplines.[5] Have no fear; A. S. Madden proposes a more robust definition. For him, information is

> a stimulus originating in one system that affects the interpretation by another system of either the second system's relationship to the first or of the relationship the two systems share with a given environment.[6]

At first, this definition seems too expansive (and perhaps too confusing) to be useful, but when you consider that Madden defines a system as "a mechanism, an organism, a community, or an organisation [sic],"[7] some familiar components appear. The stimulus starts in one system (sender) and impacts another system (receiver). How does this happen? Well, both systems are connected (either directly, or in a shared environment), allowing them to share the original stimulus.

Let's look at an example. Think of a typical classroom setting. The instructor (system) delivers a lecture (stimulus) that impacts her students (more systems). In this environment, a particular student (system) may make a comment (stimulus) that affects other students as well as the instructor (more systems). Because these people are related to each other via the course, information can be shared easily among them.

Photo-sharing websites like Flickr, Photobucket, or Picassa provide another example. One member (system) posts some interesting photos (stimulus) to the website (environment). Other members of the community (systems) are then able to view and comment on the photos. Because these people participate in the same environment, information can be easily shared (even if the individual members do not know one another).

Information is certainly a slippery term, but there are some common elements that we should keep in mind as we go forward. From our perspective, an important consideration is that information (and therefore meaning) is tied to the human experience. Information is about making an impact. It can influence others, even providing an impetus for change. We often use information to help clarify, or resolve our uncertainty.[8] It needs to be communicated to be important, which implies that information requires relationships (sender and receiver) and communities (shared environments). In other words, information does not—or cannot—exist in a vacuum. On its own, without someone to add meaning or perspective, information is lifeless.

2.2 Knowledge Hierarchy

Building blocks of knowledge

Information and communication theory can get very complex, but we're going to try to keep it fairly straightforward. We started to differentiate between similar terms like data and information (section 2.1), but now we want to make those distinctions more explicit. Data, information, knowledge and wisdom are similar but separate concepts. The most basic approach is to look at these elements as part of a hierarchy where each element is dependent on the level beneath. It might help you to think of a pyramid structure (wide at the base, culminating in a pinnacle).

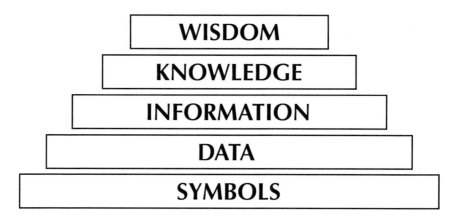

At the bottom of the pyramid are symbols, the building blocks of our knowledge hierarchy. Symbols are visual short forms that represent ideas. The Canadian flag, a red octagon, or the letter "o" would all be classified as symbols. Symbols are unspeakable; even though we might recognize our national flag, or a letter from the alphabet, the moment we speak these things we have translated those symbols. In fact, our very moment of recognition transforms the symbol into a product of observation—more aptly described as data.[9]

As we discussed earlier, data are simply a combination of symbols put together according to convention or a shared set of rules. For example, when you're driving and you see a red octagon, chances are you know that you should stop at the forthcoming intersection. You know this because red octagons are part of the rules of the road. Similarly, the letters in the Roman alphabet are symbols, which are used according to the conventions of language and grammar. Data exist in many forms (some useable, others not), but data have no real significance beyond their existence.[10] Data are our way of representing observed facts, but these facts remain largely unorganized and unrelated.

The next level up on the pyramid is information. We've already spent a lot of effort examining information, so we won't spend long here. Suffice it to say that information is ordered data—data that has been given a meaningful relational connection. It is through this organization that data transform into information. For example, imagine the daily receipts at a local restaurant. As each party settles its bill important pieces of data accumulate (food and drink purchased, method of payment, time of payment, server, etc.). But these data only become useful—and only become information—once the manager decides to organize them. For example, she may choose to view the receipt totals for each server, so that she can identify her high performers.

Information, however, is not the pinnacle of the pyramid. When information is integrated and assimilated the result is knowledge. Knowledge can be acquired through instruction (transferred from someone else) or through experience (section 4.4).[11] It might best be viewed as actionable or useful information. If we return to the restaurant example, the manager should learn from the information she has collected and make decisions to refine her business practice. She may choose to schedule her best servers during peak traffic hours to maximize profits, or she may use her knowledge to provide additional coaching to her underperforming servers. Knowledge is a deterministic process, which means that it is based on (or is determined by) things that have happened before (antecedents). In other words, knowledge is all about understanding patterns, comparing new information with old, and tracking trends to improve decision-making.

At the top of the pyramid is wisdom, but wisdom is a bit of an outlier. It doesn't rely as much on the blocks below it. Wisdom involves applying moral or ethical judgment. It's about moving beyond knowledge to a deeper under-standing of principles. As such, it is extrapolative because it expands (or extrap-olates) beyond what is known. Unlike knowledge, wisdom is non-probabilistic, meaning that it is not concerned with probabilities or predictions of specific events.[12] It focuses on bigger picture reasoning and abstract thoughts that are beyond natural laws or causes. While wisdom is generally viewed as a uniquely human characteristic, this hasn't stopped us from pursuing the idea of Artificial Intelligence (A.I.)—machines that can think and reason for themselves. However, given that most futuristic visions of A.I. lead to the annihilation of the human race, maybe we should leave things as they are.

2.3 Knowledge Continuum

Meaning + understanding

Dividing knowledge into a pyramid of building blocks is nice in theory, but not so much in practice. Looking at symbols, data, information, knowledge, and wisdom as a hierarchy is a bit of a misnomer. After all, these elements aren't clearly delineated from one another. Most of us don't consciously identify the moment when a red octagon (symbol) transforms into a stop sign (data), re-minding us to stop at the intersection (information/knowledge). Nor do we spend much time thinking about the principles behind the broader traffic sys-tem (wisdom).

Since our brains work too quickly for us to differentiate the individual stages, we might more accurately describe these elements as belonging to a continuum. By definition, a continuum involves continuous progression. In our example, symbols comprise the "simple" end of the continuum and wisdom comprises the "complex" end. In between these endpoints, each element trans-forms into its adjacent elements without much effort. Since it is often hard to pinpoint the exact moment when data transforms into information, or knowl-edge into wisdom, what holds the continuum together?

One potential explanation is that *understanding* is the glue that fuses data, information, knowledge and wisdom together. To move toward more complex phenomenon, we rely on our ability to understand. Understanding takes new knowledge, observations, and facts, and synthesizes them with previously held knowledge. As a result, understanding is more of an interpolative process, meaning that it helps us connect ideas.[13] Our restaurant manager (section 2.2) may see that total sales on holiday weekends are consistently greater than on regular weekends. From that observation, she might rightly interpolate that she should use more staff for the next holiday weekend. Understanding is also a probabilistic exercise. It helps us recognize patterns and attempt to predict the future. Since the restaurant manager knows that weekends in the summer are more popular than those in the winter, she can forecast how much seasonal help she should hire.

Understanding is often confused with knowledge, but they are different concepts. Knowledge is something that can be obtained and retained. In contrast, understanding is the process through which we attain that knowledge. This distinction is like the difference between learning and memorizing. You might *know* that $2 \times 2 = 4$ because you memorized your multiplication tables as a kid—you accumulated that knowledge through repetition. However, to prove that you *understand* how to multiply, we might ask you a question that you are less likely to have memorized, like what is 1024×768? *(786 432)*[14]

Understanding, then, is the *process* by which we learn about a particular phenomenon, not the product of our learning. In fact, the whole knowledge continuum is probably best viewed as an iterative process (one that repeats). As we learn, we move from data to information by understanding *relationships;* we move from information to knowledge by understanding *patterns;* and we move from knowledge to wisdom by understanding *principles.*[15] In other words, true understanding is about making connections between data, information, knowledge, and eventually wisdom—we need to consider the whole continuum.

2.4 Information Transfer

You tell me yours and I'll tell you mine

We've looked at knowledge as a hierarchy of elements. We've suggested that these elements are best viewed as a continuum (supported by understanding). We've even added that communication helps us form communities. But what we haven't done is examine how meaning, knowledge and understanding are actually shared between members of a given community. Information sharing is a great idea, but how does it work? It works through a process called information transfer.

At its most basic level, information transfer requires three components:

1. a source or sender (where does the information originate?)
2. a channel (what medium or method is used to communicate the information?)
3. a destination or receiver (where is the information going?)

This seems pretty straightforward. Whether you're discussing celebrity gossip with a friend over lunch, or researching used cars over your broadband

Internet connection, it's fairly easy to distinguish between the source, channel and destination.

Interestingly, the information transfer process depends almost entirely on perspective. Let me explain with a hypothetical scenario. A cultural anthropologist, a computer engineer, and an undergraduate student go into an Internet cafe. They decide to watch short pirated clips of *The Simpsons* that have been uploaded to YouTube.

To the anthropologist, the clips provide an interesting window into contemporary (American) culture, because they are full of cultural references and satirical commentary. Additionally, *The Simpsons* was the one of the first animated sitcom for adults and it was followed by countless others (e.g. *Family Guy, South Park, Adult Swim*), making it a worthwhile subject for study.

To the computer engineer, the performance of the system may be of more interest than the content itself. The group could be watching *The Simpsons*, Chocolate Rain, the Tron Guy, Numa Numa or the Grape Lady,[16] but for the engineer it is more about the quality of the video compression, the speed of the file download, and the streaming bit rate of the video player.

To the undergraduate student, the clips from *The Simpsons* are strictly for entertainment (or procrastination) purposes. The cultural references are important because they're funny, not because they provide insight into the broader human condition. And the only time the student notices the quality of the video clips is when it hampers the viewing experience.

Even though most of us who visit YouTube identify with the undergraduate student, it should be clear that people come to different conclusions about information—even after observing the same phenomena. We've established that humans are the agents who assign meaning in the information experience (and each of us does that differently), so we shouldn't be surprised that information transfer depends upon perspective or context.

Of course, information transfer is not a one-way street. Since nearly every system (recall Madden's definition from section 2.1) plays the role of sender and

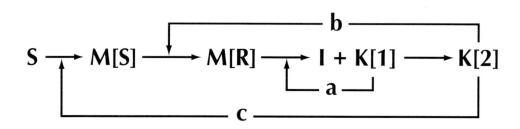

the role of receiver at some point, we need to expand our rather basic source-channel-destination model of information transfer. Fortunately, Brian Vickery and Alina Vickery have developed a more comprehensive version. For lack of a better description, we'll call it the Vickery Information Transfer Model.

Don't be alarmed, it looks more complicated than it actually is. Reading the model from left to right, you can see that the source (S) sends a message (M[S]) to a receiver through a channel (arrows). The information (I) in the message received (M[R]), affects the knowledge state of the receiver (K[1]). If the information is useful, the knowledge state of the receiver changes (K[2]). But the model doesn't stop there. It also has built-in feedback loops to inform the source about the success (or failure) of the information transmission. The first feedback loop (a) compares the knowledge state of the individual to the information received. If the information is not new, then the receiver cannot move to the second knowledge state. The second feedback loop (b) focuses on the channel of communication. It is intended to reduce the differences between the message sent and the message received. The last feedback loop (c) relates specifically to the message itself. If the message isn't getting through properly, then the source may choose to alter its content.[17]

Let's take a look at this model in action. Imagine a politician at election time making speeches around the country and presenting his platform to the public. The source of these messages is the politician himself (and, indirectly, his team of speech writers, campaign managers, and trusted advisors). The message he's sending would include the specific content of his platform (healthcare reform, tax reform, foreign policy, etc.), but it would also include more subjective messages communicated through the politician's body language and presentation style. The message received relates to the populace and what they have heard, or the impressions they have, about the campaign. Of course, each individual will have received slightly different messages, based on individual perspectives and perceptions. The information from the campaign will be added to each citizen's existing knowledge about the politician and his campaign. And if the message adds sufficient value, then the citizen moves to a new knowledge state (where she knows more than she did previously).

Throughout the campaign political strategists constantly monitor feedback. This feedback may be in the form of opinion polls, media reports, or conversations with party insiders. If the feedback is positive, the politician is unlikely to alter the message. Instead, he will attempt to build momentum by amplifying the talking points that resonate with the populace.

If the feedback is negative, the politician has two choices: alter the channel, or alter the message. The first option suggests that there is nothing wrong with the politician's message or platform. For some reason, the channels of communication (speeches, debates, political rallies, etc.) have been unsuccessful in reaching the audience; so one solution is to simply change the channel. Maybe he chooses to advertise more, or starts to get his message out using social media like YouTube, Twitter, or Meetup.

The second option suggests that the channels of communication are fine, but the message needs refining. Depending on feedback, party strategists might alter the message by downplaying ideas that are unpopular with the voters (pragmatic approach). They may choose to tweak the message for delivery to different voter groups, or choose to simplify the message altogether, making it more coherent (semantic approach). Or, they may simply attempt to clarify their message by countering the misinformation presented by opposing parties and politicians (technical approach).[18]

Of course, the principal form of feedback for the politician comes on election night. Did the public hear the message, identify with it, and vote accordingly? In the Vickery Information Transfer model, the ultimate goal for the source or sender of a message is to move the receiver to a new knowledge state. If the information is not assimilated into the knowledge state of the receiver, then the message is ineffective. However, not every shift in knowledge state is a monumental one. Advertising, for instance, is a key channel for businesses to communicate with current and potential customers. Most advertisements do not introduce the viewer to a new product and, therefore, do not signify a major change in the receiver's knowledge state. Instead, most advertisements are designed to attract attention and remind the viewer of the product's existence. This reminder represents a relatively small shift in consciousness, but if it moves the viewer even slightly toward a new knowledge state, then the message was successfully delivered.

2.5 Noise

The sound of interference

If only sending and receiving messages was as easy as it appears in the Vickery Information Transfer Model. In reality, information transfer is often complicated by noise. Noise refers to information that interferes with the original message. It's not that these additional bits of information are incorrect or false; they're just irrelevant to the task at hand. As such, they confuse the original message.

In television advertising, for example, companies try to present a clear and consistent message about their products (that's branding 101). Thousands of dollars go into professionally producing commercials, but even so, advertisers know that most viewers will not watch them with undivided attention. The average viewer will be consumed by other distractions (conversation, channel surfing, etc.), which ultimately interfere with the advertiser's message.

Interference might also be the result of the technology itself. Have you ever flipped on the radio, only to find that you're listening to what sounds like two different radio stations? This experience usually happens when you're on a road trip. You hop in the car and start by flipping on your favorite radio station, but as you drive further away from the station's broadcast center, the signal gets weaker. Depending on your location and the location of other radio stations in the vicinity, you may experience two radio stations attempting to broadcast on the same or similar frequencies.

As we've seen, noise occurs when additional information confuses the message, but noise can also refer to *missing* information. Too many gaps in the transmission and piecing together the original message becomes impossible. For instance, if I'm telling you a joke, but I forget some of the key details, then the punch line will fall flat (and you'll be confused).

Missing information might also be the result of technology. For example, when you make a call with a digital cell phone your voice gets compressed into binary packets. These packets are shuttled between cell phone towers until they're eventually beamed down to the person you called. Depending on your location, however, some of these packets get dropped and never make it to the destination. If the signal is strong, the majority of the packets get through; if the signal is weak, the packets disappear and the call may be lost altogether.

Whether we look at noise as additional pieces of information or missing pieces of information, the end result is the same. Noise is detrimental to the transmission process. In each case, noise interferes, confuses the pattern, and makes it more difficult to share knowledge.

2.6 Experiment

Explicit vs. implicit

Transferring or sharing information can be understood by examining how information travels via the available technological infrastructure. For example, we might look at how a message is delivered over the Internet, or how voices are carried over the telephone network. While this approach to information transfer is important, it tends to be overly technical—and let's face it, a little boring.

It is much more interesting to think of information transfer as a transfer of messages between people. After all, we're bombarded by so many messages every day, that we can be easily overwhelmed. Some messages are designed to educate (newspaper articles, public lectures, video tutorials), others are intended to entertain (MP3 tracks, video clips, comics), and others are invitations to interact (conversation, forums, wikis). But what do these messages mean?

The fact is that messages can be both explicit and implicit. Explicit messages are clearly expressed and readily observable. For example, the lyrics to your favorite song are explicit messages because they can be easily observed (unless you happen to like some obscure form of thrash metal). Implicit messages are not directly expressed; they are implied. Song lyrics often include metaphors, similes, and other word pictures to imply messages and meanings that cannot be easily expressed explicitly.

Of course, each of us interprets the messages we receive differently. Differences in age, gender, culture, language, sexual orientation, race and other areas make information transfer a decidedly complex operation. For example, in 1982 Mitsubishi Motors introduced a sport utility vehicle called the Pajero. According to the company, this vehicle was named after a mountain cat in southern Argentina,[19] but to Spanish speakers *pajero* is an idiom for 'wanker' or masturbating man—not the best name for a car. Fortunately, Mitsubishi was aware of the cultural differences and released the Pajero as the Montero ("hunter in the mountains") in Spain and the Americas.[20]

Advertising provides a great industry to examine information transfer for a couple of reasons. First, it is the dominant mode of communication between organizations and potential customers. Second, companies spend thousands of dollars carefully crafting the messages they send (both explicit and implicit) for desired impact (to make you buy).

For this experiment, apply the Vickery Information Transfer Model (section 2.4) to a television commercial of your choice. Use the worksheet and questions on the following page to analyze your television commercial.

Name _____ Date _____

Part A

Visit YouTube, Vimeo, or Veoh and find a commercial from a major brand in another market (e.g. A Pepsi commercial from Spain, a Nike commercial from Germany).

Part B

1. Which company is sending the message?

2. Which region of the world (market) was the commercial created for?

3. What messages are being sent? (Remember implicit and explicit approaches.)

4. What is the channel? How are they choosing to deliver this message?

5. What is the message being received? Is it the same as the message sent?

6. After receiving the message, does your knowledge state change? Why or why not?

7. How would the company evaluate the success of the advertisement? (How might the company measure feedback?)

8. If the feedback is negative, how might the source alter the message?

9. Do the messages in the commercial work across cultures and markets, or are they specific to the market the commercial was created for?

2.7 Reflect

Information + metabolism

Audrey Fenner discusses some of the difficulties with understanding and defining information in the digital age. She presents an interesting discussion about information as a commodity. Read her article (originally published in a *library* publication not a *business* publication), and consider the questions below:

Fenner, Audrey. "Placing value on information." *Library Philosophy and Practice* 4, no. 2 (2002), http://www.webpages.uidaho.edu/~mbolin/fenner.pdf

---

QUESTIONS

1. Fenner lists a number of observations when comparing information to physical inventory. Which of her statements demonstrate the *similarities* between information and physical inventory? After reading her list, what do you think of these comparisons? Should information be valued like a commodity? Is such a comparison even possible?

2. Fenner lists a number of observations when comparing information to physical inventory. Which of her statements demonstrate the *differences* between information and physical inventory? After reading her list, what do you think of these comparisons? Should information be valued like a commodity? Is such a comparison even possible?

3. In an attempt to help describe and define "information" Audrey Fenner turns to the metaphor of metabolism. Does her comparison of information to the metabolizing process make sense? Or are there obvious problems with this approach? Does the metaphor clarify your understanding of information, or confuse it? Why or why not?

2.8 Reflect

The promise of information technology

John Seely Brown and Paul Duguid discuss the nature of information and technology in their book, *The Social Life of Information* (HBS Press, 2000). In the interview cited below, they respond to a number of questions about the future of information and communication technology. Read their thoughts and respond to the questions below:

Brown, John Seely and Duguid, Paul. "The Social Life of Information." *Harvard Business School Working Knowledge Archive* (March 28, 2000), http://hbswk. hbs.edu/archive/1403.html

---

QUESTIONS

1. Brown and Duguid suggest that we have developed "tunnel vision" when it comes to new technology and design. In our haste to drive forward, we miss things like "context, background, history, common knowledge, [and] social resources." What do you think of this statement? Do we need social context to understand the information we encounter? Why or why not?

2. Futurists like to predict that the promise of technology will make the Information Age an open frontier. Brown and Duguid caution against such optimism, claiming that there will always be a place for technologies like paper and institutions like universities. What do you think? Does the explosion of information on the Internet reduce the need for educational institutions (or other organizations)? Why or why not?

3. For some time we have heard that the Internet enables people to work more easily from home—to "telecommute" to work, but statistics show that the percentage of people who work out of the home instead of the office is quite small. Brown and Duguid propose a number of potential reasons for this discrepancy. What do you think of their reasons? Would you be willing to work out of a "home-office" for your career? Why or why not?

2.9 Decide

Conflict of interest

Lori works in the Human Resources department of Echo Hearing Devices, a major hearing aid manufacturer based just outside of Toronto, Ontario. Last week, Lori's friend Bruce called to tell her that he has just been offered an engineering position with the company. Bruce is currently working in Winnipeg, Manitoba as a materials specialist for a manufacturing firm. While he likes his current job (his annual salary is $58,000), he has been looking for an opportunity to return to Ontario—and to the Toronto area in particular.

He will be working in the Industrial Products division to develop safer ear protection for workers in the airline industry. Bruce is thrilled with the new opportunity and the chance to reunite with Lori. Lori is equally excited at the opportunity to reconnect with her friend from university.

In her position, Lori is familiar with staff salaries and salary ranges across the company. During the course of their conversation Bruce disclosed his salary offer ($68,500) and Lori's heart sank. Lori knows that Bruce's salary offer is much lower than what the company traditionally pays for that position ($75,000 - $90,000).

Lori wants to alert Bruce to the discrepancy but she is worried about violating her own job obligations.

What do you think Lori should do? Four options are presented on the following page.

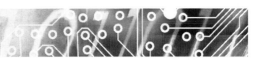

Worksheet

Name _____   Date _____

In the space provided, discuss the advantages and disadvantages of each option and make a final recommendation.

A) Tell Bruce the specific salary range he should expect for an industrial products engineering position at Echo Hearing Devices and encourage him to negotiate aggressively.

B) Respect the obligations of her job and avoid telling Bruce anything. Let him handle the negotiations on his own.

C) Speak to the director of Human Resources on Bruce's behalf and attempt to get the salary offer raised.

D) Provide Bruce with some basic salary information from the overall industry (but not specific to Echo Hearing Devices), so that he can be armed with more information during negotiations.

So, what do you think Lori should do? Why?

_____

_____

_____

_____

_____

_____

The Information Environment

3.1 What is Technology?

Technology as disruption

Like information, technology is another word that gets used carelessly (we're off to a great start here). Recently I saw a television commercial for a popular hair product. The tag line at the end of the advertisement was "Inspired by technology." But what are they trying to say? Did a computer inspire the shampoo? Was it created with fancy software? Does it contain active nanorobots? Of course, it doesn't mean any of those things. I'm guessing that the marketers used the word technology to suggest that their product is advanced, exciting, effective, efficient, and sufficiently sophisticated—words generally used to describe the latest and greatest technology. For me, the association fell flat.

It might interest you to know that the word technology was not always associated with computers, software, networks, or feats of mechanical engineering. Looking at the etymology (history of origin and usage) of technology provides some interesting insight. Technology comes from the Greek word *tekhnologia,* which refers to the systematic treatment of an art or craft.[1] Interestingly, it was often used when referring to the rules and usage of grammar (the systematic treatment of language). From there it evolved to mean "the terminology of a particular art or subject."[2] In other words, technology came to represent the set of technical terms (nomenclature) used in a particular subject. Today, technology usually refers to specific objects—things like tools, machines, appliances, networks, or computers.

It might be tempting to ignore these older definitions, but when we use the word "technology" we're often talking about aspects from each of these three definitions (whether we realize it or not). In our usage, technology can refer to a systematic approach, specific terminology, and the production of a useful end product. Don't believe me? Let's take a look at paper—a relatively simple technology, and one that we tend to take for granted. When paper was first invented in China, there were specific techniques and a systematic process for creation (suspend plant fibers in water, drain water through a screen, let fibers dry). The process of making paper (then and now) also includes unique terminology related to the process (slurry, pulp, calendaring, watermarking, sizing, etc.).[3] And, of course, the end product on which we write is an incredibly adaptable piece of technology. Whether we're describing paper or processors, these same three principles can be found in nearly everything we describe as technology.

When examining the impact of technology, observers often separate technologies into two categories: disruptive technology and sustaining technology. As you might expect, a disruptive technology upsets the current order and completely redefines the rules.[4] For an obvious example, look no further than the Internet. The introduction of the Internet changed the rules of order. It changed the way we share information, the way we conduct commerce, the way we govern ourselves, and, ultimately, the way we communicate. Most people did not predict the phenomenal success of the Internet; in fact, quite the opposite happened. An article in *Time* magazine suggested that the Internet "was not designed for doing commerce."[5] In 1995, a *Newsweek* feature simply dismissed the Internet with the word "Bah!"[6] How times have changed.

In contrast to disruptive technology, sustaining technology refers to technology that improves upon already existing technology. Sustaining technologies find ways to do things better, cheaper and more efficiently. The introduction of popular search engines like Google, Yahoo!, and AltaVista certainly made information on the web more accessible, but those services were simply improvements on previous search algorithms like Archie.[7] Search engines made searching the Internet easier and, as a result, more people used them to find information.

To be sure, there are dangers with separating technology into such categories (e.g. Did the invention of the digital camera reinvent photography, or merely improve it?);[8] however, these distinctions are particularly helpful when we look back on the impact that specific technologies have had on business and society. Technology is usually viewed as a product of the society or culture, meaning that we can understand more about a particular society by the tools and technology its citizens create.

More recently, however, theorists have suggested that we've got it backwards. It's technology that plays the primary role. In this view (known as technological determinism), it is technology that causes social change and determines cultural value. Rosalind Williams, a cultural historian of technology, phrases it this way: "technology determines history."[9] Now there's a bold statement. Certainly, technology plays a key role in our society, but is it the dominant force shaping the Information Age? That may be a stretch.

When we examined the definition of information (section 2.1) we acknowledged that information is important *because* it relates to the human experience. Can the same be said of technology? The technological determinism thesis suggests that technology is autonomous—it can be viewed independent of the human experience. But does this make sense? Is technology the cause or solution to the problems we encounter? We can argue all day about whether technology is good, bad, or neutral (and there are good arguments for each), but in the end we must acknowledge our own role in its adoption. To riff on the popular t-shirt slogan: "Guns don't kill people, we kill people." Despite our efforts, we can't escape responsibility for how we use technology.

 ## 3.2 Information Systems

The human factor

To be sure, information and technology are key components of an information system, but they're not the only elements. Databases, search engines, spreadsheets, and other tools for managing information may have incredible capabilities, but if they are unusable, they provide few advantages. Likewise, we may be able to collect vast amounts of detailed information, but if we can't manipulate the information for our needs, then we've gained nothing.

Both of these situations point to the fact that we need to consider the human factor when planning, designing, and using information systems. Whether we're using Supply Chain Management (SCM) systems to handle company inventory; Customer Relationship Management (CRM) systems to track contact with customers; or Geographic Information Systems (GIS) to map potential locations for expansion, these systems need to consider how the user will exploit the technology to interact with the information. Therefore, a well-designed system needs to consider three components: People, Technology, and Information.

Any system that focuses on just two of these three elements is limited from the outset. For example, imagine if the engineers behind Google's search engine chose to focus only on technology and people, leaving information to the side. Google's system might feature the best search technology and the most user-friendly interface (both of great importance), but if there is no information to be found, then the system will be ineffective. Fortunately for us, Google has not ignored the information component and currently holds one of the largest indexes (lists) of available online information.

Similarly, imagine if Wikipedia designed its information system around people and information, but not technology. Great effort might be spent encouraging people to contribute their ideas to a large repository of information; however, if the technology does not make contributing easy, people will lose interest, and the system will be inefficient.[10] Again, fortunately for us, Wikipedia has not ignored technology. Nearly every page on the website can be edited in real-time through the use of wiki software (interesting side note: "wiki" is a Hawaiian word for "quick" or "fast").[11]

The reality is that most information systems tend to focus on the information and the technology and forget about the people. Think of the last poorly designed website you visited, or the last time you got lost in a company's automated phone menu ("Please press one for sales … press four for service … press seven to listen to this menu again"). Too often, human factors get lost in the design process—a recipe for failure.

An information system, then, employs technology (hardware, software, applications) to manipulate information, and leverage the talents of people in pursuit of an objective.[12] In other words, information systems are designed with a purpose: to help us solve problems. Information systems that ignore people, technology, or information, greatly reduce our ability to achieve our goals or solve our problems.

3.3 Efficiency + Effectiveness

Measures of success

Information systems can help us achieve our organizational objectives (managing supplier relationships, developing product pricing), or individual objectives (planning a weekly budget, updating an address book). But how do we know whether or not a given information system satisfies our needs?

Evaluating information systems often boils down to two different concepts: efficiency and effectiveness. Efficiency is all about measuring the *performance* of a system. It's about "doing things right,"[13] and getting the most out of every resource. In an ideal world, we want the system to perform at optimal efficiency, meaning it completes tasks using the fewest resources in the shortest time possible. From a technology perspective, we would measure things like the system's performance, speed, storage, availability, and processing capabilities. From an information perspective, we would examine the system's inputs and outputs. We would measure how easily information is added to the system, or how quickly information can be extracted from the system. When evaluating efficiency we're focusing on *productivity metrics.*

In order to measure the overall performance of the system, it helps to have a standard for comparison. This standard is called a benchmark and the process of comparing the current performance of a system against its optimal performance is known as benchmarking. Clearly, if the system is underperforming, then adjustments need to be made to ensure greater efficiency.

In contrast, effectiveness is more about evaluating the *impact* of the information system. How well does the information system meet its defined goals? It's not about using the least amount of resources, nor is it about doing things in the shortest time; it is about "doing the right things."[14] To gauge whether an information system is effective, we might measure things like: customer satisfaction, usability, and return on investment. We're focusing on *quality metrics.*

If the system is not meeting its goals and objectives, then it is ineffective. Potential solutions include improving the inputs (gather better information), redefining the objectives, or even replacing the information system altogether.

Obviously, systems must strive to achieve both efficiency and effectiveness. However, a system that is highly efficient isn't necessarily highly effective, nor is an effective system necessarily efficient. For the purpose of illustration, we'll use a simple example. Think of a typical family looking to purchase a new car. The parents start by identifying their needs. Likely they need a reliable, flexible vehicle with space for kids and cargo, and one that gets decent fuel mileage.

The next step is to actually look at some cars—and there are hundreds to choose from. If money isn't an issue, the husband might start by salivating over a luxury sports car. On the efficiency scale this type of car is off the charts. Performance is its reason for being. Unfortunately, it isn't exactly the best system of transportation in terms of effectiveness, because it doesn't meet the family's stated objectives for space.

Perhaps the family also evaluates a large-scale recreational vehicle (RV). Certainly, this type of vehicle more effectively meets their space requirements than the sports car—it is a house on wheels after all. Unfortunately, this vehicle it isn't exactly efficient. Its sheer bulk means the RV gets poor gas mileage, is expensive to repair, and is much too large for driving around the city.

Clearly, the family is looking for a compromise. Chances are they'll end up with a full-sized sedan, wagon, minivan, or SUV. These vehicles have the room required for the kids, they're reliable (under warranty), and have decent fuel efficiency.

What might we learn from this silly example? First, we need to know what we need to know. Since the selection of a car (or an information system) should meet our stated objectives, we need to take the time to actually state those objectives. Second, different cars (or information systems) are designed to achieve different goals. Sports cars and recreational vehicles meet the objectives of some individuals, just not those of our hypothetical family. When we employ information systems successfully, we have defined the right goals and objectives, and we have selected best technology to meet them.

 ## 3.4 Competitive Advantage

And the winner is ...

As we've discussed, information systems are a combination of people, information and technology. But we haven't really looked at the reasons for having information systems in the first place. Why bother creating information systems? The answer to that question depends on your objective (surprise, surprise).

On a practical level, information systems help us manage and manipulate information. They help us collect, summarize, and analyze key data. But information systems are designed for more than just keeping information orderly.

Information systems are also strategic investments that can contribute real value to an organization. The primary reason we employ information systems is to give us an advantage. A well-designed information system can help us make better decisions—and better decisions mean an increased advantage (read: more profit). But it is not enough to simply stockpile information. We need to understand the information we collect, and then do something with it. We need to act. Simply put, information systems can provide us with actionable information—the intelligence required to decide.

One way to view an organization is by applying the value chain model.[15] In this view, achieving an objective is broken down into a series of discrete processes. Every step, procedure, activity, or person works together to add value, helping the organization move one step closer to producing its product or delivering its service. This approach is most evident when we imagine an assembly line. Think of Henry Ford and his Model T in the early twentieth century. The process of creating a car was broken down into individual steps, with each step moving the car closer to completion and adding value to the product in the process. Whether we're manufacturing cars, writing software code, managing guests at a hotel, or flying airplanes, most business objectives can be broken down into a series of smaller processes.

Each business process, sometimes called a "value activity," has a physical component (tasks required to carry out the process) and an information component (data required to perform, measure, and evaluate the process).[16] If utilized properly, information technology can help identify inefficient or ineffective processes. By improving or replacing these processes information systems add value to the organization. In fact, to borrow from Peter Drucker, advances in information systems and technology are important not because they deliver access to more information, but because they make traditional processes more routine.[17] They increase efficiency, allowing us to do the things we've always done, but to do them more quickly. As a result, information systems need to be designed so that they are flexible and responsive, enabling new processes to be easily integrated into the value chain.

In this environment, then, information technology is more than an operational business expense. We need to avoid viewing I.T. systems as simply "the cost of doing business." Instead, we should view them as resources to exploit advantage.

Obviously, what we're talking about here is not a secret. Every individual and every organization uses information to gain the upper hand. Why do basketball coaches spend hours watching game tape? To learn their opponents' tendencies (and win more games). Why do students spend hours studying course material? To do well on the exams (and outperform the other students). Why do top chefs spend hours perfecting their recipes? To keep their menus fresh (and attract more customers than other restaurants). You get the picture. Not only do the basketball coach, student and chef hope that they will glean some new insight; they hope this insight will proffer advantage.

Competitive advantage occurs when customers have some reason to place a greater value on one company's products over its competitors' products. For example, one furniture manufacturer might choose to compete on price; another manufacturer may compete on quality; and still another might compete with designer furniture (it's not cheap, or functional, but it's definitely sexy). In essence, competitive advantage is a value proposition to the customer.

To better understand competitive advantage, companies are increasingly turning to their information systems. Therefore, a well-designed information system needs to handle *all* of the information that is essential to the organization. This includes internal information created by the organization, and external information that directly affects the company.

A good information system should also be hard to duplicate. If your information systems are easy to copy—in terms of both the technology and the information collected—then you've lost your competitive advantage. Take Google Maps, for example. The information system behind this product handles a lot of geographic data (roads, satellite images, etc.). While much of this data are purchased or licensed from other sources, Google has integrated this information in a way that makes it easier for the user to manipulate. They've added value to the data through the application of technology. As a result, it is easier for other companies who require geographic information to simply access Google's data instead of trying to create it on their own.

Competitive advantage comes down to managing information and making good decisions based on that information. Of course, gaining an advantage is hard enough, but maintaining it may be even harder. The competition, it seems, is never over.

 ## 3.5 Technology as Utility

Oddities of commodities

In the previous section we looked at competitive advantage. More specifically, we looked at how information systems (a combination of technology, information and people) contribute to competitive advantage. Well, as it turns out, things may not be so straightforward. While competitive advantage remains an important business objective, perhaps it doesn't come from investment in technology (or information systems), like we first discussed.

In 2003, Nicholas Carr wrote an article in the *Harvard Business Review* called "IT Doesn't Matter," which caused a lot of controversy. He argued that because nearly everyone was investing in information technology (or at least had access to the same I.T.), then information technology could not be a source of competitive advantage. After all, "what makes a resource truly strategic—what gives it the capacity to be the basis for sustained competitive advantage—is not ubiquity but scarcity."[18] In other words, you can only gain an edge when you have something that others don't have.

In his argument, Carr separates technologies into two categories: proprietary technologies and infrastructural technologies. Proprietary technologies are effectively owned and controlled by a single company. The software behind the Portable Document Format (PDF) would be considered a proprietary technology because it is owned by Adobe Systems. As the sole provider of the technology, Adobe benefits when organizations or individuals use it. Providing that proprietary technologies stay protected, they contribute to sustained strategic advantage over rivals.

In contrast, infrastructural technologies, can be shared by all—and, in fact, are more effective when shared. The telephone system is a perfect example. Since nearly every organization uses the telephone as part of their communication strategy, information can more quickly flow between parties. Everyone uses the infrastructure and everyone benefits. However, the telephone network is not a strategic differentiator for most organizations and therein lays the problem. Infrastructural technologies simply don't create competitive advantage.

Let's rephrase that: infrastructural technologies don't create *sustained* competitive advantage. The window in which to capitalize on infrastructural technologies is brief. For instance, early adopters of electricity enjoyed an advantage over their competitors for a short time. But eventually the competitors caught on and began using electricity in a similar manner, eliminating the advantage.

As more people take advantage of an infrastructural technology, the cost to implement the technology falls. Falling costs mean the technology becomes more accessible and affordable, enabling even more companies to adopt the technology. Of course, as more companies adopt the technology, competitive advantage erodes even more quickly—and the playing field is leveled again.[19]

So, is information technology a proprietary technology, or an infrastructural one? According to Carr, it's the latter. Information technology is simply "a transport mechanism—it carries digital information just as railroads carry goods and power grids carry electricity."[20] Like the Internet, most information technology is more valuable when it's shared. Individuals and organizations benefit from the Internet *because* its platform is open—no single organization owns or operates it. Additionally, history demonstrates that the cost of information technology plummets due to economies of scale.

In section 1.2 we talked about information as a commodity (without much resolution), but Carr argues that it is technology—not information—that is commoditized. As we've discussed, if information technology is an infrastructural technology, then it must be widely accessible and broadly shared. But for this to happen, the technology requires some measure of standardization. To ensure interoperability of systems the technology must employ the same basic parts. Don't miss the significance of his argument: the standardization of information technology means that all of the players share the same advantage.

Technology, then, is simply an input commodity for most businesses. Carr argues that information technology functions like a utility, providing everyone with essentially the same service.[21] Put another way, information technology is like a cable TV vendor, telephone company, or electricity provider, delivering services that are nearly identical to everyone in the neighborhood. And you guessed it—identical services are not a reliable source of competitive advantage.

Many of Carr's critics suggest that he is proposing an overly simplistic (and dangerous) view of technology. One common rebuttal is that information technology cannot be examined in isolation; instead, we must acknowledge that information technology "is inherently strategic because of its indirect effects—it creates possibilities that did not exist before."[22] In other words, technology is important because it creates new opportunities. It's not the technology itself that lends an advantage; it is the ability to employ technology to improve traditional business practices.

For others, Carr's arguments ignore the human factors. If you recall our information systems discussion from earlier in the chapter (section 3.2), we cannot forget the role that human capital plays in competitive advantage. "It's not the IT that confers competitive advantage; but the people who know how to use it effectively."[23] Again, we see that people take precedence over technology and information.

A third counter-argument claims that information technology cannot be so easily lumped in with other infrastructural technologies. For example, information technology is not like electricity. The copper wires that deliver electric power to appliances are not the same as the fiber optics or Ethernet cables that connect our information technology. The I.T. infrastructure does more than transfer information, it also holds and preserves the pieces of information that are essential to the organization. Information technology is simply too complicated to be dismissed as an input commodity.[24]

Building on his IT as utility argument, Carr proposes that information technology is shifting from an asset that organizations own to a service that they purchase. Advances in virtualization technology, storage arrays, grid computing and web services mean that many information tasks (for processing and archiving) can be outsourced to computing utilities.[25] Offloading information processing responsibilities to capable providers may sound like an attractive solution, but are companies willing to loosen their control over essential information?

Clearly, there are a lot of questions surrounding this debate. Carr's views may be in the minority, but they still provide a provocative set of ideas for discussion. Should we spend less on information technology, wait before investing, and focus our attention on system vulnerabilities?[26] Or, considering that the window of opportunity is short, should we aggressively adopt information technology? As usual, the answer depends on your perspective.

3.6 Experiment

Switching costs

Humans are creatures of habit. We imagine ourselves as independently minded individuals, free to choose as we please, but the reality is we gravitate to things that are familiar. We like drinking our morning coffee and our late night beverages; we like watching our Saturday morning cartoons and our Sunday afternoon football; we like having our spot on the bus and our specific seat in the classroom. The routines and repetition provide structure and allow our minds to relax.

For many of us, our behavior in the information environment is similarly habitual. We have our preferred search engine, our preferred source for news, our preferred instant messaging application, our preferred channel for weather, and so on. Even though the Information Age is full of choice, it takes a lot of effort to move us beyond our known universe.

For example, think of the first email address you every signed up for. Do you still have it? I'm guessing, but I'd say that your employer did not provide your first email address, nor did the school you chose to attend. Instead, you probably started with an email address from a service like Yahoo! or Hotmail, because the addresses were free and you could personalize your user name. Even though you've probably acquired other email address since, I'd bet that most of you still have—and probably still use—your original address. Why is that?

One of the reasons we keep using our original email address is due to switching costs. Basically, we think it's too much trouble to switch to another service or start over with a new email address. We don't want to notify everyone, we don't want to learn a new interface, we don't want to create a new address book, and we definitely don't want to migrate our old email. Even though there are tools that will help us make the switch, we stick with our habits.

When the costs—or the perceived costs—of switching to a new supplier or provider are higher, it becomes more difficult for us to make the switch (even if the switch would be beneficial). Switching costs are related to competitive advantage. If companies can make it hard for you to use an alternative, then you'll stick with them.

For this experiment, you're going to face the issue of switching costs head on. First, you'll need to identify your current habits; second, you'll need to identify some alternatives; lastly, you'll need to spend a week using the alternatives. Use the worksheet on the following page to get started.

Worksheet

Name _____ Date _____

Part A

Identify the website you use <u>most</u> in each category.

Search engine (e.g. Google):

Online reference/encyclopedia:

Source for political news:

Source for celebrity news or sports news:

Video sharing (e.g. YouTube):

Source for new music:

Part B

Identify at least one alternative website for each category that can provide the same basic experience.

Search engine (e.g. Google):

Online reference/encyclopedia:

Source for political news:

Source for celebrity news or sports news:

Video sharing (e.g. YouTube):

Source for new music:

Part C

For the next week, use only these alternatives when you're looking for information.

1. What was the experience like? How did you adjust to the alternative web sites?

2. Did you find yourself returning to your familiar services before the week was over? If so, why?

3. Did you find the alternatives more or less useful than your preferred sites?

4. Are you more or less likely to consult some of these alternative sites in the future? Why?

3.7 Reflect

Utility computing

Nicholas Carr has made a living making controversial statements about IT. First was his *Harvard Business Review* article, "IT doesn't matter" where he claimed that IT does not provide strategic advantage. More recently, he published a book called *The Big Switch* about the future of utility computing. Read his Q&A session with *Computerworld* and reflect on the questions below:

Carpenter, Joyce. "Q&A: Nicholas Carr on the big switch to utility computing." *Computerworld* (January 17, 2008), http://www.computerworld.com/action/article.do?command=viewArticleBasic&articleId=9057379

QUESTIONS

1. Carr makes a simple comparison between the information technology infrastructure (computers, Internet, processing power, etc.) and the development of the electric grid. For him, business changed dramatically when electricity was centralized and he predicts a similar upheaval in the IT world. Does this comparison work for you? Or is it too simplified? Why or why not?

2. Carr notes, "the World Wide Web is turning into a World Wide Computer" which ultimately makes the Internet "programmable." What do you think of this statement? Are the days of personal computing numbered? Will we turn to the Internet for everything that we have traditionally done on our own computer?

3. The concept of utility computing means that companies will outsource IT tasks like storage and processing power to large IT utilities. If this is the case, then an obvious concern is security. Do you think companies be willing to store their sensitive information out on the Internet with these IT providers? Carr thinks security isn't a major problem, but what do you think?

3.8 Reflect

Outsourcing information technology

Dan Pink investigates the complaints of "pissed-off programmers" who are losing their jobs to competent counterparts in India. Shipping jobs overseas to take advantage of cheaper labor is a common business strategy in the manufacturing sector, but recently companies have started to outsource information technology work as well. While the controversy has cooled somewhat, Pink's article raises some interesting issues. Read his discussion and reflect on the questions below:

Pink, Daniel T. "The New Face of the Silicon Age," *Wired* 12, no. 2 (February 2004), http://www.wired.com/wired/archive/12.02/india.html

---

QUESTIONS

1. To some, the American programmers in Pink's article sound like sore losers, to others these programmers have legitimate concerns. If you were an IT programmer and you lost your job to a programmer in India or China, would you be "pissed off," or would you accept that outsourcing is part of the reality of globalization? Why or why not?

2. Outsourcing sounds like a good business strategy (especially when the work is equal in quality), but some people suggest that companies have the responsibility to provide and protect jobs in their home country. What do you think of this argument? Do companies have an obligation to their employees? Or, should they conduct business by the most efficient means possible? If you were a senior manager, would you consider outsourcing jobs? Why or why not?

3. Pink suggests that future IT jobs in North America will be "high concept and high touch." In other words, IT will require higher order skills like designing and strategically positioning technology—the mundane coding responsibilities can be outsourced. Creativity is the future. What do you think of this idea? Does this sound like a better future for the IT industry? Why or why not?

3.9 Decide

Internet monitoring

Carolyn is the owner of Magnate Experiences, a niche company in the travel and tourism industry. Magnate Experiences serves the vacation needs of movie stars, celebrities, business elite, and other high-profile clientele from around the world. Magnate specializes in providing unique private vacations and getaways to some of the world's most exclusive locations. Need a villa in Italy? What about a private lodge in the Swiss Alps? Want to rent a beachfront mansion in Hawaii? Magnate can make the arrangements.

Currently, Carolyn manages approximately two-dozen employees. She has a team of sales representatives who provide each client with personalized service. She also employs a pair of researchers to identify potential customers and possible vacation locations. Lastly, she has some administrative help and information technology support staff who maintain the website and information systems.

Carolyn has recently become concerned with how the company's I.T. resources are being used. Magnate employees handle most client interactions from their central office (via email and over the phone), which means that employees are online constantly. This fact also means that employees are tempted to use the company's resources for personal use. The recent economic climate has been tough on the tourism industry, so Carolyn needs her employees to stay focused on growing the business. If business gets too slow, she may have to lay off employees.

In the past few weeks, Carolyn has noticed employees spending excessive amounts of time perusing social networking sites, reading personal email, and shopping online—not to mention downloading large media files, and participating in gambling sites. To curb such behavior, Carolyn is considering installing monitoring software on all of Magnate's computers. This software would track the websites that each employee visits and monitor corporate email. Historically, Magnate has relied on the common sense of its employees to use the resources appropriately, but maybe it is time for more extreme measures.

What do you think Carolyn should do? Four options are presented on the following page.

Name _____   Date _____

In the space provided, discuss the advantages and disadvantages of each option and make a final recommendation.

A) Install the Internet monitoring software, but don't tell employees. The company's resources are precisely that—the company's—employees should know that.

B) Install the Internet monitoring software, but inform Magnate employees of the change in policy. Employees who have nothing to hide will not be worried.

C) Do nothing. In this age, employees expect to have unfettered access to the Internet. Carolyn should expect (and tolerate) some misuse of company resources.

D) Develop an acceptable use policy (AUP) in cooperation with a few employees. Since employees can be expected to follow the policy, there is no need for monitoring software.

So, what do you think Carolyn should do? Why

_____

_____

_____

_____

_____

_____

_____

Chapter 4

Information Fluencies

4.1 Information + Technology

Communication + communities

We started this book by examining the concepts of information and technology independently, but in the Information Age they are largely inseparable. So, what happens when we cross information with technology? We get something different altogether—we get communication. When it comes right down to it, humans are relational beings. We are proud of our amateur YouTube videos, rambling blog postings, and emoticon-filled instant messages—so proud that we go to great lengths to share what we have to say with the people we know (and sometimes with people we don't). In fact, the history of innovation in information technology might be understood through humankind's desire to communicate with each other.

Admittedly, suggesting that our desire to communicate is the motivation behind information technology is a gross oversimplification, but stick with me for a minute. I think there is something here that will illuminate why some technologies are adopted, some are adapted, and others are abandoned altogether.

Think about the key technologies in the development of writing. We started by using a reed stylus to mark wet clay, we moved to using quill pens on parchment, then fountain pens on paper. Now some of us have returned to the stylus, only this time we're writing on tablet computers (not tablets of clay). The development of printing (moveable type, printing press), the development of telecommunications (semaphore, Morse code, mobile phones), the development of the computer (keyboard, mouse), and the introduction of the Internet (World Wide Web, email) experienced similar innovations in information technology. Why did we invent these (and other) information technologies? It wasn't because we were bored. We pursued these advances because they improved our ability to send messages to each other.

Some inventions make previous technology obsolete (e.g. telegraph to telephone), while other inventions merely redefine the role of existing technology. For example, we still use pen and ink; we just don't use them to transcribe books. It should be clear that these technologies were invented—and, we might even say, embraced—by contemporary citizens primarily *because* they facilitated communication.

Why is this important? Communication, you see, leads to information sharing; information sharing leads to shared meaning; shared meaning leads to community building; and community building leads to identity forming. In other words, communication is at the core of our identity—it's how we learn about others, our community and ourselves.

4.2 Literacy + Competency

Learning how to navigate

Of course, communicating in the Information Age can be a challenging task. To become truly fluent in this new digital language (section 1.5), we must improve both our information literacy and our technological competency. Since technology is the mediator through which we experience information, then the two concepts are by necessity intertwined.

Developing technological competency includes skill-based improvements like learning to use a software program, or administering a Local Area Network (LAN). But technological competency is more than simply having knowledge of hardware and software; it also describes a broader understanding of the application of technology. For example, an individual who is technologically fluent has the ability to select appropriate tools for problem solving and to troubleshoot those tools.[1]

In contrast, information literacy focuses more on information. It describes the ability to "recognize when information is needed and have the ability to locate, evaluate, and use effectively the needed information."[2] Again, our discussion revolves around application; in this case, it's the application of information. Knowing how to critically select technology and information in pursuit of an objective is what makes these fluencies so important in the Information Age.

Interestingly, our notions of literacy (reading and writing) are rooted in the era of the printed word. Printing presses, typewriters, and word processing software are products of a text-focused environment. Not surprisingly, these technologies tend to emphasize a particular type of linear learning. However, "with the Web, we suddenly have a medium that honors multiple forms of intelligence—abstract, textual, visual, musical, social, and kinesthetic."[3] As more and more information is delivered via multimedia, we must adapt our concept of information literacy—or rethink it altogether.

This is not an insignificant observation. Before Gutenberg introduced moveable type to the world, people participated in a largely oral tradition. The spoken word became the primary way of knowing about culture. We learned through narrative, rhetoric, repetition—and other largely subjective experiences. Print-based culture, however, turned those values upside-down. Instead of complex narratives passed down through generations, we privilege scientifically tested facts compiled by strangers. The subjective nature of the oral tradition has been supplanted by the objectivity of the printed word.

In the Information Age, new media is transforming culture once again. Reading is out; watching is in. Our information is increasingly delivered via screens: screens on our devices (laptops, cell phones, refrigerators, etc.), and screens in our physical environment (in airports, at gas stations, on buildings, etc.). This shift may once again return subjective experiences to prominence. To hear Kevin Kelly tell it, "truth is something you assemble yourself on your own screen as you jump from link to link. We are now in the middle of a second Gutenberg shift—from book fluency to screen fluency, from literacy to visuality."[4] This shift is profound for both producers and consumers of information.[5]

It may take some time before screen culture fully replaces book culture, but in the meantime what does information literacy look like in the Information Age? Even though the information environment is increasingly diverse, the basic tenets of information literacy remain the same. First, we must understand the nature of the information needed; second, we must design an appropriate research strategy and begin collecting information; third, we must evaluate the information we find; fourth, we must organize it so that it is useful; finally, we must to apply the information to achieve our defined purpose.[6]

Put more briefly, information literacy is the ability "to know how to navigate through confusing, complex information spaces and feel comfortable doing so."[7] Don't miss this: the Information Age is about more than simply understanding information; it's about understanding how to *navigate* information.

4.3 Knowledge Creation

Collection to production

Knowing where to find information and understanding how to navigate those information environments are definitely important skills in the Information Age. After all, we use websites like the Internet Movie Database, the Internet Archive, and the Weather Network, *because* they provide rich environments of relevant information. But we want to take a step back and examine how knowledge is produced or created in the first place. Unlike data, knowledge isn't automatically generated or compiled. If we remember that knowledge is assimilated information (section 2.2), then we know that simply collecting vast amounts of information will not lead us to knowledge. We must create knowledge out of the information (and data) we accumulate.

But how does that happen? What does the process look like? Who produces knowledge from our databases of information? Who invests the required time and effort to transform information into knowledge? Why? These questions may appear to be too philosophical, but understanding the knowledge production process helps us better understand the overall information environment. Such insights can help us think strategically, improve competitive advantage, or, as we discussed in the previous section, develop our information literacy.

With a cursory glance we might observe that knowledge is produced by society's organizations: governments generate laws, policies and statistics for citizens; educational institutions produce experiments, studies and surveys for other researchers; corporations develop markets, products and wealth for stakeholders; religions contribute liturgy, music, and commentary for parishioners. In each of these examples, the purpose of knowledge production is twofold: to further the mission and objectives of the organization, and to benefit the individuals within (or affected by) the organization.

This seems like a relatively straightforward observation. Authorities and organizations (producers, distributors) invest the time and money to gather information, produce knowledge and deliver it to the people (consumers). If only knowledge production was really that simple. While governments, educational institutions, corporations, religions and other organizations continue to produce and disseminate knowledge, we must acknowledge a significant shift in knowledge production. The distinction between providers and consumers has become blurry.

In the fifteenth century, the printing press fundamentally changed the concept of knowledge production. This new tool meant that knowledge could be more easily produced—and reproduced—in tangible form quite quickly. Even though governments and authorities attempted to control the production of knowledge, ideas proliferated as printed matter became more accessible. Indeed, as use of the printing press spread across Europe, the responsibility for knowledge creation became increasingly diffused.

Fast forward to the twenty-first century. Technology has helped diffuse knowledge production even further. While the printing press made knowledge more readily available through the printed word, new information technologies put the actual tools of production into the hands of the public.[8] Digital cameras, personal computers, video editing software, desktop publishing applications and other information technology make producing knowledge a snap. These tools—once the domain of professionals and authorities—empower the public to create. In fifteenth century terms, we each have our own printing press to produce and reproduce knowledge as we please.

You may argue, however, that individuals have always had the ability to produce knowledge. And you'd be right. The real difference between the fifteenth century and the twenty-first century is that we have also democratized the tools of distribution.[9] For example, we can self-publish a book and distribute it via Lulu.com; we can write a large software application and share it via a BitTorrent stream; or, we can contribute our unique views about the world via a Wordpress blog. The Internet has become the primary tool with which we distribute such content. Indeed, the sheer reach of the Internet greatly expands our ability to communicate ideas with others.

When we have the tools to produce knowledge and the tools to distribute knowledge, our circle of influence expands. We are no longer producers *or* consumers—we are both. In the Information Age, the distinction between contributor and consumer melts away. What does this mean for the future of knowledge? What does this mean for our identity? Is this the logical extension of the printing press era, or are we experiencing a disturbing bout of dissociative disorder? Only time will tell.

4.4 Explicit + Tacit Knowledge

Product + process

As we've seen, looking at knowledge production through a strictly organizational lens is too limiting. After all, it is the intellectual capital (brainpower) of individuals that helps organizations produce knowledge. However, looking at knowledge production through the lens of individuals doesn't work either, since the knowledge production process rarely occurs through a single person.

To understand how individuals contribute to organizational knowledge creation, it might be helpful to start with a distinction between two dimensions of knowledge: explicit knowledge and tacit knowledge. Explicit knowledge describes a more systematic approach to knowledge production. It includes hard data, quantitative methods, codified processes and universal principles. Explicit knowledge can be easily expressed, recorded and evaluated (by similarly explicit means).[10]

In contrast, tacit knowledge often relies on subjective insights, intuition, and qualitative observations. Tacit knowledge is not something that can be easily produced; as a result, it is more accurately described as a way of being. It's built on experience and instinct. Since it is intensely personal, tacit knowledge is also hard to express, making it difficult to communicate to others.[11]

Explicit knowledge focuses on concepts or content (the "know-*whats*") and tacit knowledge manifests itself in actual practice ("know-*how*").[12] Explicit knowledge may be more measurable than tacit knowledge, but that doesn't make it more reliable. And even though tacit knowledge is based on individual intuition, it doesn't necessarily provide more insight than explicit knowledge. The point of this discussion is not to polarize these types of knowledge, but to view them as ends of a spectrum.[13] We want to employ a holistic analysis that incorporates both dimensions of knowledge in the knowledge creation cycle. To focus exclusively on explicit knowledge is to treat organizations (and individuals) simply as machines for processing information. By including tacit knowledge in the discussion the organization becomes a living organism—one that continually renews itself through the process of knowledge creation.[14]

To demonstrate how the interaction between tacit and explicit knowledge contributes to knowledge production for individuals and organizations, Ikujiro Nonaka proposed "the knowledge spiral." In this spiral we can imagine knowledge production happening in four basic ways: tacit to tacit, explicit to explicit, tacit to explicit, and explicit to tacit.[15] These distinctions are important so let's use a small organization—a gritty tattoo parlor—to observe the knowledge spiral in action.

One way that knowledge is produced is through tacit to tacit transfer. This process is known as *socialization*. For example, when the tattoo shop manager hires a new artist, the new artist socializes with the other artists. Together, these artists share general knowledge about the industry, or more specific knowledge about how to operate in that particular parlor. The important point here is that the artists are sharing their unique experiences and expertise within the tattoo industry.

A second example of knowledge production occurs when tacit knowledge is expressed as explicit knowledge. For example, the artists may decide to codify basic procedures for a particularly difficult tattoo technique, moving the knowledge out of the realm of individual expertise and into a more structured form. Such an expression may serve as explicit guidelines for more inexperienced artists. This process is known as *articulation* or *externalization*.

When explicit knowledge is synthesized with other explicit knowledge, the process is known as *combination*. For example, the basic procedures for tattoo techniques might be included with other explicit knowledge in the tattoo shop (e.g. health regulations, sample sketches, or safety manuals). Combining explicit knowledge with other explicit knowledge is the most common method for knowledge production.

Lastly, when explicit knowledge leads to an increase in tacit knowledge the individual experiences *internalization*. This is the "learning by doing" approach to knowledge production. As a new artist internalizes the explicit knowledge of the tattoo parlor, his tacit knowledge of the trade increases. Of course, as tacit knowledge of the trade increases, the tattoo artist then has more personal experience to share, returning to the first step in the knowledge spiral.

The key steps in the knowledge spiral are articulation (tacit to explicit) and internalization (explicit to tacit)—the two areas where knowledge changes dimension. This dynamic interaction between tacit and explicit knowledge is important because it requires the active involvement of the individual. Both articulation and internalization require commitment on personal *and* collective levels.[16]

This book, for example, can teach you *about* information issues by providing you with explicit knowledge in a structured form. But being a participant in the Information Age is more than simply memorizing the contents of this book—you have to experience it (that's why the book also includes experiments, additional reading, and discussion questions). It is through the combination of explicit and tacit knowledge that we come to truly know anything. And now you know.[17]

4.5 Evaluating Information

Context (not content) is king

Understanding knowledge production is great in theory, but in practice things get messy. Based on experience, we know that information can be found in multiple places, in many formats, and in varying levels of detail. Since knowledge is created for a variety of purposes and comes from diverse sources, we need to continually evaluate the quality of the information we encounter. Incomplete, inaccurate or irrelevant information can lead to disastrous results. It seems obvious to state that we need good information to make good decisions, but evaluating information is not always as easy we think.

Some tasks, like writing a research paper in university, call for academic articles published in peer-reviewed journals; other tasks, like locating a product review on the latest netbook, might be solved with a quick visit to a gadget blog like Gizmodo or Engadget. In these examples, the type (and quality) of information required is obvious, but it isn't hard to imagine other scenarios where the lines aren't so clearly drawn. Should students be able to quote from Wikipedia in course assignments? Should investors rely on company websites for information? Should we trust citizen journalism to present objective news stories? Should people form political opinions based on programs like *The Daily Show, The Colbert Report,* or *Saturday Night Live?* These are important questions.

To be sure, each piece of information has its purpose,[18] but information needed for one task may not be needed for another (translation: useful information is not useful in every circumstance). Likewise, information that is relevant to one person may not be relevant to the next. What determines usefulness or relevance? Two things: the quality of information and the context of the inquiry (the information need). These factors help us differentiate good information from bad.[19]

In the Information Age it is often said that *content* is king: websites and organizations that possess the best content will always attract an audience—and bigger audiences are better (section 1.4). But when it comes to evaluating information *context* is king: point of view is essential. Evaluating information may be a predominantly subjective activity, but there are criteria that can help; namely, the intended audience, scope of the work, currency, authority, and objectivity of the author.

When we're evaluating the intended audience we need to ask questions like: Who is the information for? Is the publication aimed at a specialized group or the general public? Is the information presented at an appropriate level? As we would expect, articles published in *PC Magazine* have a different readership than those published in a more technical publication like *Transactions on Neural Networks*.

We should also consider whether the article provides a general overview, or focuses on a specific aspect of the topic. In some instances, the coverage will include extensive background information; at other times, the author will assume the reader knows the background and will present a much narrower scope of information.

The third element we should evaluate is currency. When was the information published? The importance of currency may vary widely depending on the information need. For example, current information is very valuable to business, engineering, and applied science, but it is less important in history or literature.

Another key consideration is the authority of the source. Is the author a known expert in the field? Of course, most of us don't spend a lot of time examining each author's credentials; instead, we tend to rely on authority by association. We look at who published the information. Was it a reputable institution or organization (university press, government agency, advocacy group)? Was the information peer-reviewed? Obviously, accounts of the 9/11 terrorist attacks carry more weight when they are published in the *New York Times,* than when they appear on an anonymous conspiracy theorist website.

Objectivity is the final element for evaluation. Does the information appear to be well researched? Is the text free of emotional words or obvious bias? Sometimes separating fact from opinion from propaganda can be a difficult task—especially, when the information is about a controversial topic. Most of the time we're taught that biased information is bad, yet in its broadest definition bias simply indicates a particular perspective. Since individuals create knowledge, we shouldn't be surprised that knowledge is biased. The trick is to be aware of the bias or perspective of the information in question, evaluate it, and use it accordingly.

The Information Age introduces resources that are even more difficult to evaluate. Wikipedia, the open source encyclopedia that anyone can edit, is a perfect example. It's aimed at a general audience, yet the site includes relatively obscure articles with extensive detail (e.g. *Battlestar Galactica* terminology). Information changes rapidly on the site, which some consider a strength, and others a weakness. Wikipedia strives for a neutral point of view,[20] but controversial articles betray at least some contributors' biases. Anonymous authors make multiple edits and subsequent users must trust that these authors know their stuff. So, is Wikipedia reliable? Like so many issues in the Information Age, the best answer might be: "It depends." It depends on the context of your inquiry—it depends on what you need.

These five elements are not meant to act as a prescriptive list; nor should they be used as an ultimate checklist. It's simply not practical to put every new piece of information through a rigorous test for information quality. Rather, these elements are meant to be guidelines for evaluation. There is only one way to get better at evaluating information: practice, practice, practice. Through practice we internalize the criteria for evaluating information and develop habits for doing this automatically (remember our explicit-tacit knowledge spectrum from last section?). Sometimes experience is the best teacher.

4.6 Experiment

Truth is a moving target

Currently, the English version of the Wikipedia project has over 2.7 million entries. You can find information on nearly every imaginable topic. In fact, the Wikipedia project has become so popular that it is the eighth most-visited site in the United States.[21]

One of the reasons Wikipedia has grown so fast, in such a short time is its innovative application of wiki software. Wikis are collaborative applications that allow web pages to be quickly and easily edited via an Internet browser. Traditional web design requires technical skill, training, and specialized software applications, but for wikis the barrier for participation is much lower. With a rudimentary knowledge of the Internet anyone can participate—and many people do. The goal is less about achieving a perfect visual design and more about building a reliable knowledge base.

Anyone with access to the Internet can hop online and contribute to the world's largest social knowledge project. Of course, Wikipedia's greatest strength is also one of its weaknesses. When everyone approaches the project with noble intentions, the results can be incredible; however, human nature (and history) has shown that at least some people will always have mischievous intentions.

Some acts of vandalism in Wikipedia are juvenile (e.g. a company removing unflattering information about its business, students inserting random expletives, etc.) while other changes are more politically motivated (e.g. Republicans attacking Democrats). The use of wiki software means that such incidents of vandalism can be easily corrected, but every alteration remains a part of Wikipedia's history. Indeed, you can actually track the changes to each article using the "history" tab at the top of each entry.

The task for this experiment is to look at the history of some of the more controversial terms in Wikipedia. Use the worksheet and questions on the following page to reflect on your experience.

Worksheet

Name _____ Date _____

Part A

Select one of the terms below. If you don't like any of the terms that are listed, choose one of your own terms from Wikipedia's list of most vandalized pages (http://en. wikipedia.org/wiki/Wikipedia:Most_vandalized_pages). Once you've selected your term, use the "history" tab to move through the archived versions of your term. Negotiating the Wikipedia history pages can be confusing at first, but you'll get the hang of it.

Terms

Beaver	Chicago	Macintosh	Microsoft
Stingray	YouTube	Uranus	Borat
Toronto	Bitch	Cannibalism	Cheese

Part B

1. Which term did you pick? _____

2. Using the history tab at the top of the page, track your term back to its very first entry. When was the first entry for your term? (*Hint: the history section is listed in reverse chronological order, so choosing the "earliest" link will take you back to the beginning.*)

3. How does it compare to the version that is presently available? What are the differences? What are the similarities? (*Hint: clicking on the "cur" link beside an edit will provide a side-by-side comparison between the historical version and the current version of the article.)

4. Scan through the pages of history (likely, you'll see hundreds even thousands of entries) and try to find at least one act of vandalism related to your term. What was the act of vandalism? How long did it take before the entry was corrected? (*Hint: most of the entries have a brief description of the changes. If you do a page search for the word "vandalism," you might locate a sample faster.)

5. Reflect on your experience—or lack of experience—with Wikipedia. Have you ever edited an entry in Wikipedia? What information did you contribute?

6. Does this experiment make you more or less likely to use Wikipedia in the future? Do you have more or less confidence in the Wikipedia project? Why?

4.7 Reflect

A social experiment

Much has been written in the popular press about the Wikipedia project. Schiff traces the origins of the website and the culture of wikipedians. Read her article and reflect on the questions below:

Schiff, Stacey. "Know it all." *New Yorker* 82, no. 23 (July 31, 2006), http://www.newyorker.com/archive/2006/07/31/060731fa_fact

> ### QUESTIONS
>
> 1. Schiff describes Wikipedia as "an experiment in unfettered democracy," yet it also "embodies our newly casual relationship to truth." What do you think of the Wikipedia project? Is the existence of Wikipedia good, bad (or neutral) for the future of knowledge?
>
> 2. Wikipedia is one of the most popular websites in the world. The range of topics covered by this encyclopedia is truly astonishing. When (if ever) do you consult Wikipedia? Do you think it is an appropriate resource for an academic context? Why or why not?
>
> 3. Schiff highlights that "Wikipedians are officially anonymous, contributing to entries under unsigned screen names." Is anonymity a good or bad thing for Wikipedia? Do you worry about the authority or credibility of the people who are editing the entries? Why or why not?

4.8 Reflect

Textuality to visuality

Kevin Kelly's article examines the impact of technology on human culture through the ages. He suggests that the introduction of printing press transformed our oral tradition into a text-based one. But even more telling is Kelly's suggestion that the era of print is nearing an end as we embrace the world of images. Read his ideas and then respond to the questions below:

Kelly, Kevin. "Becoming Screen Literate." *New York Times Magazine* (November 21, 2008), http://www.nytimes.com/2008/11/23/magazine/23wwln-future-t.html

---

QUESTIONS

1. Kelly claims that our commitment to the print world led us to value precision, linear logic, objectivity, and authority; however, our new commitment to the screen means, "the subjective again trumps the objective." What do you think of this statement? Are images by definition more subjective than the printed word? Should we be concerned by a return to subjectivity?

2. Kelly writes, "an image stored on a memory disc instead of celluloid film has a plasticity that allows it to be manipulated as if the picture were words rather than a photo." Should we trust images (and video), since they can be easily altered? In the age of digital manipulation should we be concerned about the connection between images and truth? Why or why not?

3. "If text literacy meant being able to parse and manipulate texts, then the new screen fluency means being able to parse and manipulate moving images with the same ease." Based on Kelly's bold statement, do you think that people have—or will have—the ability to manipulate (and understand) moving images? Is "screen fluency" a coming reality, or simply an interesting idea? Why?

4.9 Decide

Reputation management

Paul is the Vice President of Marketing at Silver Wing Technologies, a manufacturer of computer accessories and peripherals (printers, specialty cables, speakers, microphones, etc.). Most of these products are sold through established retailers in physical stores, or through retailers' e-commerce operations.

In his role, Paul is responsible for the company's branding. Considering that most of Silver Wing's customers are tech savvy, Paul has focused the company's advertising campaign on Internet branding using banner and text advertisements. This strategy has allowed Silver Wing to raise the profile of its products and exchange information directly with its customers.

Last quarter, customers returned a significant number of the company's products due to various defects. Company officials traced the error back to one of the assembly plants and rectified the issue, but the Silver Wing brand has been damaged. Customer complaints—some might say "horror stories"—are popping up all over the Internet. Just last week, someone edited Silver Wing's Wikipedia entry to include an extensive list of the problems.

Paul is frustrated. He knows that most of the complaints reflect isolated incidents and not the experiences of most Silver Wing customers. But Paul also knows that bad news spreads faster than good news. In his attempt to counter this rather vocal minority and salvage the Silver Wing brand, Paul stumbled upon the website of a local reputation management firm. For a small fee, Hubbub Metrics can monitor and manage all aspects of Silver Wing's online reputation. Given the recent troubles at Silver Wing, Paul is tempted to try the service.

What do you think Paul should do? Four options are presented on the following page.

Name _____ Date _____

In the space provided, discuss the advantages and disadvantages of each option and make a final recommendation.

A) Paul should do nothing. The problem has been fixed, so the controversy will eventually blow over.

B) Paul should contract Hubbub Metrics to monitor and manage Silver Wing's online reputation. The Internet is too important to the future of Silver Wing to leave it up to chance.

C) Paul should use internal resources and in-house staff to actively manage Silver Wing's reputation and aggressively defend the company online.

D) Paul should increase his advertising budget and launch a new campaign to combat the bad publicity.

So, what do you think Paul should do? Why?

_____

_____

_____

_____

_____

_____

The Information Paradigm

5.1 Knowledge Work

Labors of the mind

Maybe you are wondering why we're spending so much time talking about data, information and knowledge. Aren't we essentially saying the same thing with different words? Sure, it's important to understand how information is transferred, or how systems contribute to competitive advantage, or even how knowledge is produced, but haven't we said enough already? Well, yes ... and no.

The reason the discussions and distinctions in these early chapters are important relates to the concept of the knowledge worker.[1] Despite the inherent problems with sweeping terminology like the Information Economy, or the Information Society, the fact remains that an increasing number of jobs focus on working with information.

It can be difficult to specifically characterize knowledge work, but at a basic level it involves acquiring, organizing and analyzing information. These tasks may seem rather ordinary to us, but they signify a fundamental shift in the way we work.[2] To be sure, our economy still includes traditional sectors like mining, manufacturing, and farming, but more and more we contribute labor by applying our minds. In fact, in many developed nations the proportion of knowledge workers has risen to over 30% of the workforce.[3]

Key decision-makers have traditionally wanted unfiltered access to information; however, as information increases (and attention decreases) there is a developing role for information intermediaries. These intermediaries, we might call "knowledge workers," can filter out unnecessary information and provide the decision-makers with information that they can easily focus on.[4]

Interestingly, the primary challenge for knowledge workers relates to the nature of information itself. As Frederick Hayek pointed out:

> The problem of a rational economic order is determined precisely by the fact that the knowledge of the circumstances of which we must make use never exists in concentrated or integrated form, but solely as the dispersed bits of incomplete and frequently contradictory knowledge which all the separate individuals possess.[5]

In other words, knowledge never exists in the form that we need. The "knowledge of circumstances" needed to make decisions is incomplete and comes from multiple perspectives. The task of the knowledge worker is to find patterns among these seemingly random pieces of information. But how do we do this? Making sense of knowledge comes down to three ways of knowing: knowing-what, knowing-how, and knowing-whom.[6]

We discussed knowing-what and knowing-how extensively when we looked at explicit and tacit knowledge (section 4.4), so it is knowing-whom that we want to focus on here. Returning to Hayek's thoughts for a second, we see that no single individual possesses knowledge in its totality. Despite our best efforts, it is difficult to compile all of the knowledge we need in one location. It simply cannot be centralized.

By its very nature, knowledge is possessed by separate individuals (or organizations). It is decentralized. If information is distributed across multiple individuals and organizations, then how do we acquire the knowledge we need to achieve objectives? We do so by bringing these separate parties together in collaboration.

Collaboration is about actively building something together. It means more than simply sharing information; it means sharing purpose. Put simply, collaboration means united labor.[7] For knowledge workers, collaboration occurs in four areas: among individuals, communities, organizations, and within the broader industry.

For example, think of a blog website like TypePad. Making this service available to the public involves collaboration of all four types. Programmers need to collaborate and share knowledge with other programmers. But they also need to collaborate across communities, drawing on expertise from people in business development, marketing, and human-computer interaction. TypePad may work with other firms to develop and host the website, so collaboration also occurs among organizations. Lastly, for TypePad to fully integrate features like embedded video, active polling, or widget integration, collaboration must occur across the industry (or industries).

To conclude, the three ways of knowing (knowing-what, knowing-how, knowing-whom) remind us of the three fundamental considerations for any information system (information, technology, people). Again, we cannot ignore the human factor. The key to knowledge work is building relationships and making connections to other individuals, communities, organizations and industries. Perhaps the Information Age is not so complex after all.

5.2 The Information Revolution

The revolution will not be verified[8]

There are many ways to describe this current period of human history. In economic terms, we're often said to be living in the Digital Economy, the Knowledge Economy, the Internet Economy, the Virtual Economy, or, as we looked at earlier, the Information Economy. If you find these terms too focused on commerce, there are terms like Information Society, Network Society, or the Information Age (the term used in the title of this book), which are a little broader. Each of these descriptions refers to the same set of ideas (with slightly different emphasis); namely, that developments in information and communication technology have changed the way we live—and that those changes are significant enough to redefine our collective identity.

It is definitely hard to understate the impact of technology on our current age. If you listen close enough you will hear people claim that we are living during a revolution. But, you might ask, where are the marching soldiers, powerful leaders, and flashpoints destined to overthrow the established order? You know, like the storming of the Bastille during the French Revolution, or the Boston Tea Party from the American Revolution? Well, this revolution has had no such events—yet. The revolution I'm talking about isn't a political revolution, even though it has already challenged and changed governments around the world. Of course, the revolution I'm referring to is the Information Revolution.

The Information Revolution may not have overthrown a government, but it has certainly changed the social order. In that sense, the Information Revolution is probably more like the Industrial Revolution. The socioeconomic and cultural changes first experienced in Britain in the early nineteenth century are not unlike the changes we're experiencing now. In fact, it might be instructive to compare and contrast the two revolutions by examining their key networks: the railway system and the Internet. Even though there is over a century between these two revolutions, a short history lesson should provide some insight and may even help us understand the present revolution better.

First and foremost, we should acknowledge that the railway system and the Internet each developed in response to society's needs. Railways were improved to transport raw materials (gold in the United States, coal and iron-ore in Europe) and they were also used tactically for war. The Internet improved the transport of information and had its roots in American military technology (section 5.3).[9]

Both technologies created an expansive network. Railways created a complex transportation network that connected places geographically, while the Internet created a complex communication network that connected people (irrespective of geography). In fact, the design of these networks is remarkably similar as both utilize hubs, switches, routers, main lines, branch lines, and other essential features.[10]

Another key factor is that both of these technologies enforced new standards. The development of railways led to the standardization of time. Since trains couldn't easily travel to and from places that operated on different time schedules, countries needed to synchronize their clocks. In comparison, the introduction of the Internet led to standardized protocol. Computers couldn't share information unless they had a shared language and set of rules, so the TCP/IP protocol was adopted (section 5.4).[11]

Most obviously, these technologies increased efficiencies and created new opportunities. The railways meant that people had new territories for habitation and increased mobility. This system also meant that products could be transported further and more quickly. The introduction of the Internet opened up new opportunities for communication and commerce. Electronic commerce, in particular, created one market and one economy.[12]

Today, the Industrial Revolution is usually reserved for the history books, but evidence suggests that the Industrial Revolution changed the social order every bit as fast as the Information Revolution.[13] Our tendency is to evaluate the Information Revolution through the lens of technology (as we've just done), when in fact it may have little to do with technology at all. Peter Drucker, the influential management theorist, suggests that the *next* information revolution (or the next phase of the current Information Revolution) will be more about meaning and concepts. Essentially, the future will be about the "I" in I.T.[14] Technology will continue to advance, and information will continue to accumulate, but our challenge is to find meaning, understand patterns, and anticipate potential changes.

People living during the Industrial Revolution probably knew that times were changing. Examples were everywhere. But did they foresee the full impact that steam power, railways, and eventually the internal combustion engine would have on subsequent generations? Probably not. Like those nineteenth century British citizens, we want to believe that we are living during a turning point in human history. After all, examples are everywhere. But can we foresee the full impact that current technology will have on future generations? Probably not.

5.3 Birth of the Network

Your own personal library

For many people the Internet is a symbol of the Information Revolution (and it's the one we used in the previous section). Indeed, it is hard to find a corner of the world that has not been impacted by the development of this global network. It has become the primary medium through which we understand our world, fundamentally altering the way we interact with friends, conduct business and engage with government. But where did this network come from? How did it come to be the way it is today?

A quick search online will retrieve many websites that detail the history of the Internet. Certainly, these timelines are important, but we want to step back a little and approach the story of the Internet from a people perspective. While this isn't a history book, it is important to have some background for one the most transformative technologies of the Information Age.

The public first learned of the Internet in the mid-1990s, but its roots go much deeper than that. In fact, many historians suggest that the key elements of the modern Internet can be found in an article published way back in 1945 called "As We May Think." In this article, Vannevar Bush, an American engineer and computing pioneer, dared to imagine what the future might look like. At the time, many of America's brightest minds were directed at the war effort, but as World War II drew to a close, Bush wondered: "What are the scientists to do next?"[15]

Bush felt that the country's leading researchers should turn to the problem of information. They should attempt to help make the huge store of human knowledge more accessible. Bush focuses mostly on the technology of the day, but he concludes his article by introducing an intriguing concept: the memex.[16] For him, the memex was a "device in which an individual stores all his books, records, and communications, and which is mechanized so that it may be consulted with exceeding speed and flexibility."[17] In other words, the memex posed as a repository for key pieces of information, but it was also organized and "mechanized" in such a way that it could retrieve the information easily. The memex was like having your own personal library at your fingertips.

For Bush the future also meant that information would be easily connected and associated: "Wholly new forms of encyclopedias will appear, ready made with a mesh of associative trails running through them, ready to be dropped into the memex and there amplified."[18] With the benefit of hindsight, these ideas do seem to describe many information systems in use today—in particular, the Internet. Bush was painting a picture of our potential information future, but since he was writing over 60 years ago, he was a little sketchy on the details.

A couple of decades later, a man named Ted Nelson attempted to put Bush's idea of the memex into practice. Working on the belief that every document was a footnote to another document, Nelson developed hypertext, a protocol that enabled users to jump from one document to another.[19] At the time, Nelson's work was relatively unknown, but hypertext altered the way we relate to information. Now we easily jump from website-to-website, or link-to-link, without a second thought, In fact, hypertext remains one of the underlying paradigms of the Internet (it's the "h" in http).

The memex and hypertext are intriguing ideas, but they don't tell the whole story of the Internet. For another perspective, we need to turn to the political climate of the post World War II era and the rising tension between the Soviet Union (USSR) and the United States.

On October 4, 1957, the USSR became the first nation to launch a man-made satellite into space (Sputnik). This single act caused a lot of consternation for the American public. Some wondered how a communist country could have more advanced science and technology, while others worried about their national security.[20] In response, the United States formed the Advanced Research Projects Agency (ARPA) within the Department of Defense to reestablish America's prominence in the fields of science and technology.

In 1969, ARPA was commissioned to do research into networking. The intent was to create a robust communications network so ARPA-sponsored researchers could collaborate and share resources more efficiently.[21] After a slow start, academic researchers and government scientists eventually developed a reliable network called ARPANET. This research network used packet switching, employed a decentralized design, and developed a web-like structure—innovations that can still be found at the heart of today's Internet (section 5.4).

It is often claimed that ARPANET was designed to withstand a nuclear attack from the Soviet Union, but this was simply not the case. ARPANET was an open project, not a military secret. That being said, ARPANET was used as a test case for networking. Once the technology was mature, the Department of Defense went on to build similar networks for military purposes.[22]

The technology continued to mature in the 1970s and 1980s as other research organizations began experimenting with networks. In 1984, the National Science Foundation (NSF) built a high-speed network to connect its research centers. Shortly after NSF and ARPA discussed merging the two networks, agreeing to replace the aging infrastructure of ARPANET with the much faster NSFNET. Just like ARPA, however, the NSF was primarily interested in the using the network for research. Universities, research laboratories, and government agencies were allowed to connect to the NSFNET backbone, but not private interests or commercial interests.[23]

Of course, such restrictions were hard to enforce and didn't last for long. In the early 1990s, the National Science Foundation lifted the restrictions on commerce and transferred responsibility for the Internet to the private sector—effectively, ending government ownership and direct regulation of the Internet.

Since the network was built on open standards, its primary users were also contributors to its development. For example, in 1991 Tim Berners-Lee was frustrated with the text only nature of the network, so he developed the World Wide Web. This platform provided more tools for organizing and presenting information, improved access to multimedia data, and linked content sites around the globe.

Shortly after, a team in the National Center for Supercomputing Applications (NCSA) began developing an improved web browser. The browser further enhanced the user experience and quickly became the standard for navigating the World Wide Web.[24] Eventually, the team left NCSA to create a commercial browser known as Netscape—the browser through which most of the public first experienced the Internet.

When the National Science Foundation stepped back from the Internet fully in 1995, a number of Internet companies were poised to take advantage of the new frontier. Netscape in particular did exceptionally well in their initial public offering (IPO) with stock peaking at $75 dollars on its first day of trading. This seems insignificant to us today, but many people point to this moment as *the* moment when people suddenly noticed the Internet.[25] And the rest, as they say, is history.

5.4 How the Internet Works

Communication to participation

Today, we regularly use the Internet for commerce and communication, but the Internet was not initially conceived for either. As we just discussed, it was intended to be a research network, empowering scientists in different locations to collaborate and share access to expensive resources (i.e. computers and processing power). As such, the Internet pioneers made careful design considerations to achieve their objectives.

One of their first decisions was to develop a decentralized network. This meant that there was no central control or command center. Responsibility for controlling network traffic would be distributed across the entire network. This design reduced bottlenecks (delays due to the large volume of information) and ensured that each node (point on the network) had multiple connections. This design redundancy ensured that nodes would still be connected to the broader network, even if one of the connections experienced technical difficulty.[26]

To improve the efficiency of the network even further, information was transferred according to a method called packet switching. This approach breaks information into smaller pieces (called packets) and ships them along different communication paths to their destination. Since each packet was small the network could more easily route pieces to under-utilized portions of the network—and thus speed delivery. Remember that the Internet has roots in the United States military, so it was important to develop a reliable network that could deliver messages even if a portion of the system went down.

Packet switching greatly improved the efficiency of transmission, but for computers to share packets they needed protocol—a shared set of rules and procedures. The Transmission Control Protocol/Internet Protocol (TCP/IP) provided instructions to computers for transmitting and transferring information, and is still in use today. The TCP portion of the protocol manages the disassembling and reassembling of packets, while the IP portion of the protocol establishes the connection between computers. The advantage of a shared protocol (or language) means that different types of hardware and software can interact with each other.

For TCP/IP to be effective, the protocol needs to know the *location* of the computers on the network that are exchanging messages. On the Internet, each computer is given an Internet Protocol address, which is written as a series of four numbers separated by dots. For example, "69.63.176.11" is the IP address for Facebook. (Go ahead, type those numbers into the address bar of your favorite browser and see what happens). Computers handle IP addresses quite easily, but this numerical system doesn't work so well for humans. Since we aren't particularly good at remembering numbers, the Domain Name System (DNS) was invented to make browsing easier.[27] Basically, the DNS system matches IP addresses to their more familiar text equivalents. This means we can type www.facebook.com or another familiar text address (also known as a Uniform Resource Locator (URL)) into our browser instead of having to remember its numerical address.

Packet switching, protocol, and location information are essential to the functionality of the Internet, but so is the physical infrastructure over which the information travels. As information traverses the planet, it travels over a pastiche of fiber optic conduits, telephone lines, coaxial cable, and Ethernet connections.

In fact, the Internet infrastructure functions much like the transportation infrastructure, except it is information—not cars and trucks—that travels from place to place. Just like the transportation network consists of interconnected highways, roads, and neighborhood streets, the Internet features main trunk lines, branch lines and tertiary lines. Each of these communication channels has specific capacity to carry information (known as the bandwidth). When the information in transit exceeds this capacity, the traffic slows down (just like commuting during rush hour). To help mitigate bottlenecks the transportation infrastructure uses signals and signs to control traffic. Similarly, hubs, switches and routers manage the flow of online information, directing information from one computer to the next using the most efficient means possible.

Even though the Internet was initially designed to address the unique circumstances of a relatively small number of government researchers, it's obvious that some of their early design decisions led to the maturation of today's Internet. Without their commitment to an open, decentralized network, or their development of packet switching, protocol, and the domain name system, the Internet would not be the powerful network it is today.

5.5 The Internet is Broken

Creativity thrives, but so does crime[28]

We've just seen that the Internet was designed to facilitate communication between government agencies and researchers. As such, the early designers made a couple of key assumptions. First, they assumed that everyone on the network could be trusted. They believed each individual who contributed to the network understood its importance and worked to preserve it. Secondly, the designers assumed that each node (computer, router) on the network was a fixed object in a specific physical location. These assumptions made sense in the early stages when a handful of people shared information via large mainframe computers, but they don't work so well now.[29] Today, over a billion people are online and many of us access the Internet via wireless signals and mobile devices.

Not surprisingly, one of the main concerns with the current state of the Internet is security. Because security was not viewed as a necessity in the early stages, it was not built into the original design. Current strategies for protection like firewalls, virus protection, and authentication measures are all "add-ons." Unfortunately, this patchwork of security solutions is far from comprehensive, leaving numerous vulnerabilities. Indeed, the proliferation of spam, viruses, worms, botnets, and other malware puts the entire network at risk (more on that in Chapter 9). And that risk is real—as John Zittrain states, "Take any of the top ten viruses and add a bit of poison to them, and most of the world wakes up Tuesday morning unable to surf the Net—or finding much less there if it can."[30] The promise of living in a globally connected world is great, but so is the peril.[31]

In section 5.4, we implied that Internet's decentralized design led to its widespread acceptance, but this global network is not as decentralized as we first thought. After all, someone (or some organization) needs to oversee the Domain Name System; someone needs to carefully allocate the IP addresses to avoid duplication; someone needs to maintain the root servers that match domain names to IP addresses; and someone needs to shepherd the technical standards which ensure the interoperability of the network.[32] As the Internet entrenches itself into modern life, the "who" behind each of these responsibilities becomes even more important.

Some nations believe the current system of Internet governance is problematic because it favors American interests[33] (which is partially excusable considering American researchers played a primary role in its development). However, even though nations want more control over the Internet, their ability to wield power may be largely illusory. The Internet ignores borders and territories. Laws and regulations, which are enforceable inside national boundaries, don't translate to the border-less Internet frontier.

Others warn that the rise of private interests and the broader commercialization of the Internet pose a greater threat than government control. Even though commerce is a relatively new arrival to the Internet, many fear that corporate interests will dominate the infrastructure and potentially restrict free speech.[34] By some estimates we're already there. Such an observation should give us pause—even the early pioneers, saw the Internet "as an open commons, not to be undone by greed or commercialization."[35]

Big Crime, Big Politics, and Big Business are important considerations for the future of the Internet, but they're certainly not the only ones. Privacy issues (surveillance and anonymity), access issues (censorship and the digital divide), intellectual property issues (file-sharing and copyright), and other considerations also need to be addressed. But how might we do this? Should we rebuild the Internet from scratch based on what we know now? Should we hand over regulatory responsibilities to a single international governing body? Should we carve up the Internet and allow individual governments to police their own nations? Should we abandon regulation altogether? Should we trust private interests and free market capitalism to bring us the Internet we want?

Posing these questions is much easier than answering them. And if you think about it, doesn't whole-scale tampering with the Internet clash with the original collaborative ethos of the Internet's design? We would do well to remember that "the hardest thing to grasp about the Internet ... is this: It isn't a thing; it isn't an entity; it isn't an organization. No one owns it, no one runs it."[36] Traveling on a ship without a captain can be fun, but it can also be dangerous.

In the early days of the Internet it was easy to bring key decision makers to the table on matters of technology or standards. Now, of course, there aren't enough seats at the table for every interested party. Keeping the Internet on track will involve everyone: governments, international organizations, concerned societies, businesses, and people like you and me. How will we collectively shape the future of this global network? With the Internet of course.[37] Yes, you read that right: we'll use the Internet to solve the Internet—now there's a solution for the Information Age.

5.6 Experiment

Clients + servers

On the Internet there are two basic types of machines: servers and clients. Clients request information from other machines (usually servers) and servers provide requested services. For example, when you access your email your computer (client machine) requests information that is stored on the server. The server finds the pages you've requested and serves, or delivers, them to you.

Of course, for clients and servers to share information they must have Internet Protocol (IP) addresses (section 5.4). For servers, IP addresses are static—or at least stable. If you think about it that's a good thing. We wouldn't want our email provider to jump around the Internet, changing IP addresses each day. Having consistent, dedicated online addresses for servers are a key component of the information infrastructure.

In contrast, many client machines rely on dynamic IP addresses. This means that each time the user goes online their computer may be assigned a different address. Since client machines are not usually destinations for information, having a dedicated address is less important. As long as the IP address stays consistent for the session (as long as you're online) information can be exchanged.

The global IP address system is managed by the Internet Assigned Numbers Authority (IANA) and is the ultimate responsibility of the Internet Corporation for Assigned Names and Numbers (ICANN). This system ensures that numbers and domain names are unique and helps resolve any disputes between registrants.

Most of the information related to IP registration is publicly available, so for this experiment we're going to see what we can dig up. We'll start by identifying the IP address for your session and end by look at the people behind some specific websites. Use the worksheet provided on the following page.

Worksheet

Name _____ Date _____

Part A

Go to http://www.whois.net/. This "who is" service is one of many websites that offer domain name and IP address information. For future reference: typing "who is" into your favorite search engine, will retrieve a handful of similar websites.

1. Under the "Domain Tools" heading below the search boxes on http://www.whois.net/ find "Your IP address" and click on the link. The number that you see is your IP address for the current session. What is it?

2. Return to the Domain Tools section on http://www.whois.net/ and find the "Whois By IP Address" link. Type in the IP address for your session (the one that you just found in question 1). The website should generate some information about the institution or organization providing your Internet service. List the NameServers associated with your IP address.

Part B

Whois.net sells domain name services, so you may have to scroll down below the "available domain names" feature to see your search results to answer the questions below.

1. Domain name services can be used to identify the people and organizations behind specific websites. In a separate browser window, find the government website of the town or city in which you were born. Using the "WHOIS Lookup" feature on http://www.whois.net/, see what information you can find about that city's website. Who registered the domain (the registrar)? Who is the domain registered to (registrant)? Are they the same organization?

2. Experiment with the "WHOIS Lookup" feature. Search for domain name information on three websites that you visit often. Are you surprised by the information that you can find?

3. Just for fun, go to the Random website generator (http://www.randomwebsite.com). Click on the "random link" button until you find an interesting website. Using the web address (URL) of this random website, return to http://www.whois.net/ and see what information you can find? What website did you choose? Did the IP information provide any new, or interesting, information?

5.7 Reflect

Cyberspace + independence

In the early days of the Internet, John Perry Barlow (of Grateful Dead fame) drafted a radical document about the independent nature of Cyberspace. The article tackles the role of government on the Internet—as in, the government has no role. Read his thoughts from the mid-1990s and respond to the questions below:

Barlow, John Perry. "A Declaration of the Independence of Cyberspace." (February 8, 1996), http://homes.eff.org/~barlow/Declaration-Final.html

> **QUESTIONS**
>
> 1. Barlow argues that governments, which have dominion over the physical world, should not have any control over virtual spaces. What do you think of this claim? Is there a role for governments on the Internet? Is government regulation inevitable? What should the role of government be online?
>
> 2. Barlow says that governments "do not know our culture, our ethics, or the unwritten codes that already provide our society more order." What do you think of this statement? Are governments hopelessly behind in the Information Age? Do they lack the ability to understand the force of the Internet? Why or why not?
>
> 3. "We are creating a world where anyone, anywhere, may express his or her beliefs, no matter how singular, without fear of being coerced into silence or conformity." Such was the great promise of the Internet (e.g. the democratization of knowledge), but has such a claim become a reality? Is free speech really as free as we'd like to believe? Do you think people can use the Internet to express their beliefs without fear of retribution? Why or why not?

5.8 Reflect

More than a revolution

Peter Drucker tackles the Information Revolution and compares it to the Industrial Revolution. For him, the development of e-commerce and the explosion of the Internet as the major network for the distribution of goods and services are essential parts of the Information Revolution. Read his discussion and respond to the questions below:

Drucker, Peter F. "Beyond the Information Revolution." *The Atlantic.* (October 1999), http://www.theatlantic.com/doc/199910/information-revolution

---

QUESTIONS

1. What do you think of this comparison between the Information Revolution and the Industrial Revolution? Drucker suggests that due to the Internet and e-commerce "every business must become globally competitive, even if it manufactures or sells only within a local or regional market." Do you agree with this statement? Why or why not?

2. Toward the end of his article, Drucker claims that "the key to maintaining leadership in this economy and the technology that are about to emerge is likely to be the social position of knowledge professionals and the social acceptance of their values." What do you think of his statement? Has our culture embraced the "knowledge profession?" Why or why not?

3. Drucker suggests that e-commerce opens new distribution channels, and he argues that these distribution channels "change not only how customers buy, but what they buy." Do you agree? Has buying things online changed your buying habits? Are we likely to see more of that in the future? Why or why not?

5.9 Decide

Taxing work

Rosa is a part-time elementary school teacher. When she's not teaching, she can be found on the Internet with her second love: online shopping. Since money is tight, Rosa spends most of her time looking for bargains, regularly frequenting online auction sites like eBay and Bidz. Over the years she has learned to be disciplined, refusing to pay more than an item is worth.

Rosa's extensive experience has turned her into an auction veteran. In fact, she has such a knack for recognizing deals that she decided to become an online retailer herself. She started by selling stuff she didn't need, then she moved on to selling items on behalf of her friends. Now Rosa makes regular trips to yard sales and second hand stores to find items that might turn a profit on eBay. For example, just last week she found a pair of vintage jeans at a local consignment store for $8 and managed to sell them on eBay for $125.

Currently, the laws for personal e-commerce are muddy. Technically, each person should report their income from online auctions under the "other income" category on their income taxes, but most people don't bother—or don't remember. For years the government has paid little attention to online auction websites. These sites are particularly hard to regulate and most people do not enjoy huge capital gains from selling items online.

As online auctions and personal retailing becomes a bigger business online, the government is starting to pressure sites like eBay, Zazzle, CafePress, and Etsy to reveal the identities of their power sellers for income tax purposes. It is only a matter of time before the government closes the loophole.

Last year, Rosa did not sell enough items to become a power seller, but she's not an occasional user either. In fact, when she looked at her records from the last 12 months she was amazed to find that she had made almost $7,000 dollars.

Next month Rosa has to file her income tax return and Rosa isn't sure what to report. The extra cash has nicely supplemented her teaching salary, but it hasn't made her wealthy.

What do you think Rosa should do? Four options are presented on the following page.

Name _____ Date _____

In the space provided, discuss the advantages and disadvantages of each option, and make a final recommendation.

A) She should declare all of the earnings from her online retailing activities, and include her account statements from eBay.

B) She should only report about half of the amount ($3,500) on her income tax return.

C) She shouldn't report her income at all. The laws aren't clear, so why help the government out?

D) She should declare her earnings but not specify how she obtained the additional money.

So, what do you think Rosa should do? Why?

_____

_____

_____

_____

_____

_____

_____

Chapter

Findability

6.1 Organizing Information

Lumping + splitting

If information is everywhere in this age, then how come it can be so hard to find? Even knowledge workers with expertise in information retrieval and research have trouble finding what they need. Some estimates suggest, "knowledge workers spend at least 20% of their time each day searching, and the majority of those searches fail or do not provide complete results. That costs companies thousands of dollars per worker and, more significantly, delays the completion of work."[1] Obviously, these failed searches lead to lost productivity for organizations and for individuals. We may have access to more information than ever before, but searching for the specific piece we need, can be like looking for that proverbial needle in a haystack.

All is not lost, however. In our attempt to make large bodies of information usable, we have invented various strategies for organizing information. Some approaches to organization are quite simple. For example, we use lists to help us keep track of important items. Your "to do" list, your grocery list, your playlist of favorite songs, even David Letterman's famous Top Ten Lists are collections of related information. They are important for what they include and for what they leave out.

Lists work well for relatively simple organizational tasks, but for more diverse collections of information we need more complex solutions. Take this book, for example. The content covered between these covers is related to the Information Age, but this book wouldn't read too well if it was structured as a list—the material would still be included, but it would be missing context and meaningful connections. Instead, this book is organized into chapters as main headings, and within each chapter the content is broken down into subsections. If we want to go even further, each subsection is broken down into individual paragraphs, with each paragraph contributing a unique perspective on the issues of the Information Age (at least that's the intent).

This type of organization is more accurately described as a hierarchy. Hierarchies generally utilize parent-child relationships to structure information. Just like in a biological parent-child relationship, the "child" part represents a component of the "parent." For instance, Chapter 5 was called "The Information Paradigm" which is a broader term (parent) than the subsection called "Birth of the Network" (child). Of course, parent-child relationships depend on where you are in the hierarchy. When comparing "The Information Paradigm" to the entire book, *Exploring the Edges of the Information Age,* the chapter becomes the "child" not the "parent."

Hierarchies—or, more accurately, nested hierarchies—should be quite familiar to us. After all, the directory structure on your computer works this way too. When you put files in folders, and folders in other folders, you're setting up a hierarchy (even if you don't call it that). In each of these examples, however, the hierarchy primarily serves the individual user. The particular parent-child relationships with which you have chosen to organize your computer make sense to you. Similarly, the way that I've chosen to organize this book makes sense to me. Most of the content in this book is not original. I'm building on ideas that I've heard filtered through other people. What is original, however, is how I've chosen to order the information. In part, the hierarchies and organizational structure that I've chosen mark my unique contribution.

Of course, there are times when we need to organize information beyond any single individual. If we are going to understand our world, then we need to develop systems and structures of information that we can share. In computer science and information science, this type of organization is called an ontology. An ontology is "a rigorous and exhaustive organization of some knowledge domain that is usually hierarchical and contains all the relevant entities and their relations."[2] Here are just a few examples of ontology:

- Biologists use the Linnaean classification system to identify plants and animals. Each living thing is classified according to a basic nested hierarchy (domain, kingdom, phylum, class, order, family, genus, species).[3]

- Librarians use the Dewey Decimal System to organize knowledge. Each published resource belongs to a major class (e.g. Philosophy), a division (e.g. Ethics), a section (e.g. Ethics of consumption)—and some sections are divided even further.[4]

- Politicians and business professionals rely on the North American Industry Classification System (NAICS) to organize industries. Each company belongs to a major industry category (e.g. Information and Cultural Industries), a sub-category (Publishing Industries), and a further subdivision (e.g. Book publishers).[5]

Ontologies like the previous three are sometimes described as taxonomies because they group—or classify—content based on similar attributes.[6] Ultimately, that's the key to categorization. Whether we're organizing living things, industries, information, or anything for that matter, we're looking for similarities.

In fact, the process of categorization can be ultimately reduced to two concepts: lumping and splitting. Lumping is the term used when we group information together based on similar attributes. For example, when the average person uses the term "computer," they are referring to a particular category of machine (one for information processing). The term itself lumps together parts of the machine (the Central Processing Unit, operating system, keyboard, etc.) and different types of machines (servers, laptops, desktops, etc.).[7]

The problem with lumping is that the lumps of information can grow too large, or become too diverse. For a computer technician, using the term "computer" as we've just described is much too general. A technician would need to parse our definition further and reorganize the concepts. In other words, he would need to split the information into finer categories. Splitting, therefore, describes the process of separating the information and recombining it according to a more specific set of criteria. Splitters tend to see differences before they similarities.[8]

At first glance, the mechanics of organizing information seem mundane. Lumping and splitting information, classifying living things, or categorizing industries sound more like elaborate methods of filing—glorified strategies for reducing chaos—than essential components of the information environment. However, taxonomies like these underpin everything we know about the natural order of the world.[9] Without these systems in place, the meaning of information shrinks into obscurity. In fact, the manner in which we organize information can tell us more about our broader information environment (and inherent biases). Think about the choices you make when you classify things in your life (tasks, emails, music, friends, etc.). What do your choices say about you? What are your preferences? Are you a lumper or a splitter?

6.2 Browse + Search
Information wants to be found[10]

Hierarchies, taxonomies, and ontologies are great in theory, but how do these ideas inform our practice? The previous section presented a fairly high-level view of organizing information. Now we want to turn to the technology that we use to help us handle all of that information. In particular, we want to focus on directories, search engines and databases. Each of these tools uses different strategies of organization to facilitate better searching and information retrieval.

A directory is a relatively common tool for organizing information. The information is collected, grouped, and presented according to a particular convention, making browsing easier. The phone book provides the most obvious example of a directory. Each telephone directory contains various pieces of information (names, addresses, phone numbers, businesses, government listings, maps, etc.). This information is easy to use because it is organized consistently: people are grouped by city and listed alphabetically, and businesses are grouped by service and organized alphabetically. In fact, even if you weren't familiar with a phonebook at all, it wouldn't take you long to figure out its organizational structure.

When information is collected for directories, it's collected and presented consistently. In a phonebook each resident has her name, address and phone number included. Usually, the content of a directory is selected, edited and organized by humans. This may seem like a trivial matter, but even the slightest human involvement suggests that conscious choices have been made regarding the quality of information. Most often the information is structured using a hierarchy (section 6.1), which facilitates quick browsing. When users know what they're looking for, a directory provides an expedient path. When users would prefer to explore categories, a directory provides a defined structure of broad and narrow topics to browse.

Directories aren't limited to the telephone books or to the print world. In fact, there are many examples of online directories: Yahoo's home page includes browse-able categories of content (entertainment, sports, shopping, etc.); the Librarian's Index to the Internet evaluates useful websites for public libraries; the Open Directory project is building a human-reviewed directory of the Internet; and Business.com provides a portal to business and management information.

If directories are designed for browsing, then search engines are optimized for searching (obviously). Search engines consist of long lists of information that have been collected and arranged in a large database (more on databases in a second). Since this content is generally selected by computer applications (section 6.3), search engines are largely indiscriminate when they collect information. They compile what they can find from multiple sources and make little attempt to evaluate the quality of what they find. In comparison to directories, search engines usually provide a much larger "universe" of information to search and they are capable of more in-depth searching.

Examples of search engines can be found all over the Internet: some are household names (Google, Yahoo!, MSN, Ask); others combine results from multiple search engines (SurfWax, Dogpile); others search for specific content (Blinkx, IceRocket); and still others attempt to visually cluster similar pages (Kart00, Clusty, Cuil). Since the information collected by search engines isn't filtered in advance, or organized like a directory, then the key to success for a search engine is to retrieve *relevant* information from its vast storehouses quickly and efficiently.

But we can go deeper. Behind most directories and search engines sits a database. A database is a collection of data that has been organized to facilitate collecting, searching, and retrieving information. This definition doesn't sound like much, but databases are the dominant method by which we organize information in the Information Age. In fact, databases are tools built specifically for digital information. While it is beyond the scope of this book to cover every aspect of database mechanics, it can't hurt to peek under the hood.

The major advantage of a database is how it connects pieces of information. The power of a database is not in the amount of data, but in the relationships of that data. Take the Internet Movie Database (IMDb) for example. Currently, the IMDb includes information on over 430,000 theatrical releases, over 1,000,000 actors, and almost 600,000 actresses—not to mention the information on made for TV movies, TV series, directors, cinematographers, and costume designers.[11] The collection of information is truly astonishing, but it would be unusable if it weren't for the database behind the IMDb.

To understand how databases work we need to remember three basic concepts: entities, attributes and records. While each database will differ in its overall organization, these three elements help classify the information that is being collected. An entity is something that you collect data about. If this were an English grammar class, an entity would be a noun. It would be a person, place, or thing. The IMDb, for example, collects information about movies, actors, awards, and directors—nearly anyone and everything connected with the production of a movie.

An attribute is an individual piece of information about an entity. To return to our English class, an attribute is an adjective; it describes a particular characteristic of the thing we're collecting data about. For example, when the IMDb is collecting information about actors (entity) they collect the actor's name, birth date, biographical details, which movies he acted in, and his character name in those movies. All of these characteristics would be considered important attributes.

The last important element for database design is a record. A record is a collection of related attributes. For you grammarians, a record would be like a proper noun. All of the attributes combine to describe a single item in the database. For example, looking at the IMDb page for *Sneakers* (a classic hacker film, and the source of the epigraph to this book) we would see a lot of attributes. We would see that Robert Redford and Ben Kingsley star in the film. We would see that it was directed by Phil Alden Robinson and released in theaters in September of 1992 by Universal Studios. All of these attributes combine to uniquely describe one movie—or one record—in the Internet Movie Database.

By separating entities, attributes and records, databases can more easily connect discrete pieces of information and reduce the duplication of data. The particular methods by which these pieces of data relate together is mostly beyond the scope of this discussion. Suffice it to say, that the structure of these relationships allows us to jump from the IMDb page for *Sneakers,* to Robert Redford's page, to the awards he has won. A properly designed database can effectively accommodate new information and integrated it with existing information.

6.3 How Search Engines Work

The quest for relevancy

In the Information Age the search engine is our dominant tool for finding information. Whenever we need an answer we look for the nearest search box and try typing in some words. Search engines have become such an essential part of the Internet ecosystem that we tend to take them for granted. In this section we want to take a closer look at how search engines actually work.

Search engines have three basic tasks. First, they search the information universe—which, in most cases, refers to websites on the World Wide Web. Search engines may be directed to troll the entire Internet, or to focus on a subset of the Internet based on predetermined criteria (topic area, media format, etc.). Second, search engines keep an index (think: list) of the words that they find and where they find them online. This index is constantly changing and shifting because the information on the Internet is constantly in flux. Lastly, search engines permit users to search the index. When the user finds an interesting result, the search engine directs the user to the information via an available link.[12]

These three tasks seem rather elementary, but did you catch the subtlety? When you're using your favorite search engine, you're not searching the entire Internet; you're searching that particular search engine's index of the known information universe. It's a small but important distinction. Since every search engine accomplishes these tasks differently, the results that you will find with one search engine will differ from those found in another. Simply put, their information universes are not the same. That is why it's a good idea to use multiple search engines when you're using the Web for serious research.

Search engines build their indexes with robots, which are sometimes called spiders (it was only a matter of time before the World Wide Web had spiders). These robots are actually software programs that crawl the Internet and report back on what they find. For each page that they land on, they send important content and location information back to be compiled in the search engine's index. Spiders surf from page to page, just like we do: they follow the embedded links in each page. Of course, as automated programs, they're able to do it much faster. Since the Internet changes so rapidly, spiders work continuously to add new pages to the index and to update pages that already exist in the index—a spider's work is never done.

Listing all of the available information is only the beginning. The real work of the search engine is trying to solve questions or information needs. Even though we don't phrase most of our searches as questions, the search engine interprets the words that we type into the search box as a request for information. To use appropriate parlance, these search words are called a query. Search engines are mechanized to solve user queries through a series of mathematical rules, called algorithms.

The specific algorithm behind each search engine is a closely guarded secret. After all, better algorithms produce better results, and better results leads to more users (and, more users means more profit). Essentially, these algorithmic equations form the basis for each search engine's competitive advantage. While it difficult to know precisely which elements are factored into a search engine's algorithm, we can make some educated guesses. As spiders leap from page to page, they examine the page address or URL, incoming links, outgoing links, page title, headings, keywords on each page, even the user's IP address. Since spiders are engineered to read the code behind each web page, they can also uncover key pieces of information in the page code. This category of information is not visible on the page itself and is usually referred to as metadata. Each of these factors (and many others) combine to determine which web pages rise to the surface, and which are buried deeper in the pile for each user's query.

At the risk of oversimplifying, we might look at the rise of Google as an indicator of the importance of developing a good algorithm. Before Google, the search industry was dominated by companies like Yahoo!, Lycos, and AltaVista. But in 1995, two computer science students at Stanford University, Larry Page and Sergey Brin, developed a new approach for ranking results. By 1998, the pair had refined their unique algorithm (called PageRank) and had a working prototype named Google. Their innovative search technology worked so well, that Google quickly stole market share from the established players.[13] Now, just over a decade later, estimates indicate that Google handles over 75% of global Internet searches.[14]

What was their innovation? Interestingly, their unique insight came from the world of academic research—not a particular area of research, but the process of research itself. They understood that new knowledge builds on previous knowledge (remember section 2.4?). Authors who write in scientific and technical journals tend to build on work that has been published by other authors and researchers. When an author chooses to reference the work of someone else, the author sends two messages: first, the author validates the previous studies; second, the author situates her current research in the field. In fact, by examining the references in a given body of literature you can quickly determine who the most influential thinkers are in the field. This process is sometimes known as bibliometrics or citation analysis.[15]

In other words, Brin and Page recognized that a research paper's reference list forms an important network of influence. And this network mirrors the basic structure of the World Wide Web. If you're paying attention at home, you'll note that this sounds a lot like Ted Nelson's idea that every document should be a footnote to another document (section 5.3). Google's innovation, then, was to translate the connections between academic researchers to the world of the broader Internet. They tweaked their algorithm to emphasize the connections between pages. When a reputable content provider (e.g. *The New York Times*) links to external content, it lends some credibility to those outside pages. As a result, Google tends to ascribe a higher measure of relevance to those pages when users search for them. By considering the links to and from pages, Google's algorithms produced better results.

Obviously, providing relevant results is an important function for any search engine; however, relevancy is about more than simply satisfying user needs. Relevancy is also a big business. Studies show that almost 90% of searchers will click on a result within the first three pages of results. If we don't find what we need within those three pages, we refine our search by adding more keywords, or by switching search engines.[16] Why does this happen? Without putting too fine a point on it, it comes down to user behavior—we are lazy. Even though search engines present thousands of hits nearly every time we search, most of those pages are invisible because we don't go beyond the first few pages of results.

To cope with our information overload, we offload responsibility for sifting and sorting information to our technology. We assume that the search engine has done the hard work for us. This fact alone has led to an entire cottage industry called Search Engine Optimization (SEO), where organizations hone their websites so that their placement in popular search engines becomes more prominent.[17] Clearly, being ranked on the first page results, as opposed to the fifth page, can mean the difference between fame and obscurity. The quest for relevancy—as defined by the search giants—cannot be understated.

6.4 Information retrieval

Lost + found

As we saw in section 6.3, search engines do not index the entire Internet. In fact, there is a very large portion of the web that search engines cannot access at all. The websites and web pages that cannot be found via general search engines are part of the invisible (or deep) web. If you think Google will find everything that's available online, you're wrong.

What type of information is considered part of the deep web? For one, search engines do not generally record dynamic content. For example, if you search for "pink haired troll dolls" on eBay, the auction site will generate a unique page based on what's available for sale at that particular moment. The results are served up dynamically—they don't exist until you type your query. Since the results page is important to a small audience (i.e. you), and performing another query can easily duplicate the results, search engines tend not to bother with these types of web pages.

Search engines also have trouble accessing private content (this is by design). As a general rule, content that is posted behind user login pages are off-limits to search engines. For example, corporate intranets, subscription databases, social network pages, and personal email are not accessible via search engines like Google or MSN Live Search (whew!). Some of this content is private (e.g. email), and some of this information is proprietary (e.g. databases). In either case, most search engines avoid this category of material.

Search engines also struggle to index unlinked content (without links the spiders can't find the pages), multimedia (non-text formats are hard to accurately index), and pages buried deep within databases.[18] Why is this important? Well, the deep web is the largest growing category of information on the Internet. It experiences much more Internet traffic than the surface web, which should make sense. While we use the Internet regularly to search for information, the majority of our online activities consist of reading personal email, browsing social networks, and accessing private networks (all components of the invisible web). Since search engines do not—and cannot—index everything that is online, then we will inevitably miss some information that is available to us.

Perhaps you remain unconvinced. You're more than satisfied with your search engine results. Even I have to admit I rely on search engines for the majority of my information retrieval tasks; however, they're not perfect. You see, search technology is quite good at following instructions, but it isn't so good at anticipating needs. For example, if I type the word "atlas" into a search engine, I will retrieve thousands of results. But, am I looking for a map, the god from Greek mythology, the particle physics experiment at the Large Hadron Collider in Switzerland, or something else altogether? Chances are that I can find links to all of these ideas in my results, but the search engine doesn't know which one I'm most interested in. Don't get me wrong, I'm not claiming that the search engine is faulty—it did exactly what I told it to. I'm merely suggesting that the tools for information retrieval can only take us so far.

Like most human activities, research and information gathering is a social experience (section 5.1). When it comes to solving an information need, we rarely use the same approach. We try multiple methods and angles. We start with one question and then jump to another. We follow link after link until we're miles from where we started. We begin by trying to find one thing, but based on the results we retrieve, we realize that we really want something else. Information retrieval is a product-oriented activity (focused on the end result), but it is also a process-oriented one (concerned with the steps in the journey).

Technology can be counted on to behave consistently and deliver predictable results (i.e. match the user's term "atlas" to occurrences of the word "atlas" in the index). Our behavior, by contrast, is not so consistent. We each handle information tasks differently, choosing different strategies for negotiating the information environment. We rely on our instincts to lead us to the content, gravitating toward familiar methods. Sometimes we are fortunate enough to stumble upon relevant information inadvertently (serendipity), other times we rely on advice from other people (social recommendation), and sometimes we navigate based on our knowledge of the environment (orienteering or wayfinding).[19]

Serendipity, social recommendations, and orienteering are borrowed from the study of how humans interact with each other and with their physical environment. We've all experienced random situations that lead to new insight, or stopped to ask a stranger for directions, or relied on maps and signs to get us to our destination. The strategies we use to find our way represent important concepts in the theory of information retrieval as well. In fact, it is these very behaviors that enable us to recognize meaningful patterns in the data and information we retrieve. We may not possess the calculated precision of search engines, but our chance encounters, our instincts, and our knowledge of context help navigate to the information we need.

Perhaps the day is coming when innovations in interface design, usability, and search technology will anticipate our needs, but for now we have to work with what we've got.[20]

6.5 Digital Disorganization

Categories don't work

In section 6.1 we talked about specific ways to organize information. We looked at the structures of categorization (e.g. taxonomies), and we looked at tools that employ those structures to help us find what we want (e.g. directories). We even went so far as to suggest that ontologies and taxonomies were essential to understanding our world because they provide context. They provide a place where old and new knowledge can be situated.

Our discussion implied that taxonomies and organizational schemes make finding information a straightforward process. We like to believe that information retrieval is simply a matter of asking the right question, employing the appropriate technology, and selecting the best quality information. But, in reality, our carefully contrived taxonomies may not be the best tools for the Information Age. To some degree these artificial structures are remnants of a time before the Internet. We're operating on an assumption that comes from the physical world. We believe that in order for something to be found, it needs to be part of something bigger. It needs to belong somewhere. It needs to be filed. It needs to be defined by neighboring pieces of information. In short, it needs to be organized.

If we take a closer look at taxonomies, however, there are some significant disadvantages to structuring information according to rigid categories. First and foremost, such elaborate systems of classification are inflexible. They don't easily adapt to changes, nor do they age very well. For example, the Dewey Decimal system used in public libraries was intended to categorize all known knowledge *and* all areas of future knowledge. The original design, however, did not anticipate the huge growth area in computer science and information technology and so those topics have been awkwardly squeezed in. Similarly, the Dewey category for religion is almost exclusively about Christianity (as if other world religions did not exist). When the world changes, taxonomies have trouble keeping up.[21]

Classification systems also rely on experts to steward the system. For example, to classify living things in the Linnaean system, one needs to have a general knowledge of the system's structure, and specific knowledge of the distinctions, which separate one category from another. Without an authority in place to make key classification decisions, the system breaks down. Expertise is not always a disadvantage for taxonomies, but when experts control the tools and language for organizing items the system becomes less accessible.[22]

By design, taxonomies also favor a binary ("either-or") approach. To classify something means deciding what that something is, *and* deciding what it is not. Problems arise when that something can be situated in more than one place in the taxonomy. Imagine you're trying to categorize a company like Procter & Gamble (P&G) in the North American Industry Classification System (NAICS). P&G is a large multinational company that operates in a number of industries. Do they fit under "soap and detergent manufacturing," "sanitary paper product manufacturing," or "pharmaceutical preparation manufacturing?" The reality is that P&G fits into all three categories (and others). So what should we do? We could list P&G under its primary industries only, but then we'll lose the full scope of its activities. We could list P&G under each relevant category, but then we lose the ability to focus on its primary business. As you can see, special cases cause all kinds of problems for taxonomies.

To sum up, taxonomies fail to adapt to change, rely on authorities to steward development, and do not handle special cases well. The pursuit of organization is a laudable ideal, but no taxonomy is perfect.

Perhaps we can re-imagine the problem of organizing information by looking through the lens of information technology. As we saw in Chapter 5, the Internet turns organization on its head. Everything can be linked to everything else. From afar, the Internet looks like an incoherent mess of links, but if we look close enough, there is order under the chaos.

Taxonomies provide a place for new items by including room in the design; however, it is too hard to plan for every potential item that will need to be categorized. Instead, we might learn from the Internet and allow our organizing principles to develop more organically. When categories aren't structured according to a rigid set of rules, they more directly reflect reality. As knowledge shifts, so does its organization.[23]

Taxonomies require well-defined terminology and vocabulary to ensure that items are described consistently; however, the development of tagging suggests an alternative approach. Tagging is the act of labeling items based on individual user preferences. It puts the power of description and classification into the hands of the user. For example, the photo-sharing website Flickr, allows photographers to describe their photographs with keywords. This might seem like a foolish endeavor, but as more people contribute tags, a more flexible set of categories (descriptive terms) evolves. If photographers want others to find their work, they would do well to tag their pictures with meaningful keywords.

We take linking and tagging for granted because they are germane to the Information Age. But they signify a fundamental shift when it comes to organizing information. These strategies put the user at the center of their information environment. By using tags and labels that make sense to them, users contribute both content and classification. There are no experts, there are no nested hierarchies, and there are no categories limited by binary thinking. The absolute elements of taxonomy give way to relativity as the system evolves. In the Information Age, information is more likely to organize itself organically, than artificially.

6.6 Experiment

Image searching

Search engines work wonderfully for finding text-based information, but they're less successful when it comes to image searching. Images and other multimedia materials are particularly hard to incorporate into a text-based index. Of course, this doesn't mean that visual information cannot be found via a search engine, only that it's more difficult.

Since search engines cannot identify the contents of a picture like you and me (at least not yet), they have to infer the content of the image from the surrounding text. For instance, we might immediately recognize a photograph of Niagara Falls (or at least identify that it's a picture of waterfall), but a search engine is not capable of such a revelation. Instead, the search engine will rely on the image's context for identification. It will look at the content of the webpage, it will look for a caption associated with the photograph, and it will look at the file name of the image. Based on these details, the search engine will assume that the photograph is a picture of Niagara Falls.

As long as there is enough contextual information, search engines can retrieve a reasonable set of results for most queries. The problem occurs when the images are out of context, or not described with enough detail. One solution for improving image searching is to allow users to submit additional keyword tags (section 6.5) to describe the images, essentially assisting the search engine. It's a hybrid approach to organizing visual information. People provide the meaningful tags and the search engine optimizes retrieval.

Allowing users to describe their images as they see fit is not a perfect solution to image retrieval. After all, people use different languages, different spellings within the same language, and different words for the same thing. In the United Kingdom, for example, "garden" is used to describe a backyard, not a place for flowers or vegetables.

The solution to this problem is to make tagging a social activity. Let me explain. When enough people tag their photographs, the search algorithms are able to cluster similar tags together and disambiguate different contexts.[24] For instance, when you search for "Paris Hilton" the search engine can separate results for images of the hotel in the French capital from images of the celebrity.

When people start tagging their images so that other people can find them, an organic taxonomy develops—or as some call it a "folksonomy" (because it's created by the people—the "folks"—not experts).[25]

Worksheet

Name _____ Date _____

Part A

For this experiment, you are going to explore image searching with tags using Flickr, a popular photo-sharing service, You will compare your results to those from a general image search engine. Use the worksheet below as a guide.

Fill in the blanks below with the first term that comes to your mind.

Noun _____

Verb _____

Adjective _____

Emotion/Mood _____

Color _____

Famous person _____

City _____

Mode of transportation _____

Book Title _____

Movie Title _____

Part B

Open two browser windows (or two tabs). In the first browser window, open up an image search engine like Yahoo! Image Search (http://images.search.yahoo.com/) or Google Images (http://images.google.com/). In the second browser window, open the Flickr advanced search (http://www.flickr.com/search/advanced). Underneath the search box, click the button that says, "Tags only" (this will ensure that you're only searching the keywords provided by the community). Plug the terms you selected in Part A into each search engine and compare the results. Reflect on the questions that follow:

Part C

1. Which of your terms retrieved better results in Flickr?

2. Which of your terms retrieved better results in the general image search?

3. Did any of your searches retrieve unusual images that didn't seem to match your search term? Provide one brief example. Why do you think your search retrieved the image?

4. If you were submitting images to a photo-sharing service like Flickr, would you tag your images? Why or why not?

5. Provide any additional comments

6.7 Reflect

Search engines + bias

Most of us assume that search engines retrieve results without bias, but evidence suggests that search engines may not be so neutral. Eric Goldman takes a closer look at the nature of bias in online search engines and how it affects the user experience. Read his overview and respond to the questions below:

Goldman, Eric. "Search Engine Bias and the Demise of Search Engine Utopianism." (September 22, 2006), http://www.informit.com/articles/article.aspx?p=607376

QUESTIONS

1. Goldman argues "search engines make editorial judgments just like any media company." After reading his article, does the potential for search engine bias bother you? Why or why not? Are you concerned that some information will not be available to you because of decisions made by an editorial team?

2. Goldman states "to maximize search perceptions of search success, search engines generally tune their ranking algorithms to support majority interests." Are you worried that minority views and smaller independent websites will be drowned out by mainstream websites? Is ranking search results based on popularity or prominence a good thing? Why or why not?

3. Goldman suggests that technological evolution will eliminate search engine bias as search engines develop the ability to retrieve results based on "personalized ranking algorithms." What do you think of this idea? Is it a good idea for search engines to target individual people? Will the results be better or worse than search engines now? Why or why not?

6.8 Reflect

Online user behavior

In April 2006, iProspect, a search engine marketing firm, published a report on search engines and user behavior. The research team used a survey instrument to ask people about their online behavior and interactions with search engines. Although the report is a few years old, it is still widely cited online. Read the report and respond to the questions below:

iProspect. "Search Engine User Behavior Study" (April 2006), http://www. iprospect.com/premiumPDFs/WhitePaper_2006_SearchEngineUserBehavior. pdf

---

QUESTIONS

1. Based on the results from the first two survey questions (see the report's pie charts), it looks like a high percentage of search engine users rarely go past the first three pages of results. Do these findings surprise you? Do they reflect your experience with search engines? Why don't users go beyond the first few pages? How do these findings affect companies hoping to get noticed on the Internet?

2. Question #3 of the survey asks users about their behavior once they get a bad set of results. Over 80% of people stick with the same search engine and simply type in additional search words. Does this finding surprise you? Does it reflect your experience with search engines? Does this finding suggest that we have more trust in search engines than in our own ability to search? Why don't users switch to a different search engine and try their search again?

3. Based on this report, it appears that most search engine users don't have the time or patience to sort through long lists of results. We seem to leave the majority of the work to the search engines. Do you see any problem with this approach? Do you think we might become too shallow or too superficial in our search for information? Or, do you trust search engines to bring you the best available information? Why or why not?

6.9 Decide

Information migration

Cindy manages a small childcare operation called Silly Monkey Day Care. She started by looking after children in her home while their parents went to work, but she loved it so much that she decided to start her own business. With a small business loan, she was able to lease a child-friendly location, get proper certification, hire specially trained staff, and advertise her services to the community.

Since the demand for childcare services is high in her region, the number of children enrolled with Silly Monkey continues to rise. In fact, in her current facility, Cindy cannot meet the demand. She has started a waiting list and is thinking about expanding to a second location to accommodate the number of applications.

Her more pressing need, however, is to overhaul the way that Silly Monkey organizes its information. When the service started over ten years ago, Cindy interacted with most of the parents and the children directly. Now that Silly Monkey has grown, such personal relationships are more challenging. It is becoming imperative for Silly Monkey to have a more flexible information system.

Currently, Cindy's information system is strictly paper-based. All of Silly Monkey's key documents (child applications, allergy information, employee details, parent contact information, government policies, etc.) are kept on file in her office. She knows that keeping a paper-based system won't work well if she expands to multiple locations, so she is investigating other options.

She is aware that most companies have moved to database-driven systems because the information is easier to retrieve, but she isn't sure it's worth the investment. While Silly Monkey is doing well, Cindy doesn't have a lot of extra cash to invest in information systems or office management—she would rather pour the money back into programming.

If she does move to a computer-based system, she's not sure what to do with her existing paper system. The government requires that Silly Monkey keep all records—even after children have graduated from the program and started elementary school—so she can't just throw the old information out.

What do you think Cindy should do? Four options are presented on the following page.

Worksheet

Name _____ Date _____

In the space provided, discuss the advantages and disadvantages of each option and make a final recommendation.

A) Cindy should implement a database-driven system. In addition, she should migrate all of the information from her paper-based system into the new database.

B) Cindy should implement a database-driven system from this point forward. She should keep the paper-based system intact for the government, but not worry about adding all of that information to the new system.

C) Cindy should leave the information system as it is. A computer-based system will be too expensive and too much work to be truly valuable—Silly Monkey is still a fairly small operation.

D) Cindy doesn't need a database-driven system. She should simply move the information she keeps in paper format to electronic format. Electronic documents could be more easily stored and organized using file directories on her computer, eliminating the space required by the current paper-based filing system.

So, what do you think Cindy should do? Why?

_____

_____

_____

_____

_____

Chapter

7

Information Ethics

7.1 Ethics for the Information Age

Right + wrong

Ethics is the philosophical investigation of right and wrong. It is the branch of philosophy that examines the nature of moral virtue and evaluates human actions (and the motivations behind those actions). The ultimate goal, of course, is to develop a way of thinking and acting that improves life for all. Stretching back thousands of years, we can find philosophers, religious leaders, and government officials proposing various ethical systems designed to increase human happiness.[1]

Some ethical systems are deeply rooted in cultural traditions and religious ideologies. While these approaches can be valuable, the study of philosophical ethics is separate from religious ethics (or religious morality). Instead of trusting that ethical directives come from God (or some other higher power), the brand of ethics we're interested in here is based in human rationality. We want to apply reason to the secular study of right and wrong.

Philosophical ethics are also different than legal ethics. We live in a civilized society, so it is tempting to believe that the law will dictate how people should act; we expect the legislative authorities to help guide our behavior. The problem with this approach is that there simply aren't enough laws for every circumstance. And when there are laws, they are often in conflict and open to interpretation. The reality is that law usually lags behind the rest of society—even more so in the Information Age.

The law certainly plays an important role in how people behave, but it is not enough. We need a better foundation for making ethical decisions. We need to focus on moving beyond the letter of the law to embracing the spirit of the law. Making good ethical decisions requires the ability to recognize principles and extrapolate beyond what is known. Simply put, ethics is about that uniquely human trait: wisdom (section 2.2).

We don't have time to examine every philosophical approach, but a basic introduction to ethics with a particular focus on information and technology ethics should prove enlightening. The Information Age poses some unique ethical challenges:

- Do managers have the right to monitor their employees' behavior on the Internet?

- Is file-sharing of media files using peer-to-peer networks stealing?

■ Should software developers be liable for damages caused by bugs in their software?

■ How far should companies go to gain intelligence on their competitors?

The answers don't come easily.[2]

The volume of available information combined with rapid technological advances further complicates ethical matters. Since the world relies on computers and the broader information infrastructure, decisions made locally can have an impact globally. For this reason, it is important for us to develop a solid understanding of information and technology ethics.[3]

Let's start with a classic definition: "*computer ethics* is the analysis of the nature and social impact of computer technology and the corresponding formulation and justification of policies for the ethical use of such technology."[4] This definition is computer-centric, which is understandable because it was first published in 1985, but we might broaden it to include information technology and information systems. We might say, then, information ethics deals with dilemmas where information systems and technology are "*essentially* involved and there is an uncertainty about what to do and even how to understand the situation."[5]

Technology is a fairly broad term (section 3.1) so we need to identify what makes technology in the Information Age different than in previous eras. First, computers and information technology are everywhere. Second, this particular type of technology connects us. Diverse communities can thrive despite the geographic separation and distance of members. Since technology mediates nearly every information exchange, the potential impact of information technology is both personal and public.[6] Third, computers have moved beyond simply computing; they have become more than just number crunchers. Activities that were not possible decades ago can now be completed with the click of a button. Of course, the question now is should we click it?

Yes, information technology is ubiquitous, but that is not enough to make it unique from previous technologies. Instead, information technology is unique because it is an exceedingly flexible—almost universal—tool. Nearly every task we have can be augmented with application of information technology. As long as a series of instructions (software applications) can process inputs and create outputs in a logical fashion, information technology represents a significant break from past technologies.[7]

In the Information Age, work becomes less about doing physical labor and more about instructing computers to do work for us (section 5.1). Implementing information technology is more than simply doing the same tasks with new tools. The application of technology redefines the tasks themselves. Here are just a few examples: teaching courses via course management software changes the nature of education for the teacher and the student; banking electronically affects the definition of money for both the customer and the bank; using instant messaging and chat applications to talk to friends changes the nature of personal communication.

I'm not suggesting that these changes are negative, only that technology alters our expectations and behavior.[8] Technology has the potential to become a tool for enlightenment or a weapon for destruction. Since we can instruct computers to commit acts on our behalf, we are able to distance ourselves from the consequences of our actions—even when our actions affect those half a world away. It is for these reasons that we need to carefully consider the nature of information and technology ethics.

7.2 Consequence-based Reasoning

Quantity + quality + pleasure

One way of approaching ethical dilemmas is to focus on the consequences of decisions. Basically, you take what you know about a particular situation, identify your options, try to predict what will happen with each option, and then choose the one with most desirable consequences. For most of us, this is a practical, common sense approach to decision making. Decisions that produce more benefit are right; those that produce more hurt are wrong. Evaluating our moral character depends strictly on whether our decisions help or hurt people. It's that simple.

During the European Enlightenment philosophers like Hobbes, Locke and Rousseau began writing about human nature (are we inherently good or bad?) and introduced new ideas like the social contract. Rather than submit to nature or to a divine power, these thinkers asserted the independence of humankind. They recognized that each human being was a freethinking, independent individual (at least in the Western tradition). In order for civilized society to function, they felt we needed a social contract. In this arrangement, we, the people, freely gave up some of our rights to an authority (e.g. government) in exchange for protection and provision.[9] Note that this contract is both rational and relational. It is rational because it is for the greater good; it is relational because it is an agreement among groups of people in the name of maintaining social order.

These ideas about how society should order itself spread quickly (with the help of the printing press) and provided the foundation for further thinking about ethical systems of behavior. Jeremy Bentham, for example, proposed a consequence-based system, also called the teleological approach. Bentham was interested in developing a "moral science" that was separate from the religious traditions of eighteenth century England. The church claimed that sacrifice and suffering were good examples of moral character, but Bentham didn't agree. In his view, two forces motivated human behavior: pleasure and pain. Pleasure makes life happier; pain makes it worse.[10]

Pleasure and pain are not just motivators; they are also the primary standards for evaluating right and wrong. "According to Bentham, utility is the property of an object whereby it tends to produce pleasure or prevent pain. The utility of any action can be measured in terms of the amount of pleasure it tends to produce and pain it tends to prevent. Hence, determining what should be done is a matter of calculating the utility of actions."[11] Actions with higher utility produce more pleasure and, therefore, are morally desirable.

To help measure pleasure and pain Bentham developed a number of parameters. For example, pleasure could be measured according to its intensity (strength of pleasure), duration (length of pleasure), extent (number of people affected), fecundity (chance that pleasure will lead to more pleasure), and other factors.

Bentham's consequence-based reasoning strives for the greatest good for the greatest number of people, but there are some key oversights with this approach. First, for complex ethical dilemmas there are potentially an infinite number of options to consider. Measuring the pleasure and pain for each person involved with each option available can be a daunting task. Even if you limit the potential outcomes to the immediate future (short-term consequences rather than long-term consequences) there are still many variables. Second, Bentham's theory sees pleasure as the only good and pain as the only evil. This binary approach can be rather restrictive. Lastly, Bentham largely ignores the notion of rights and duties. He points to the consequences as key factors for ethical decision-making—not the inalienable rights of humankind, or our obligations to authorities.[12]

In an attempt to improve on Bentham's work, John Stuart Mill suggested that there should be a measure of quality to pleasure and pain. Instead of something being strictly pleasurable or strictly painful, there should be a way to distinguish between types of pleasure. For Mill, high quality pleasure included things like intelligence, education, sensitivity to others, morality, and physical health, while low quality pleasures arose from selfish indulgence, stupidity and sensual delights. Pain worked on a similar scale.[13]

John Stuart Mill turned Bentham's approach of quantifying consequences into one of qualifying consequences. Introducing pleasure and pain scales allows for more flexibility when examining ethical dilemmas. For instance, a small amount of high quality pleasure can outweigh a larger amount of low quality pleasure (or even pain). But this approach too has its limits—it can be ruthless. For example, suppose you were rushed to the hospital after a serious car accident. In the hospital, the doctors decided that it would take a lot of effort to save your life and even if they managed to do that your quality of life would be very low. Instead, they decided that the greater good would be to harvest your internal organs and provide transplants to six other people, essentially saving their lives. Your life is lost, but half a dozen others are saved.

Qualifying pain and pleasure means that any moral action is defensible as long as it produces enough high quality pleasure. Another issue with this approach comes down to who gets to decide what is pleasurable and what is painful. According to Mill, the person with the most experience is in the best position to assess the situation. But by making personal experience the deciding factor some participants are excluded from ethical reasoning. This situation is also vulnerable to the subjective whims of the judge. While subjective judgments are not inherently bad, there is potential for abuse.

Ultimately, teleological reasoning requires a keen sense of observation, an ability to forecast or predict the future, and an understanding of how people respond to various circumstances. To be sure, the simplicity of measuring pleasure and pain is attractive—it provides a very practical approach; however, it isn't hard to imagine scenarios that quickly become too complex or too ruthless for analysis.

7.3 Action-oriented Reasoning

The end never justifies the means

The problem with evaluating ethical behavior based strictly on consequences (or potential consequences) is that it ignores the actions required to make particular decisions. Consequence-based reasoning may be practical, but most of us instinctively realize that the moral virtue of the actions themselves should also be considered. Even the Golden Rule (Do unto others as you would have them do to you) puts the emphasis on action-oriented thinking. Before we make a decision, the Golden Rule implores us to put ourselves someone else's position.

Another action-oriented approach to ethical reasoning is called the Rule of Change. Simply put, if an action cannot be taken repeatedly, it is not right to take it at all. This is sometimes called the "slippery slope" principle. If you start with small indiscretions (e.g. taking office supplies), you may eventually end up compromising on much larger indiscretions (e.g. embezzling money). Clearly, examining our actions is also essential for sound ethical reasoning.

If teleological ethics focuses on the end result (consequences) of decisions, then deontological ethics focuses on the actions themselves. Actions like telling the truth, keeping promises, and respecting the rights of others are inherently good; others like lying, stealing, and murder are inherently bad. In other words, no matter how much good might come from lying or stealing, those acts are never right.

The primary philosopher behind actions-based reasoning was Immanuel Kant. Kant was influenced by many of the same thinkers as Jeremy Bentham (section 7.2), but ultimately arrived at different conclusions on the nature of ethical behavior. Kant preferred the deontological approach, focusing on the actions themselves (or motivations behind those actions). He felt that right and wrong actions are fundamental laws imprinted on human nature.[14]

Since humans are rational beings with inalienable rights, Kant believed that ethics should be universal and consistent. The study of ethics could be as logical and rational as the study of mathematics.[15] If an equation like $2 + 2$ always equals 4, then ethical behavior could be similarly predictable. Murder, for example, is inherently bad and therefore can never be justified.

Kant's concept of the categorical imperative described the fundamental moral law of human existence that holds true no matter what the consequences are. The categorical imperative is based on our obligation, or duty, to moral action. An ethical action, then, is one that is committed by a rational and free being and is in accordance with the moral law. It considers things like fairness, equality, justice, and dignity—the good things in our nature—and avoids things like manipulation, dishonesty, and indecency.

Sometimes the categorical imperative is phrased like this: If an action is not right for everyone to take, then it is not right for anyone. For instance, imagine you overstate your qualifications on your resume. To put it up against the categorical imperative test, we need to determine whether social order could be maintained if everyone else followed your lead and embellished their resumes. It shouldn't take long to realize that if doctors, lawyers, electricians, and crane operators lied on their resumes, then we would have some serious problems on our hands; therefore, overstating your qualifications on your resume is wrong for everyone. Not only is it dishonest, it potentially destabilizes trust in the entire job application process.

The deontological approach provides a much more focused discussion of ethical behavior. Instead of trying to predict the outcome of our decisions, we simply need to evaluate our motives and actions. However, the major issue with the categorical approach is its inflexibility.[16] The end never justifies the means, but it wouldn't be too difficult to imagine a scenario when stealing might actually be defensible. Do we really believe that lying is *always* wrong? Despite Kant's efforts, ethical dilemmas in the human experience are a little more complex than mathematical equations.

7.4 Ethics in Practice

Consequences + actions

While teleological reasoning (section 7.2) and deontological reasoning (section 7.3) conflict in theory, they complement each other in practice. Most of us use a combination of these approaches when we face an ethical dilemma. In some cases, our decisions may weigh consequences more heavily than actions, and in other scenarios the opposite may hold true. However, nearly every decision we make requires a closer look at both consequences and actions.

For example, suppose you're an investor. When choosing which stocks to buy you need to decide how comfortable you are with risk (especially when it's your own money). You need to balance your risk tolerance with your risk aversion. If you're risk averse you might choose to keep your money in the currency markets. Your return on investment may be low, but it's relatively safe. If you're more risk tolerant, you might choose to keep your money in a hedge fund or real estate markets. Your return on investment can be quite high, but these markets are much more volatile.

From the teleological perspective, investments that bring in bigger returns are better decisions. These returns improve your quality of life and give companies more money to deliver their services, so there is more pleasure than pain. But investing money is about more than simply weighing risks. If we consider the act of investing in a company or idea an act of implicit support for that company or idea, then we should also apply the deontological approach. According to this approach, you might choose to avoid companies with frequent human rights abuses, crimes against the environment, or companies in "unethical" industries (pornography, gambling, tobacco, weapons, etc). For socially responsible investments, each investor must weigh both the return on investment (consequences) and the nature of the companies being invested in (actions).

When it comes to ethical practice many professions use codes of conduct or codes of ethics to help guide behavior. Doctors, for example, are mindful of the ancient Hippocratic Oath when it comes to practicing medicine. Knowledge workers are guided by similar codes when it comes to the use of information and technology.

A typical code of conduct for information professionals requires members to protect the reputation of the broader profession. In other words, it is the members' collective responsibility to ensure that the industry has good standing in the community. This commitment goes beyond just being honest; it also requires members to be competent. In addition, codes typically describe how members work with information. Professionals ensure the accuracy and reliability of the information they collect and create, while respecting the confidentiality and the intellectual property rights of sources. Lastly, members are instructed to use technology appropriately, respecting the rules of access to acquire necessary information. Ultimately, a code of conduct reminds members of obligations to their employer, to their fellow members, and to society as a whole.[17]

Ethical dilemmas often arise due to conflicts of interest. Such conflicts might occur between private interests and official duties (e.g. accepting bribes in exchange for business), or they might occur between people with competing claims (e.g. customers versus shareholders). Codes of conduct provide a helpful starting place, but they are hardly sufficient to deal with every ethical scenario. For that reason, it might be helpful to cover some basic steps to resolving an ethical dilemma. Remember, these steps are not presented as a formula for sound ethical reasoning, they are intended as a guide only.[18]

For the purposes of this discussion, let's imagine that a clothing store wants to implement a Radio Frequency Identification (RFID) system. In this system, a unique radio tag will be affixed to each item of clothing and will transmit the garment's location to the store's RFID readers. Such a system will greatly improve inventory management, deter theft, and allow the store to collect incredible amounts of consumer data. The benefits to the customer, however, are less clear.

At first glance, this seems more like an operational issue than an ethical one. But one of the primary complaints against RFID technology from consumer advocates is that RFID systems are potential invasions of privacy. So, the first step in resolving an ethical dilemma is to recognize its moral dimension.

Once an issue has been identified, the next step is to identify the key stakeholders. Who has an interest in the outcome? In our RFID scenario, there are a number of interested parties. Employees, managers, the Board of Directors, investors, and customers will all be affected by the new system.

Step three is to gather the facts of the case. These are the facts that all sides agree on. For implementing RFID systems, all sides might be able to agree on how the technology works and how much it costs. The goal here is to reduce the areas of disagreement.

After the basic facts have been agreed upon, it is time to figure out what the conflict is really about. What are the higher order values at stake? Is the company most concerned with making processes more efficient, protecting property, or collecting data? Is it about personal privacy? Is it about control? Is it about technology for technology's sake?

The next step is to examine the possible options. Which potential solutions can address the key issues in the debate? In the case of RFID, options might include implementing the technology, avoiding the technology, or introducing a compromise; for example, the company may choose to implement RFID in the supply chain side of the business, but not in the retail side.

Once the reasonable options have been identified, it is time to speculate about the consequences of each option. For example, we could postulate that if the clothing store implements RFID, customers might get upset and shop elsewhere. But we might also reason that RFID will make the clothing store's operations more efficient, enabling the store to lower prices, and ultimately make the customer happier. For each option, we need to examine the most likely consequences.

Of course, we need to follow up the consequence-based reasoning with a look at the actions required for each action. For example, if the company chooses to implement the technology without informing the customers, that action might be considered a breach of customer trust. If the clothing store chooses against implementing RFID, then how will it increase shareholder value, or reduce the theft of property?

Taking all of the previous steps into consideration, it is time to make a decision. Obviously, the entire reasoning process will also include consideration of the law. Does the law allow for RFID in retail environments? If so, what are the restrictions? It may also look for similar cases. Have other clothing stores implemented the technology? What have their experiences been? When it comes right down to it, the clothing store needs to weigh the potential consequences and the motivation behind implementing RFID before making a final decision. You can't have one without the other.

7.5 The Future of Information Ethics

Toward a global ethic

Despite our philosophical reasoning, laws, regulations, and codes of conduct, unethical behavior persists. Not surprisingly, the reasons for unethical behavior are many and varied. Some suggest that we commit unethical acts, simply

because we are competitive. Whether we're businesses competing in the marketplace, or students competing in school, we do what we need to do to win.
Our urge to come out on top causes us to compromise our behavior.

Another argument for unethical behavior is that we're lazy. We prefer to
take the path of least resistance. Often, doing what is right translates to taking
the much harder path, so we stick with the crowd and carefully avoid difficult
choices. Our inaction creates a moral vacuum. For example, it is easier (and
cheaper) to download vast libraries of music, ignoring the musicians' right to
compensation, than it is to purchase those same songs legally.

Perhaps we act unethically because we rationalize our choices with rela-
tivism. We convince ourselves that everything is relative and adapt our ethics to
the particular situation. For instance, we may use our company resources to
check personal email, but as long as other people are participating in greater
acts of unethical behavior, we let our own ethical standards slide.[19]

Understanding the reasons why we make poor choices as individuals is
only half the story. What about the behavior of others? Why don't we hold others accountable to a higher ethical standard? One potential reason is that power
becomes a substitute for trust. In other words, we feel forced to trust (or tolerate)
decisions made by people in authority even when we believe those decisions
are unethical. We fear retribution, so we choose not to speak.

Another reason why we allow unethical behavior in others is that we have
short memories. We believe that people can change. For example, when a man
leaves his wife for a lover, the lover chooses to believe that same man won't
ever leave her (even though his past behavior suggests this is at least a possibility). We convince ourselves the events that conspired in our favor won't con-
spire against us.

Lastly, unethical behavior persists because situations are too complex for us
to understand fully. Since we have trouble calculating the interests of all parties
involved, we end up giving people the benefit of the doubt. Since we can't distance ourselves far enough from the situation to reliably judge someone else's
actions, we remain silent.[20]

This last reason, the complexity of ethical scenarios, provides foundation
for an interesting thought experiment: could technology be applied to help us
make sense of moral dilemmas? Will sheer processing power allow us to make
more ethical choices? The idea may not be as crazy as it sounds; after all, computers manage to handle complex tasks like playing chess fairly well.

Both Bentham (section 7.2) and Kant (section 7.3) took rational, mathematical approaches to evaluating ethical behavior. For Bentham, it was simply a
matter of weighing the quantity of pleasure against the quantity of pain; for

Kant, actions were universally good or universally bad. Since machines excel at mathematics and logic, we may not be too far off. If we feed computers with enough inputs about a given scenario, can we construct an application that will help us calculate consequences and analyze actions? In other words, could we teach machines to reason ethically?

One obvious problem with this approach is that computers are not free moral agents (they are slaves to the tasks assigned by humans). As such, they are ineligible for ethical reasoning, as we've been describing it. The other obvious problem is that computers lack experience and true cognitive abilities. Computers lack our ability to understand context and our capacity for imagination. They remain confined to rule-based programs, rarely making innovative leaps in judgment.

For technology to truly reason ethically we will have to make huge advances in artificial intelligence (AI) research. This is not to suggest that technology cannot be applied to ethical thinking. We might, for instance, employ computers to analyze vast quantities of data, producing recognizable patterns from which we can make good decisions. This seems far-fetched, but computers already help us make good decisions. They analyze customer purchase data to predict future demand, they analyze weather data to predict the next natural disaster, and they measure economic data to predict risk. Computers do the computing, and we do the reasoning. It's a true division of labor.[21]

While the ethical systems proposed by Bentham and Kant are still relevant, perhaps we need to refine our understanding of ethics for the Information Age. After all, Bentham and Kant's perspectives are rooted in the intellectual tradition of the Enlightenment and the social upheaval caused by the Industrial Revolution. In today's world, actions can be committed anonymously and are largely untraceable. We simply cannot evaluate the motive or intentions behind each action. Similarly, the consequences of those actions may not be immediately apparent or measurable. How, then, can we effectively apply these two approaches? Is it possible to redefine our ethical approach based on the impact of information technology? If so, what would it look like?

7.6 Experiment

Codes of conduct

When companies hire new employees one of the first tasks is to introduce the company's code of conduct. These codes of conduct do two things: first, they communicate the company's expectations for ethical behavior; second, they protect the company in the event that employees act counter to the code.

While each company's code differs, there are some common themes that emerge. In their *Harvard Business Review* article, "Does Your Company's Conduct Meet World-Class Standards?" Lynn Paine, Rohit Deshpande, Joshua D. Margolis and Kim Eric Bettcher endorse eight ethical principles that all codes of conduct should include. Their perspective is summarized below for reference:

1. **Fiduciary Principle:** Employees should be diligent and loyal, promoting the company's legitimate long-term interests.
2. **Property Principle:** Employees should protect company assets (intellectual and physical) and respect the property rights of competitors.
3. **Reliability Principle:** Employees should honor all commitments, fulfilling obligations to key stakeholders.
4. **Transparency Principle:** Employees should conduct business in a truthful manner, refraining from deceptive practices.
5. **Dignity Principle:** Employees should acknowledge the dignity of all people, promoting human rights and preventing abuses.
6. **Fairness Principle:** Employees should engage in free and fair competition, avoiding discrimination with all stakeholders.
7. **Citizenship Principle:** Employees should act as responsible citizens, obeying all applicable laws and regulations.
8. **Responsiveness Principle:** Employees should be responsive to concerns and complaints raised about company activities, protecting the public interest.

These all sound like great principles, but the question is: do companies actually incorporate these ideas into their codes of conduct? For this experiment, you're going to find out. You'll be asked to find a corporate code of conduct (sometimes called a code of ethics) and rate it according to these eight principles. Use the worksheet on the following page to get started.

Worksheet

Name _____ Date _____

Part A

Find a company code of conduct online (it can be from any company).

1. Which company did you choose?

2. What do they do?

Part B

Read the code of conduct that you selected and try to identify aspects of the eight over-arching ethical principles. Evaluate how well you think they addressed each principle on the scales below (1=poor; 5=excellent) and provide a brief explanation for each.

Fiduciary Principle   1   2   3   4   5

_____

Property Principle   1   2   3   4   5

_____

Reliability Principle   1   2   3   4   5

_____

Transparency Principle   1   2   3   4   5

_____

Dignity Principle   1   2   3   4   5

_____

Fairness Principle   1   2   3   4   5

_____

Citizenship Principle   1   2   3   4   5

_____

Responsiveness Principle   1   2   3   4   5

_____

3. Do you think the code of conduct is clear for current and future employees? Is there room for improvement? If so, what would you change?

_____

_____

_____

_____

_____

_____

_____

_____

7.7 Reflect

Ethical challenges

Mason is writing well before the widespread explosion of the Internet, but he anticipates a number of challenges brought on by the Information Age. Issues of privacy, accuracy, property and accessibility remain issues for us today. Read his article and consider the questions below:

Mason, Richard O. "Four ethical issues of the information age." *Management Information Systems Quarterly* 10, no. 1 (1986): 5-12, http://www.misq.org/archivist/vol/no10/issue1/vol10no1mason.html

---

QUESTIONS

1. One of the ethical issues that Richard Mason discusses is the accessibility of information. What do you think of his explanation and examples? Do you believe that accessibility is still a major concern in the Information Age? Why or why not?

2. After reading Mason's four ethical issues (privacy, accuracy, property, accessibility), which one poses the least difficulty in the era of the Internet? Why? Explain your reasons and if possible provide examples.

3. Richard Mason discusses privacy and property as two key ethical issues in the Information Age. Which one of these issues is more concerning in the age of the Internet? Why? Explain your reasons and if possible provide examples.

7.8 Reflect

Competitive intelligence

Companies regularly collect information to improve their business practices. Conducting competitive intelligence, or systematically gathering information on competitors and markets, is an essential business strategy in many industries. Most companies realize this is part of the business, but occasionally some companies go too far and participate in acts corporate espionage. Jennifer Jordan and Sydney Finkelstein examine a fairly well known case between two industry giants, Procter & Gamble (P&G) and Unilever. Read the case and respond to the questions below:

Jordan, Jennifer and Finkelstein, Sydney. "The Ethics of Competitive Intelligence." Tuck School of Business at Dartmouth, http://mba.tuck.dartmouth.edu/pdf/ 2005-1-0095.pdf

QUESTIONS

1. According to the case, Procter & Gamble was accused of having "their competitive intelligence operatives misrepresent themselves to Unilever employees, claiming that they were market analysts, journalists, and students." Is this a serious breach of ethical behavior, or is it a savvy business strategy? Why or why not?

2. One common competitive intelligence/corporate espionage practice is to troll for information in the public arena. This might include dumpster diving (searching through trash), or eavesdropping on executives while they're on the telephone. Based on what you've read in the case, should this type of information gathering be illegal? Why or why not? Is there a difference between overhearing sensitive information and digging through the garbage?

3. The case concludes with Chairman Pepper's dilemma. If you learned that your employees had gone against your ethical code to acquire sensitive information on a competitor what would you do? Would you discipline your employees? Would you make a public statement? Would you inform your competitor? Would you use the information? Explain your rationale.

7.9 Decide

Corporate secrets

Naomi is a project director in the research and development department at Hygea Pharmaceuticals. She and her closely-knit team of researchers have been working on developing antiretroviral drugs to help combat HIV/AIDS. Despite a number of important breakthroughs, her team has yet to produce a drug that is ready for market.

Millions of dollars and many years of research are required for even the simplest of drugs, making pharmaceutical R&D an expensive, time-consuming process. However, when drugs can successfully deliver on their promises, they improve the quality and length of life for the user—not to mention, make their manufacturer incredible amounts of money. Considering the number of people affected with HIV/AIDS around the world, nearly every pharmaceutical company has at least one team devoted to researching the condition.

Last month, Naomi received a strange email from an anonymous source, claiming to have information that might help the team's research. This source supposedly works for Stockham-Given-Aldrich (SGA), a rival pharmaceutical firm. This week, Naomi's industry brief reported that SGA is trimming down their R&D portfolio and has decided to halt their AIDS research for the foreseeable future.

The anonymous source that contacted Naomi claims the SGA HIV/AIDS team was closer to a breakthrough than the executives realized. Rather than wait for SGA to revive their research, this source is offering to send the information to Naomi and her team at Hygea. There is a possibility that the source has approached other companies with the same offer, but it doesn't look like the source is seeking monetary compensation for the information.

Naomi is unsure of how to proceed. Senior directors at Hygea are getting restless and are putting intense pressure on Naomi's team to deliver something that can be sent to drug trials. She knows that the information from SGA might give them a new research angle, but she doesn't want to compromise her ethics or research program.

What do you think Naomi should do? Four options are presented on the following page.

Name _____ Date _____

In the space provided, discuss the advantages and disadvantages of each option and make a final recommendation.

A) Naomi should try to obtain the information.

B) Naomi should take the entire situation to the senior executives of Hygea and let them decide how to proceed.

C) Naomi should tell the source that Hygea is not interested in the information.

D) Naomi should bring the issue to the members of her research team so they can make a group decision.

So, what did you think Naomi should do? Why?

_____

_____

_____

_____

_____

_____

_____

Chapter

Privacy

8.1 Identifiability

On the Nature of Identity

Who are you? Seriously, who are you? There are over six billion people on this planet. How are you distinguished from everyone else? How can we tell you apart from your friends, relatives or co-workers? The answers to these questions are more integral to our society than you might think.

On a basic level, we're all the same. Being human means that we are similar physiologically and psychologically. Yet upon closer inspection, we're also quite different. Even among relatively homogenous groups (people who share similar characteristics) individuals exhibit different traits, preferences and behavior. Of course, it is precisely these differences that make each of us unique.

Behavioral characteristics describe one way to differentiate ourselves, but there are other methods. For example, your name differentiates you from the others around you. While someone somewhere may share your name, we can reasonably assume that those people do not share the same birth date or the same parents. If it's not names, it's numbers. Your driver's license number, for example, separates you from the other drivers on the road.

The collection of biological attributes, cultural traditions, observable circumstances, and institutional attachments that you acquire over your lifetime combine to form your identity. In fact, civilized society requires that people be identifiable to function properly. Governments need to differentiate their citizens, employers need to differentiate their employees, banks need to differentiate their patrons, schools need to differentiate their students—you get the idea. When it comes to personal identification, there are many ways to uniquely identify people. In his comprehensive discussion on the nature of identity, Gary Marx proposed the following seven methods:[1]

1. **Name.** As we've already mentioned, legal names distinguish us from each other; however, a name is more than just an arbitrary label. Names also connect us to our biological or social lineage. For example, your name identifies your family and potentially reveals your cultural background.
2. **Location.** We can be identified by our addresses. Location information might describe the physical location where we live, but it could also relate to places we frequent. As more and more devices are equipped with Global Positioning Systems (GPS), it is increasingly possible to locate someone in real-time with startling accuracy. Location no longer requires fixed addresses. Personal identification is easier, because our mobile technology (which we take great pains to personalize) continually broadcasts our location.

3. **Traceable alphanumeric symbols.** We can be identified via numbers and other identification symbols that we acquire through the normal course of life. Phone numbers, credit card numbers, social security numbers, bank account numbers, application numbers, and even biometric patterns like fingerprints distinguish us from the crowd. Usually these numbers are administered and controlled by a trusted intermediary (e.g. governments, financial institutions, etc.) and are not linked or revealed except under restricted circumstances.

4. **Untraceable alphanumeric symbols.** Sometimes we acquire numbers or symbols that are not linked to our identity, but serve to distinguish individuals from one another. For example, many law enforcement offices operate anonymous tip lines for people to report crimes. Each call or caller might be assigned an identification number, but that number is not connected to the identity of the caller. For all intents and purposes, the identity of the caller remains unknown to law enforcement.

5. **Pattern behavior.** Whether we realize it or not, we can be identified by the patterns in our lives. Purchase habits, daily schedules, and online communication can all be analyzed to distinguish individuals. For example, if you go to the gym regularly, chances are you will start to recognize other people who frequent the same gym at roughly the same time. While you may not know the other patrons by name, in some sense they are still identifiable.

6. **Social categorization.** We differentiate people based on social categories like gender, age, sex, religion, class, employment status, language, and culture. These categories might even be expanded to include leisure activities, social clubs, sporting events, or educational endeavors.

7. **Certification and Eligibility.** People can be identified by their possession of knowledge, artifacts, or skills. For example, employees with proper passwords can access the company's secure information systems, those without cannot. Similarly, artifacts like badges and uniforms separate police officers from regular citizens. Even Olympic athletes must meet basic performance benchmarks in their respective sports before they're allowed to compete internationally. All of these methods are ways we distinguish the eligible candidates from the ineligible.

Why is the nature of identity so important? Because identity is closely tied to privacy. If we want to respect the privacy rights of individuals and organizations, we need to know what factors can identify those individuals and organizations. At its core, privacy is the ability to be left alone, undisturbed, and free from public attention. We have a right to freedom from interference or intrusion.[2] Privacy is more than simply the right to remain unidentified, it is also the right to choose when identity should be concealed or revealed. True privacy, then, grants control to the individual or organization over identifiability.[3]

The Information Age further complicates the matter of privacy rights. Before the widespread use of information technology for communication, people confirmed identities face-to-face. To be sure, it was still possible to misrepresent yourself or impersonate someone else, but it was more difficult. In the Information Age knowledge of someone's social security number and mother's maiden name means that misrepresentation, fraud, and impersonation are much easier acts to commit.[4]

"In face-to-face interaction we have visual and auditory cues to assess strangers; even then, common sense advises caution. How much truer that is when we lack these in cyberspace and have even less grounds for knowing the identity of strangers and if they are who they claim to be."[5] Information technology has created a communication environment where we are incredibly cue-deaf—or, at the very, least cue-deficient.

8.2 Anonymity

Pseudonymity + Confidentiality

Related to privacy is the concept of anonymity. In its simplest definition, anonymity describes conducting yourself without revealing your identity. When no one knows who you are—and when its essentially impossible for people to find out who you are—you act anonymously. In the Information Age, this means you can participate in discussion forums, complete transactions, and visit websites without your identity being revealed.[6]

Online anonymity differs from offline anonymity in two ways: dissemination and persistence. First, our information infrastructure makes it much easier to broadcast information. Information can be disseminated far and wide at relatively low cost. With such distribution, anonymity becomes harder to protect. Second, information remains archived for much longer. Evidence simply doesn't disappear easily. Companies keep terabytes of consumer data, governments keep decades of personal records, and websites keep clickstream data on millions of visitors. In many cases all of these data are backed-up multiple times on multiple servers. Again anonymity becomes more difficult to ensure as we lose control over our information.[7]

There are at least two other types of anonymity that are relevant to the Information Age: pseudonymity and confidentiality. Pseudonymity involves conducting affairs under an assumed name. It might be a nickname, a pen name, or even a symbol. Think about all of the web services you use on the Internet (email, social networking, etc.). Many of them require a user name and password to access their websites. For each of these services the screen names we choose act as stand-ins or pseudonyms for our legal names. When we choose our screen names, we also choose whether or not to link our real names to our online pseudonyms. In essence, we have some control over our identifiability.

Confidentiality is another type of anonymity. Confidentiality means that identity is known, but such knowledge remains protected and is not made public. Anonymity and confidentially are often used interchangeably, but they describe different situations. Suppose researchers were conducting a survey on attitudes toward personal financial planning. If the researchers guarantee anonymity, they are not recording identifiable information. In this situation individual responses to survey questions cannot be linked the respondents who made them. If the researchers guarantee confidentiality, then identifiable information is collected and individual responses can be linked to individual respondents. The difference is that the information is protected from dissemination. Any identifiable information is concealed and kept in confidence. The difference between anonymity and confidentiality is subtle, but important.

Anonymity, pseudonymity and confidentiality are important because they give us a better range of communication options for controlling our individual privacy. Depending on the circumstances, of course, protecting identity and preserving confidentiality can be negative or positive. Such are the trade-offs in the Information Age.

8.3 Privacy Legislation

Anonymity + Accountability

In a democratic society, our right to privacy is closely associated with similar rights like freedom of the press, freedom of speech, or freedom of assembly. In fact, we might even argue that privacy is implicit in various iterations of the modern social contract (section 7.2). Let me explain. We regularly surrender personal identifiable information to governments, companies and other organizations. We give up our information to these institutions in exchange for goods, services, or some other perceived benefit. Similarly, organizations agree to protect our information and respect our privacy in return for the right to provide us with those goods and services.

Unspoken social contracts might work well in theory, but legislating the negotiations between public and private interests, or individual and collective interests, can get messy. On the one hand, protecting privacy certainly encourages people to be more forthcoming in their interactions and contributions. By concealing personal identity we provide "improved freedom from detection, retribution, and embarrassment."[8] On the other hand, protecting privacy also opens the door for deception, impersonation, misrepresentation, fraud and other illegal activities.

The law represents our best attempt to reconcile the individual's need for anonymity with society's need for identifiability. Ultimately, privacy legislation is designed to balance the individual's right to privacy with the organization's right (and need) to collect personal information to conduct its affairs. If the laws favor the individual, then organizations cannot collect the information they need to run their businesses efficiently. If the laws favor organizations, then privacy of individuals is potentially compromised.

It shouldn't surprise you to learn that there is no shared standard for privacy laws. In fact, regulations vary widely around the globe. Some types of information, like personal health records or financial information, are more sensitive than others and warrant extra legal protection. And some types of organizations, like schools, hospitals and other public institutions, require more transparent collection processes. Laws might also vary based on the technology used to obtain the information in the first place. But perhaps the main reason for different laws is that nations have different cultural traditions and expectations of privacy.

In the European Union, for example, member nations must follow the Directive on the Protection of Personal Data.[9] This piece of legislation relates to the processing of personal data and the free movement of such data within the EU. The directive has three basic principles: the reasons for collecting information must be transparent, the purpose for collection must be legitimate, and the use of the information should be proportional to its purpose for collection. Like all EU Directives, however, it stops short of telling countries how to achieve these principles.

On the other end of the spectrum, the United States relies on a combination of laws and self-regulation to enforce personal privacy rights. Federal legislation like the Children's Online Privacy Protection Act (COPPA), which provides restrictions for websites that collect the personal information of children, tends to be fairly limited in scope. Instead, privacy legislation in the United States is primarily a state responsibility. This is not to suggest that there aren't federal recommendations or related pieces of legislation, only that there isn't a single comprehensive legislative act related to privacy rights. For example, the Federal

Trade Commission recently adopted the following standards for regulating the collection of information:[10]

1. Individuals should be given notice that information is being collected about them and be aware of what information is being collected.
2. Individuals should provide consent and should choose how they want their information to be used or distributed.
3. Individuals should have the right to view data that has been collected, and have the right to challenge inaccurate or incomplete information.
4. Organizations that collect data should provide safeguards and secure the information accordingly.
5. There should be an enforcement mechanism in place to ensure organizations comply with these standards.

These standards may not have found their way into a unified federal act in the United States, but they can be found in the foundation for Canada's national privacy legislation. In Canada, organizations involved in commercial activity must adhere to the Personal Information Protection and Electronic Documents Act (PIPEDA).[11] This act requires organizations to be accountable for their information gathering practices. They must protect the data in their possession, identify the purpose for collection, limit how the information is used, enable individuals to access their information upon request, and discard the information when it is no longer useful. Companies that fail to comply with these principles face fines and penalties.[12]

While the letter of the law differs for national directives in the European Union, federal legislation in Canada, and state laws in the United States, the spirit of the law is the same: provide organizations with good standards for information management. In the Information Age, even small companies have the ability to attract customers from other parts of the world; as a result, organizations need to be aware of international privacy legislation. Of course, enforcing these regulations is another matter.

8.4 Data Mining

Anonymity by Aggregation

Sometimes organizations protect privacy and ensure the anonymity of individuals by aggregating the data they collect. This strategy lumps data together according to similar characteristics, making it difficult to identify any one individual. The advantage to aggregation is that it allows organizations to recognize key patterns. For example, most governments conduct a national census survey every five or ten years, which each citizen is required to complete. Even though the government collects information on every single citizen, it is more useful for the government to look at the data from a broader perspective.

Grouping people together based on similar characteristics (age, ethnicity, income level, neighborhood, etc.) will reveal trends more quickly than focusing on each individual. Of course, governments also have a commitment to protect each citizen's privacy, so the aggregated approach enables them to get meaningful information for policy development without compromising individual identity.

Companies also spend a lot of effort gathering and analyzing customer data. Typically, companies collect two types of data: subscription data and transaction data. Subscription data are personal details. Consumers submit this data willingly at the time of purchase or when they register for a service. For example, when you buy a book from Amazon, you provide Amazon with a number of personal details (name, address, email, etc.). Transaction data are preference details. Consumers create this activity data while they interact with the company. To use the book example, each title you buy creates transaction data (type of book, chosen method of payment, preferred shipping option, etc). Over time, Amazon compiles this information and learns what you like (and what you don't).[13]

By pooling enough consumer data companies can use a technique called data mining to identify important patterns. Data mining applies sophisticated statistical models to aggregated data in order to predict consumer behavior. Some typical applications of data mining include analyzing:

Propensity to Buy.   For a movie rental store, analyzing past rental patterns will improve inventory management. Managers can use past data to anticipate the demand for the next blockbuster action movie, and stock the appropriate number of copies. Will customers prefer Blu-Ray or DVD formats?

Next sequential purchase.   For a bank, analyzing customer data will help deliver promotional offers at the appropriate time. Managers can use past data to determine which products consumers are likely to purchase next. If a customer opens a savings account, how long will it be until they open a checking account?

Product affinity.   For a drug store, analyzing purchase patterns will help identify common product combinations. Managers can use past data to pair products for special promotions. If a male customer purchases a package of diapers on a Friday afternoon, what other products is he likely to have in his cart?[14]

Price elasticity modeling.   For an airline, analyzing customer data will help optimize pricing and maximize profits for individual flight routes. Managers can use supply and demand data to tie seat pricing to circumstances. If a customer needs to fly from New York to Toronto last minute what is she willing to pay?

As you can see, using aggregated customer data can deliver incredible insight. Anticipating what your customers want before they know they want it is simply good information management. However, for some organizations identifying patterns isn't enough. Organizations also want the ability to identify individuals. After all, what good is identifying patterns and changing your business practices, if you can't market those new promotions to individual consumers?

This is where the idea of anonymity by aggregation begins to break down. "Even where fragments of information do not lead to information that is uniquely identifying, people may be identified with a high degree of probability when various properties are compounded to include a smaller and smaller set of individuals who satisfy them all."[15] In other words, by cross-examining available data or by querying for multiple criteria, we can uncover the secrets of aggregated data. With enough data manipulation individual identities become known.

While using aggregated data to mask individual identities is a decent strategy, it is not entirely fail-safe. When data are refined to such precise levels of detail there is potential for the information to be abused. The abuse might be relatively harmless, like organizations using their data to send targeted marketing messages. The messages are unwanted and unsolicited, but they're a fairly minor nuisance.[16] Or, the abuse might be more serious, like organizations using their data to discriminate against groups based on certain characteristics (age, race, income, etc.). In the Information Age, even something as simple as using a credit card means that we are subject to surveillance by a variety of public and private organizations.

8.5 Privacy Doesn't Exist

Anonymity is an Illusion

Is privacy even possible in the Information Age? "As the Internet evolves into a mass medium, users are finding it increasingly difficult to preserve the right of autonomous choice in concealing or disclosing personal information, and may have to live with the erosion of their informational privacy."[17] Over a decade ago, Scott McNealy put it even more bluntly: "You have zero privacy anyway. Get over it."[18] But is he right? Is privacy gone for good?

To be sure, information technology has forced us to redefine privacy. For example, the introduction of Caller ID features for telephone users initially raised a lot of privacy concerns. People were accustomed to making phone calls without having their phone number revealed. Some customers were so upset that they started filing lawsuits against the telephone companies.[19] Clearly, people felt that their telephone number was private personal information. Now, of course, we expect to be able to see the phone number of the person calling us. If we don't, we don't answer the phone. We've done an about-face and there's no going back.

While most of us support privacy rights as an abstract concept, we are not so vigilant when it comes to protecting our privacy.[20] We readily surrender personal information in exchange for goods, services, or even free t-shirts. As more organizations collect our information, there are many points of entry to our identities. With sophisticated database-driven systems our identities can be found through our names, street addresses, emails, phone numbers, credit card numbers, passports, employee identification, travel history, level of education, purchase history, and magazine subscriptions—just to name a few. We say we value our privacy, yet we give it up so easily.

Of course, sometimes we are not presented with a choice. We are required to give up personal information. In Western society, nearly every major experience we have is logged into a database somewhere. "Our presence on the planet, our notable features and momentous milestones, are dutifully recorded by agencies of federal, state, and local government, including birth, marriage, divorce, property ownership, drivers' licenses, vehicle registration, moving violations, passage through computerized toll roads and bridges, parenthood, and, finally, our demise."[21] Even after death, information delivers evidence of our existence, eroding any hope we had for anonymity. You can't go through life without leaving a mark—our public institutions make sure of that.

It is tempting to think that using the Internet makes our activities anonymous. Since most of our actions are mediated by machine we separate our behavior from our bodies. When we hop online, we believe we're joining the millions of other unidentifiable individuals surfing the Internet. Unfortunately, surveillance activities and data monitoring turn this vision into an illusion. With access to the right information, every single thing you do online can be tracked, logged and retrieved at a later date.[22]

Maybe you don't care if organizations track what you do online. Why should you be worried? After all, you're not surfing for illicit images of child pornography, or reading instructions on how to build a pipe bomb. You have no reason to be concerned, right? In fact, you might even argue that if your online preferences are known, then organizations can deliver more relevant services. This argument makes sense in the short term, but what about the long-term? Your Internet searches, your purchases, your conversations aren't a concern for now, but they might be in the future.

Don't get me wrong; I'm not trying to be alarmist. Nor am I suggesting that we are victims of a larger conspiracy to undermine our privacy rights. I'm merely warning against developing a false sense of security. "Sir Francis Bacon, the Elizabethan father of inductive science, wrote optimistically that 'knowledge is power.' But in our contemporary digital age, it is information, rather than knowledge, that lends power. And the more personal the information, the more power it promises to those who hold it."[23]

Finally, we've arrived at the crux of privacy in the Information Age: information is personal. Each time we surrender personal information we leave ourselves vulnerable to exploitation. Remember that privacy rights grant us control over when we want to be identifiable and when we want to be anonymous. Can we really exercise this control when we don't know where our information is or who possesses it?

8.6 Experiment

Online confessions

For thousands of years, confessing wrongs has been part of religious traditions around the world. Penitent parishioners bring their sins to the religious establishment and appeal for forgiveness. In some traditions confession is an essential part of living a holy life. It is an act that transcends the human experience to reunite the believer with the divine. In other traditions, confession is simply an act of acknowledging wrongs and asking for gentle correction. Confession becomes an opportunity for further spiritual development.

Most traditions require the parishioner to bring his misdeeds to a priest or religious authority; however, some approaches remove the mediator and allow for the faithful believer to confess his sins directly to the divine. Regardless of the requirements of tradition, we can observe that confession usually happens in an anonymous (or semi-anonymous) environment. This condition of anonymity enables the person confessing to speak more freely, presumably providing a more truthful confession.

While religious confession isn't for everyone, many of us have experienced the desire to confess at some point in our lives. The particular circumstances may vary, but we all hope confessing our actions will help us clear our conscience. By admitting our motives, revealing our thoughts, and speaking the unspeakable, we hope to relieve some of the guilt and tension.

We tend to think that confession happens on a face-to-face basis, but information and communication technology provides another medium for confession. The Internet can easily provide partial anonymity and, as we'll see, confessional activity thrives in such an environment. Even churches are taking advantage of the Information Age. Welcome to the era of the e-confession.[24]

For this experiment you will look at some of the popular places for posting online, anonymous confessions. Some of the postings are silly and some are serious, some are unique and some are universal, but all are interesting. Use the worksheet on the next page to get started.

Worksheet

Name _____ Date _____

Part A

Spend some time exploring some of the following projects. Be sure to read at least a dozen confessions on each site:

Group Hug.us (http://grouphug.us/)

Experience Project (http://www.experienceproject.com/confessions.php)

Unburdened (http://www.unburdened.net/)

Post Secret Blog (http://postsecret.blogspot.com/)

Part B

1. Which website was the most interesting? Why?

2. Did you find any of the confessions amusing or entertaining? If so, provide a couple of examples.

3. Were you disturbed by anything that you read? If so, provide a couple of examples.

4. One of the goals of religious confessions is to encourage the person confessing to change their behavior. Could the same be said of these secular, online confessionals? Why or why not?

5. Would you ever consider confessing online? Why or why not?

6. Some say that reading confessions online is essentially voyeurism (getting satisfaction by watching others). Although the confessions are anonymous, did you feel strange reading them? Did you feel like you were invading someone's privacy? Discuss.

8.7 Reflect

Radio frequency identification (RFID)

Josh McHugh travels to Germany to visit the RFID-equipped Future Store. In this grocery market, nearly every item is tagged using Radio Frequency Identification tags, enabling the store to manage its inventory in real time and collect vast quantities of data. Not surprisingly, RFID technology has caused some controversy (so much so that Future Store has since dropped their RFID program). Read the article and respond to the questions below:

McHugh, Josh. "Attention, Shoppers: You Can Now Speed Straight Through Checkout Lines!" *Wired* 12, no. 7 (2004), http://www.wired.com/wired/archive/12.07/shoppers.html

---

QUESTIONS

1. McHugh's experience at the RFID-equipped Future Store in Germany includes products that trigger advertising, pricing that varies depending on inventory levels, and shelves that notify employees when product is needed. After reading his article, do you think RFID technology will create the revolution in retail that its supporters promise? Why or why not?

2. McHugh describes his grocery shopping experience as "a multimedia scavenger hunt. It's as though the store is reaching out to help me, entertain me, and, yes, take my money." What do you think about the future of RFID? Will it make experiences like shopping for groceries easier? Will RFID complicate the shopping experience and compromise consumer privacy? Why?

3. In addition to helping companies manage their supply chains more effectively, RFID technology has the potential to provide retailers with vast amounts of data about their consumers. Many companies regularly measure and analyze consumer behavior, but some consumers object to this practice. Whose rights are more important in the RFID technology debate: the company or the consumer? Why?

8.8 Reflect

Consumer data

Constance Hays discusses the amount of consumer data collected by the world's largest retailer (Wal-Mart). In her article, she provides a number of scenarios where Wal-Mart capitalizes on their information assets. Of course, not everyone loves how Wal-Mart uses the information to its advantage. Read the article and respond to the questions below.

Hays, Constance L. "What Wal-Mart Knows About Customers' Habits." *New York Times,* (Nov 14, 2004), http://www.nytimes.com/2004/11/14/business/yourmoney/14wal.html?ei=5094&en=4600bf878b8f7db8&hp=&ex=11004

QUESTIONS

1. Katherine Albrecht, a consumer privacy advocate, says "people don't know that Wal-Mart is capturing information about who they are and what they bought, but they are also capable of capturing a huge amount of outside information about them that has nothing to do with their grocery purchases." What do you think of this statement? Do you worry about the information collected about you by retailers? Why or why not?

2. Retailers, like Wal-Mart, claim that collecting so much customer data protects them "from a retailer's twin nightmares: too much inventory, or not enough." After reading the article, does this sound like a reasonable argument? Should there be a limit on how much information retailers should be able to collect? Why or why not?

3. Wal-Mart has chosen not to implement a loyalty card program, deciding instead to compete on low prices. Other companies have chosen to implement a loyalty card strategy, providing points for customers who shop at their stores. Do you think it is a good idea for companies to use rewards programs to differentiate themselves from competitors? Do customers decide where to shop based on loyalty programs? Why or why not?

8.9 Decide

Customer privacy

Tech Garden Electronics is a retailer of consumer electronics, computers, home office products, software, music, videos, appliances, mobile phones, satellite television and related services. It operates retail stores and provides commercial tech-based services. In addition to selling products, Tech Garden Electronics offers installation and maintenance services as well as technical support through its Cyber Crew service.

Amar was hired two months ago to join the company as a Cyber Crew technician. Amar's knowledge of personal computing made him a perfect candidate for Tech Garden's residential services division. Amar's employment contract has a standard three-month probationary clause. This clause allows either the company or the employee to terminate employment within the first three months if either party is unsatisfied with the arrangement. To date, Amar has done an admirable job in his position, and has every intention of continuing employment with Tech Garden Electronics.

Last week, Amar overheard some fellow technicians talking about a few of their recent service calls. Given the nature of the Cyber Crew service it is not unusual for technicians to visit a customer's residence to solve the problem on-site. What disturbed Amar was he heard his co-workers taking about how they routinely scan customers' hard drives for private information (personal data, passwords, even pornography). According to these technicians they don't plan to use the data, they just want to see what they can find. For them, finding information that people want to keep hidden is kind of like a treasure hunt—it makes the job "more interesting" as one co-worker put it.

While these accounts certainly make for entertaining stories around the office, Amar does not believe that Cyber Crew technicians should be operating in this manner. Amar is considering reporting what he heard to his manager, Kevin, but Amar is still within his probationary term and his long-term employment with Tech Garden Electronics is not yet guaranteed.

What do you think Amar should do?

Name _____   Date _____

Four options are presented on this page. In the space provided, discuss the advantages and disadvantages of each option and make a final recommendation.

A) Amar should bring the issue to his manager, Kevin.

B) Amar should keep quiet and pretend that he did not overhear his co-workers talking.

C) Amar should address the issue with his co-workers directly.

D) Amar should keep quiet until his employment is guaranteed, then he should approach Kevin.

So, what do you think Amar should do? Why?

_____

_____

_____

_____

_____

_____

_____

Security

9.1 Surveillance

The Little Brothers are watching

For many people privacy is inextricably linked to security. We imagine privacy and security at opposite ends of a scale. If we swing too far toward privacy, it becomes too hard to tell the good guys from the bad, and our sense of security plummets. Likewise, if we swing too far toward security, it grants too much power to the state, and our right to privacy disappears. To be sure, privacy and security are related, but they're not opposing concepts. The reality is that you can't have security without privacy. "Security is vital to survival, not just of people but of every living thing. Privacy is unique to humans, but it's a social need. It's vital to personal dignity, to family life, to society—to what makes us uniquely human—but not to survival."[1] One area where the dichotomy between privacy and security plays out nicely is the act of surveillance.

In the Information Age we are accustomed to being watched. Security cameras regularly track us as we ride the bus, shop at the local mall, or run a red light. One recent study estimated that the United Kingdom has over 4.2 million closed-circuit cameras and the average Londoner can expect to make 300 appearances per day on various closed-circuit television networks.[2] Ironically, the surveillance society has arrived and we barely noticed.

Surveillance is more than simply watching others with cameras. More accurately, surveillance describes the moments "where we find purposeful, routine, systematic and focused attention paid to personal details, for the sake of control, entitlement, management, influence or protection."[3] Pay close attention: surveillance activities have a motive (purpose), they occur during the normal course of life (routine), they are planned (systematic), and, most importantly, they are detail-oriented (focused). Surveillance isn't about looking at the aggregated data of the masses. It's about looking at the particular data of individuals.

This definition expands acts of surveillance to include things like: locating people by mobile phone signal, tracking purchases through credit card transactions, tapping telephone lines, scanning landscapes with global satellites, or monitoring Internet traffic.[4] Surveillance includes acts of face-to-face monitoring and acts of electronic monitoring, but it can also refer to acts of data monitoring. Purchases, telephone calls, banking transactions, television viewing habits, even changing the oil in your car can be logged and analyzed to track behavior. In some circles, such data mining practices have been described as "dataveillance."[5]

Of course, surveillance isn't a new concept—people have always watched over others. Parents monitor children, managers monitor employees, guards monitor prisoners, and governments monitor citizens. Most of us understand that surveillance helps keep society safe and secure. We even accept that companies have the right to monitor employees to ensure productivity, and that retailers have the right to monitor their customers to protect their property.[6]

The difference in the Information Age is that information technology makes surveillance much easier. Automated computer processes are quickly replacing monitoring people in person through face-to-face interaction. Managers can install keystroke programs that record everything employees type or monitoring software that logs every website they visit. Parents can use GPS-equipped cell phones and mobile gadgets to track their children. Governments can install security cameras with facial recognition technology that automatically identify each citizen within view. Note the shift: surveillance is aimed at everyone, not just a few suspects. We've moved away from "follow that individual," to "follow every individual."[7]

Surveillance in the Information Age is a lot like the concept behind Jeremy Bentham's Panopticon. In the late eighteenth century, Jeremy Bentham (section 7.2) designed a prison that optimized prisoner surveillance. The prisoners' cells were arranged in a circular design with the guards' station situated in the center. Through clever architectural features, Bentham ensured that the prisoners could never determine when the guards were watching. The guards could observe the prisoners, but the prisoners couldn't observe the guards. Since the prisoners could never be completely sure when they were being watched, they had to assume that they were *always* being watched. This uncertainty enabled the few guards to appear omnipresent—even omniscient. In fact, Bentham's name for the prison means "all-seeing."

While prisoners in the Panopticon didn't know *when* they were being watched, they certainly knew *who* was watching them. In the Information Age, however, we're not so lucky. We have a hard time determining when we're being watched and an even harder time determining who is watching. Since the tools of surveillance are accessible and affordable, such activities are no longer limited to authorities. Equipped with camera phones, MP3 recorders, nanny cameras, snooping software, and listening devices, we can spy on any one we please—including the authorities.[8]

With each act of surveillance there is a risk that we will become desensitized to the privacy implications. To be sure, we need to guard against authoritarian, Big Brother approaches to surveillance, but we should be equally concerned with the Little Brothers we encounter every day. Perhaps it goes without saying, but suspicion is at the heart of surveillance. We simply don't trust each other. In the Information Age, we cannot afford to take surveillance lightly.

9.2 The Hacker Ethic

White hat vs. black hat

So far we have focused a lot of attention on the advantages of the Information Age. We've discussed the impact of the Internet on communication, commerce and culture. And while we may have some concerns, most of us are quite satisfied with life in the Internet era. Unfortunately, one of the major drawbacks to living in a globally connected world is information security.

Remember the architects of the Internet chose a decentralized design to make the network more efficient and ease the burden of information sharing (section 5.4). The beauty of this design meant that if a portion of the network went down, messages could still reach their destinations. Unfortunately, without a central authority to oversee the development of the Internet, there was no comprehensive strategy for information security. What we have today is a patchwork of security efforts, which creates loopholes and security risks across the entire system. Exploiting the network's vulnerabilities may require significant technical skill and experience, but it can be done.

In the early 1960s, the term "hacker" was a positive term used to describe programmers who possessed an incredible mastery of computers.[9] These individuals were motivated by their curiosity; they wanted to find out how computers and networks worked—and then devised ways to do things better. Their reason for accessing unauthorized networks and computers was to learn more about these systems, not to tamper with data they contained. In fact, many hackers had unwritten rules against damaging or stealing information. These were the early days of computing and the geeks were fascinated.

As the information infrastructure evolved, so did the motives behind hacking. Instead of being motivated by curiosity, an increasing number of programmers were tempted to use their newfound knowledge for selfish interests. Some hackers performed relatively harmless pranks intended to demonstrate their abilities and gain credibility within the hacking community. Other hackers used their skills to participate in illegal activity and benefit financially. For example, one of the first known hacks was committed against the telephone network. John Draper used a child's whistle from a cereal box to imitate a tone used by the automated phone system. Duplicating the tone opened up a phone line and allowed Draper to make long-distance calls for free.[10]

Ultimately, hackers fall into two camps: the white hats and the black hats. Just like the stereotype predicts, the people wearing white are the good guys. When it comes to computers, white hat hackers are experts who test information systems to ensure that they are secure. They help organizations identify system vulnerabilities before the hackers with more malicious intentions find them. In contrast, black hat hackers (sometimes called "crackers") attack information systems with the intent of committing a crime. Black hat activities include everything from unauthorized system intrusions to outright data theft, and from spam proliferation to virus creation. Occasionally, hackers will dabble in both ethical and unethical hacking; not surprisingly, these hackers are known as grey hat hackers.

Classifying hacking as either good or bad is too simplistic, especially when we examine the foundation of hacker ideology. In *Hackers: Heroes of the Information Revolution,* Steven Levy describes the developing philosophy behind the marriage of man and machine as the "hacker ethic." Without a formal declaration or manifesto, hackers slowly developed a way of life and an unspoken method of operation for the technologically curious.[11]

The first tenet of the hacker ethic is that access to tools and technology should be unlimited. Since hackers learn by taking things apart and reverse engineering them, then computers, systems and networks should be open to such manipulation. "Imperfect systems infuriate hackers, whose primal instinct is to debug them."[12] Moreover, having access to technology allows hackers to build on their existing knowledge and develop new technology.

The hacker ethic also claimed that information wants to be free. This statement actually referred to three similar but separate ideas. Hackers felt that information should be free from restrictions (no censorship), information should be free from control (no intellectual property), and information should be free from cost (no monetary value).[13] For hackers, creativity is enhanced when they have complete access to the information they need to improve technology. Allowing information to flow freely also reduced the duplication of effort. "Instead of everyone writing his own version of the same program, the best version would be available to everyone, and everyone would be free to delve into the code and improve that."[14]

There should be no barriers between the hacker and the information or the technology needed to do the job. As such, the hacker ethic also promoted an open system. Authorities and bureaucracies hampered creativity with their arbitrary rules and insufficient understanding of technology. Instead, hackers adopted a near-anarchist approach that embraced the full extent of decentralization.

Traditional markers of success and impressive credentials did not matter in the hacker world. The inherent anonymity of hacking made it possible for hackers to be evaluated strictly on their abilities. Within the hacker community, hackers were judged by one standard: how good they were at the computer console. Credibility was merit-based and hackers cared more about how to advance the practice of hacking than they did about superficial qualifications of individual hackers.

Not surprisingly, hackers appreciated the beauty of the underlying code. For them a well-written application was like a work of art. Unlocking the computer's magic was a constant pursuit. With each line of code, hackers instructed computers to do new and wonderful things. Underlying the entire hacker ethic was the promise of technology. Hackers maintained that the computer and associated technologies could change society for the better—and the hackers expected to play a primary role. Interestingly, this part of the hacker ethic elevates hacking from a mere pragmatic activity (improving poorly designed systems) to a philosophical one (pursuing the good, the true, and the beautiful).[15]

Reflecting on the hacker ethic for a moment, we can see that it is individualistic, libertarian and very hacker-centric. Every system and each circumstance is viewed (and evaluated) from the hacker's perspective. As such, the ethic is incredibly liberating. If a hacker feels that a system needs improvement, then he improves it. Of course, by attempting to improve the system without permission, he completely ignores the rights of the system's owner. This is where things get complicated. The ethic is easy to promote, but it's just as easy to pervert.

The information technology industry has matured considerably from those early days of computing, but the core components of the hacker ethic remain strong. Without the hackers' tinkering spirit, commitment to sharing, open collaboration and community building, what would the Internet look like today? Maybe their craft with computers and code really did show us the promise of new technology and usher in the computer revolution.

9.3 Computer Crime

Tricks and tools of the trade

At first glance, the hacker ethic sounds a lot like a professional or corporate code of conduct (section 7.4), but there are a few problems with this comparison. First, the hacker ethic was an unspoken code. It was understood but not explicitly expressed or explicitly agreed upon. Second, codes of conduct are communal, but most hackers are individualistic. Since hackers are judged on merit, they tend to evolve their own personal ethic regarding acceptable behavior. Third, ethics are often tied to professional standards, but hacking is defined by its anti-establishment, even anti-professional stance. To formalize an ethical code for hackers would mean the end of hacking, as we know it.[16]

Adopting an individualistic ethic means that there is potential for increased liberty *and* for increased anarchy within the broader online community. Therein lays the problem: because the hacker ethic is constantly shifting, each hacker is free to decide what is right and what is wrong. The personal computer revolution may have wrested the information technology from the hands of business and government, but putting programming power into the hands of individuals also has its risks.

Since technology holds incredible power over modern society, there is even greater incentive for hackers to ply their trade and subvert or corrupt the system. Computers are more powerful, more numerous, and more networked, so an individual hacker can inflict more widespread damage. Here are just a few examples of hacking behavior that satisfies personal interests at the expense of the public:

Data diddling.   Essentially, hackers use remote computers to penetrate security and break into an information system. Once they have access to the system, hackers are free to copy, steal, or manipulate the data as they see fit.

Salami slicing.   Hackers break into a financial system and install an application that allows them to take small bits of money from multiple accounts and deposit those miniscule amounts into a single account.

Phreaking.   This is an encompassing term for hacks committed against the telephone networks. It might include activities like scamming free long distance calls, impersonating operator services, or cloning cell phones.

Piggy-backing.   This hack (sometimes called "shoulder surfing") involves trying to steal a Personal Identification Number (PIN) by looking over the victim's shoulder. Although this seems fairly low-tech for a computer crime, hackers know that learning a PIN can gain access to other confidential information.

Social engineering.   This term describes any activity where the hacker misrepresents himself to get the information he needs. Social engineering is a specific type of fraud, where the hacker manipulates technology to exploit human weaknesses. For example, an attacker might impersonate his victim in a phone call to the victim's insurance company, in an attempt to get the company to release confidential information.

Phishing.   This hack (sometimes called spoofing) might fall under the category of social engineering because it fools victims into revealing confidential information. In fact, phishing is actually short for "password harvesting." Phishing attacks tend to focus on victims who are less technically savvy. For example, unsuspecting users might be directed to verify their account number and password on a website that closely resembles their bank's website; however, the website is actually run by criminals who use the sensitive information provided to clear out the victim's bank account.

Cyberstalking.   This is a general term used to describe harassment conducted via information technology. Usually, cyberstalking activities are directed at specific individuals and include more than one incident. Such incidents include, but are not limited to: derogatory comments, obscene speech, and unsolicited or inappropriate advances.

Spam.   Most of us are so familiar with the nuisance of unsolicited electronic communication that we hardly need a definition. But what you may not know is that sending spam is illegal in most developed countries.

This list isn't meant to be comprehensive. As technology becomes more sophisticated, so will the nature of criminal activity. The Information Age has become more complex than it was in the 1960s. The original hacker commitment "to remove barriers, liberate information, decentralize power, honor people based on their ability, and create things that are good and life-enhancing through computers"[17] is eroding slowly—but, if we're honest, the hacker ethic probably was a little more idealistic than realistic.

 ## 9.4 Malicious Code

Attacking the infrastructure

In the previous section we listed examples of computer crime where information technology facilitates illegal activity. Gaining unauthorized access, intercepting sensitive communication, and interfering with information systems, all require the creative application of computers and networks. However, computer crimes can also target the information systems themselves. For example, hackers might craft viruses, worms, and other malicious code to hamper—even destroy—key pieces of information infrastructure. On a global network like the Internet, this type of computer crime is especially frightening.

A virus is a program that infects a computer without the owner's permission (or knowledge) and attempts to copy itself to other computers. While computer viruses are not the same as biological viruses, they certainly share similarities. Since viruses cannot copy themselves on their own they need help with reproduction. In our bodies, viruses hijack the cell's ability to reproduce itself in order to spread. In our computers, viruses piggyback on other applications in order to transfer from machine to machine.[18]

Both types of viruses have damaging effects. Included in each computer virus program is a payload, or attack phase. This is the part of the executable code that activates once the virus has successfully lodged itself in a new system. The impact of the payload varies. Sometimes the virus is programmed to display a simple pop-up message, other times it is designed to corrupt a popular application, and in the most damaging cases, the virus destroys data and renders the machine inoperable.

Generally speaking, viruses can only spread when the host machine directly interacts with the target machine. Such interaction might occur via an email attachment, via a shared network application, or via corrupted physical media (CD, USB drive, etc.).[19] In contrast, computer worms have the ability to replicate themselves around a network. They are standalone programs that can send copies of themselves without user intervention.

Like viruses, worms can be programmed to destroy data, but more often they are used to open up backdoor access into the infected user's system. Because worms copy themselves and send themselves around the network, another side effect to computer worms is clogged memory and bandwidth. The volume of traffic generated by worms can effectively halt network activity. In January 2003, for example, the Slammer worm made parts of the Internet go dark in less than 15 minutes.[20]

In addition to viruses and worms, computer users should be wary of Trojan horses. This type of code enters the user's system under the guise of a useful program, but underneath the surface the program is performing a number of potentially undesirable (and undisclosed) operations. The system appears to function normally, but the program has opened backdoor access for hackers to store things on the user's machine or seize control over the machine altogether. Technically, Trojan horses are not viruses because they don't replicate themselves and users consciously download the original program, but they are considered malicious code because they execute unauthorized code.

It is important to remember that malicious code is not the result of software bugs or programming errors. Programmers with specific intent create viruses, worms, and the like. Why do hackers program such damaging code? Their reasons are as many and varied as the hackers themselves. Some do it for the sheer thrill. Like vandals or arsonists, there is excitement in the act of destruction: the better the virus, the bigger the explosion. Others do it for bragging rights. By performing a clever hack and exploiting a vulnerable loophole, the hacker's credibility rises within the community.[21] Another potential reason is anarchy. Some hackers are committed to disrupting the system and will do anything within their control to undermine the established order.[22]

9.5 Cyber-terrorism

Extortion on a global scale

Malicious code can be detrimental to individual systems, but the real problem is how such code can wreak havoc on entire networks. The risk occurs not when infected computers act independently, but when they act together. As we've already discussed, the Internet is a distributed network, designed from the beginning to sustain periodic outages. As more and more machines get added to the Internet, the network becomes increasingly robust. Currently, there are millions of machines online, so it takes a significant army of computers to create chaos on the Internet.

The most common form of coordinated hack is called a denial of service (DoS) attack. As you might expect, the goal of the denial of service attack is to deny service. Hackers attempt to make a web resource unavailable to its desired users. The strategy behind a DoS attack is deceptively simple: flood the web server with so many requests for information that the server cannot distinguish the legitimate requests from the false requests. The volume of Internet traffic overwhelms the website, overloading and crashing the server—effectively disabling the website. In a typical DoS attack the data isn't destroyed, but the crippling effect of thousands of simultaneous requests means that requested data cannot be delivered. [23]

But how do hackers direct thousands of requests at a single website? The answer to that question reveals the real danger of malicious code. While some hackers are really just juvenile pranksters showing off for their friends, other hackers are plying their trade for political, criminal, or anarchist ends. The intent behind many viruses, worms, Trojan horses and other hybrid approaches is to gain unauthorized access to the victim's machine. Once a user's machine is compromised, the hacker opens a backdoor, granting himself perpetual access to the computer—usually without the user's knowledge.

In information security circles, an infected computer is often called a zombie and a collection of zombie machines is called a botnet. Such machines function normally for their users, but can be instructed to commit any number of acts in the background. Botnets are often behind the proliferation of denial of service attacks, spam, adware (unwanted advertising), and spyware (unwanted behavior tracking). While it is difficult to estimate the number of compromised machines, some experts claim that almost 20% of computers on the Internet are actually zombies.[24]

When botnets aren't sending spam, attacking websites, and delivering unwanted pop-up ads, they can be used for extortion. Let's try a brief thought experiment. Suppose you own your own mid-sized business. Like most businesses your website is an essential tool for advertising and communicating with your customers. One day you get an email from a potential attacker threatening to direct a botnet at your website. He claims he will crash your website with a basic denial of service attack unless you pay him $10,000 by the end of the week. What do you do? You have no way of knowing whether or not the hacker has the capability or not. If you pay him, you've set yourself up as an easy target. If you don't, you may temporarily disappear from the Internet (and lose a lot of business).

Corporate extortion is one thing, but what about when botnets are directed at entire countries? It sounds crazy, but there have been a number of examples in the past few years. The most obvious event happened in the northern European country of Estonia. Estonia has been called the most wired nation in Europe. Its population of over 1.3 million people practically lives online. More than any other European country, Estonians use the Internet to make telephone calls, to read the news, to conduct banking, and even to vote. In fact, most citizens enjoy free access to the country's wireless Internet network. Clearly, to disrupt the Internet, is to disrupt the entire way of life for Estonians.

To fully understand the significance and reasons behind the botnet assault on Estonia we need to take a brief history lesson. Estonia was occupied by Germany during WWII, but toward the end of the war the Soviets drove the Germans out. Unfortunately, instead of returning the country to the Estonians, the Soviets decided to stay. With the collapse of the Soviet Union, Estonia finally regained its freedom in 1991.[25] Of course, political friction between the two nations and within Estonia (between ethnic Russians and Estonians) still exists.

Tension between Russia and Estonia came to a head in April 2007 when Estonia decided to move a statue that the Soviets had erected after WWII. For the Russian people, this statue commemorated their fallen soldiers from the war. For Estonia, the statue symbolized the oppressive Russian occupation after the war. When Estonia moved the statue from the capital city of Tallinn to a military cemetery in the suburbs, there were brief bouts of violence in the street, but the protests settled down after a few days.

Estonia wasn't prepared for what happened next. A few short days later the entire nation was attacked by a series of rogue botnets, which targeted government websites, newspaper websites, bank websites, and telecommunications

websites—nearly every essential service struggled to keep their websites functional during the attack. In fact, just to restore service security experts started to
block all international traffic coming into Estonia. This strategy worked, but it
had a major side effect. While Estonians could access the banks and media out-
lets, news of what was happening in Estonia couldn't get out of the country. By
severing their key connections to the Internet, Estonia became a virtual island.[26]

Fortunately, "the major botnet attacks stopped as suddenly as they started.
The bots appeared to have been set to run for exactly two weeks. After that, the
infected computers abandoned the attacks and reverted to more traditional botnet pastimes, like spamming and extortion."[27] It's difficult to determine who
was responsible for the attacks. Given the political history between Russia and
Estonia, many suspect the Russian government, or the Russian mob. Regardless
of who orchestrated the attacks, it should be noted that the majority of the computers participating in the attack were based in the United States—and it's a safe
bet that most Americans had little idea of what was happening half a world
away. These American computers were infected with malicious code that turned
them into zombie computers free to do someone else's bidding.

Some say that Estonia's infrastructure is more vulnerable than other nations
because it's a small country with relatively few major connections to the
Internet. That may be true, but Estonia's plight should provide a visceral warning
to all of us: the future may be less about World Wars and more about Web Wars.

9.6 Experiment

Strategies for protection

We all have a responsibility to reduce the impact of computer crime and malicious code. While there is no need to panic, it is imperative that we take security seriously. There are three basic strategies for protection: 1) authentication and authorization; 2) prevention and resistance; 3) detection and response.[28]

Authentication describes the process of confirming that people are who they say they are. Often, this confirmation is performed with a user name and password. Once the user has been properly authenticated, the user is authorized to access certain resources. The beauty of this approach is that network administrators can more easily differentiate users and grant permissions based on the user's status. For example, faculty and students logging on to their campus network require different resources, so administrators can easily set the appropriate levels of access.

The second strategy for Internet security is prevention and resistance. Prevention simply puts the appropriate roadblocks in place to make the system difficult to penetrate. It's a proactive strategy intended to anticipate and resist potential attackers. For example, network administrators use a combination of firewalls (both hardware and software) designed to keep unauthorized users out of the system. Administrators need to block unauthorized users, but they shouldn't be so aggressive that they block legitimate users too.

The third strategy for Internet security is detection and response. Users need to be vigilant and regularly test for malicious code and malware. Antivirus software is a common way to detect threats and protect information systems. Once a threat has been identified, it needs to be eliminated and the system needs to be patched to prevent such threats from reoccurring. Virus protection is like a game: virus-writers constantly program new viruses that avoid detection, and virus-scanners are constantly updating their definitions of existing viruses. That's why it is important to should keep virus protection software as current as possible.

For this experiment you will look at the global distribution of viruses and test your computer for spyware. Use the worksheet on the next page to get started.

Worksheet

Name _____   Date _____

Part A

McAfee is a major provider of virus software and network security tools. They also offer a suite of free tools for Internet protection. Visit their free services page (http://us.mcafee.com/root/catalog.asp?catid=free) and open the McAfee World Virus Map (about halfway down the page). This map is an interactive look at the impact of viruses on computers around the world. Take a moment to examine the map. Be sure to select different options from the drop-down menus. Reflect on the questions below:

1. Are you surprised by the number of machines infected with viruses? Why or why not?

2. Which countries have the most infected computers? Why do you think that is?

3. Did you notice any global trends related to viruses? Provide examples if you can.

Part B

Most compromised machines are infected with spyware (unauthorized applications that spy on the users activities) not viruses. Spyware is a nuisance because it can hamper system performance and execute actions that the user did not authorize. There are a number of free tools for spyware detection; we're going to use one called Malwarebytes. To complete this activity you will need to download a small program to a Windows computer (Malwarebytes is not designed for Apple computers or Linux-based machines). Follow the instructions below and then reflect on the questions.

Visit: http://www.malwarebytes.org/ and follow the prompts to download the free trial version (Note: you may be taken to another site to download the program, this is a common strategy for downloading freeware). Install the application on your Windows system and then perform a quick scan. Depending on how much information is on your system, the program may take five or six minutes to scan.

1. According to the report, how many objects did Malwarebytes scan? How long did it take?

2. Were you surprised by the outcome of your spyware scan? Why or why not?

3. Did you have any infected files? If so, please provide one or two examples.

4. How did the spyware get on your machine? Do you have any idea?

9.7 Reflect

Data retention

Bruce Schneier is a well-known technology expert who writes regularly on privacy, security and cryptography. In this particular article, he focuses on the concept of data pollution. More and more moments in our lives are recorded and kept for posterity, effectively eroding our privacy in the name of security. Read the article and respond to the questions below:

Schneier, Bruce. "The Tech Lab: Bruce Schneier" *BBC News,* http://news.bbc.
co.uk/2/hi/technology/7897892.stm

QUESTIONS

1. Schneier claims "you leave a trail of digital footprints throughout your day. Once you walked into a bookstore and bought a book with cash. Now you visit Amazon, and all of your browsing and purchases are recorded." Are you concerned that companies collect this type of information? Are you worried that it could be used against you in the future? Why or why not?

2. Schneier imagines a "life recorder" that will record everything that we see and hear, keeping track of our life experiences. He suggests that such an invention could be positioned as a security device. Do you think a "life recorder" is a good idea? Will it improve security? Do you think such a device will be necessary in the future? Why or why not?

3. According to Schneier, "Society works precisely because conversation is ephemeral; because people forget, and because people don't have to justify every word they utter." Do surveillance technologies threaten our basic liberties? Or, is Schneier exaggerating the issue? Do you worry casual conversations you've had over the telephone or on the Internet can be recorded? Why or why not?

9.8 Reflect

Surveillance society

Adam Penenberg talks about the current and future state of surveillance. In particular, he discusses society's tolerance for surveillance technology after the 9/11 attacks on the World Trade Center and the U.S. Pentagon. Read his article and respond to the questions below

Penenberg, Adam L. "The Surveillance Society" *Wired* 9, no. 12, December, 2001, http://www.wired.com/wired/archive/9.12/surveillance.html

---

QUESTIONS

1. Penenberg reminds us that public and private institutions (government and business) conduct surveillance activities. "And this raises a disquieting possibility: Will the disparate elements of our surveillance society be assembled into the surveillance web?" What do you think of this statement? Do you think private companies and the government will come together to create a single database for surveillance? Are you worried about that possibility? Why or why not?

2. After the 9/11 attacks airports improved security systems to include things like iris scans and facial recognition technology. These systems were then linked to "a government database of known or suspected terrorists." Do you think biometric technology like fingerprints, iris scans, or facial recognition improves security? Should they be more widely implemented? Why or why not?

3. Despite all of the advances in monitoring technology, video cameras still form the cornerstone of surveillance strategies. The argument is that cameras bring accountability to both the watcher and the person being watched and a transparency to the entire process. What do you think of this statement? Do cameras really keep people accountable for their behavior? Why or why not?

9.9 Decide
Risk + vulnerability

Blue Moose Computer Systems builds customized web-based database applications for corporate clients. In addition to designing and building these information systems, Blue Moose signs many of its customers to service contracts for database maintenance—ensuring a dependable revenue stream. Since Blue Moose does quality work and provides a full-service guarantee, they're an attractive option for many corporations.

Six months ago, Blue Moose landed a contract to rebuild some information systems within the Department of Immigration. Immigration officials wanted to make it easier for citizens to track the status of their paperwork online. Blue Moose's proposal included industry-standard security features like data encryption, robust authentication processes, redundant servers, and restrictive firewalls. The company also proposed to handle the maintenance of these systems for a two year period. This project marks the first time Blue Moose has landed a government contract.

The project was progressing quite well until a few weeks ago when the project manager, Avery, took an extended leave from Blue Moose to resolve some family matters. Without Avery around to motivate the team, production has slowed and now the team is in danger of missing its deadline. Teresa, a promising young programmer, has taken over for Avery, but she is relatively inexperienced with project management. To make matters worse, the team recently reported some errors in the database code. These bugs do not impact the functionality of the database, but they could affect the security of the data. It would take a fair amount of technical expertise for a hacker to exploit these vulnerabilities, but the risk is real.

Teresa believes that it will take the team an additional two weeks to fix the bugs and properly test the system, but the team is running out of time. The project is due in four days. Teresa knows that the current design of the information system does not meet the standards defined in the original contract. She also knows that if Blue Moose completes the project on time and on budget, then other government departments will be interested in Blue Moose's data management services.

What do you think Teresa should do?

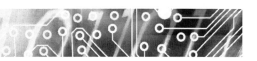

Worksheet

Name _____ Date _____

Four options are presented on this page. In the space provided, discuss the advantages and disadvantages of each option and make a final recommendation.

A) Teresa should deliver the project on time and not mention the security vulnerabilities.

B) Teresa should contact the Department of Immigration, providing them with detailed information on the situation and plead for an extension.

C) Teresa should inform the Department of Immigration that the project will be two weeks late and give Avery's sudden absence as the reason for the project falling behind schedule.

D) Teresa should deliver the project on time and let the Blue Moose employees who handle the database maintenance portion of the contract fix the bugs over the next few months.

So, what do you think Teresa should do? Why?

_____

_____

_____

_____

_____

_____

Chapter 10

Property

10.1 Ideas + Ownership

Protecting the intangible

Intellectual property is the term we give to the creative output of individuals or corporations. We consider such creations "intellectual" because they originate in our minds as intangible ideas; we label these creations "property" because they point to ownership. Basically, intellectual property falls into one of four main categories: copyright, trademarks, patents, or trade secrets.[1]

Copyright protects the expression of an idea, not the idea itself. For example, Al Gore's film *An Inconvenient Truth* is protected by copyright, but the copyright is granted for his particular expression and presentation of global warming and climate change ideas. Al Gore has not been granted the copyright for the idea of climate change itself. Copyright is relatively easy to attain because it exists the moment an idea is fixed in tangible form and it does not have to be registered with a governing authority.

The only requirement for copyright protection is that the expression of your idea needs to be original, but the bar for originality is quite low. This means that you are free to create your own documentary about climate change and, as long as it differs from Al Gore's version, you are granted the same protection under the law. Creators are granted exclusive rights to their work, meaning that they can determine how and when it can be used. These rights are generally protected for a predefined amount of time (varies by country). Once the copyright expires, the work becomes part of the public domain, essentially meaning that it becomes public property—free for anyone to use.

In current practice, however, creators often surrender their copyright to the publisher or distributor of their work. For instance, even though I'm the author of this book, the copyright for its content actually resides with the publisher (Kendall Hunt). The contract I signed before writing this book grants the publishing company control over the material in these pages. Admittedly, this seems like an unequal arrangement. Why would an author invest so much time and effort into writing a book only to lose control over its reproduction to corporate interests? The simple answer is that the publishing company is in a better position to distribute, market, and protect the content than the author. By transferring copyright, authors potentially reach a bigger audience and allow the publisher to assume the risks associated with publication. In return, publishers receive intellectual property rights and a share in the profits.

Trademarks are another type of intellectual property. We're conditioned to think that trademarks are simply company names and logos, but they're more significant than that. Trademarks are often described as a "designation of source."[2]

They tell you where a good or service comes from by pointing to the original owner of a brand name or product. For example, the label on your shirt tells you which company was responsible for its creation or distribution.

Unlike copyright and patents, trademarks are not limited in term; they do not expire. As long as companies like Levi's, Microsoft, Apple, and Coca-cola continue operating, their trademarks will remain part of their intellectual property portfolio. Trademarks highlight the intangible nature of intellectual property because they aren't particularly valuable on their own. What good would it be to own Ford's blue oval trademark if you don't make cars? However, trademarks often signify or represent something that is quite valuable. The trademarks associated with Coca-cola, for instance, represent the broader market or brand value of the company as a whole.

Patents are a third example of intellectual property. Like copyright legislation, patent law protects unique processes or products for a limited amount of time. For patents, however, the bar for originality is much higher. While copyright exists the moment you fix the idea in physical form, patents require an extensive application and examination process through a regulating body (e.g. Government). When applying for patent protection the creator must adequately demonstrate to patent examiners that the idea is non-obvious and original. Failure to do so will result in a failed application.

Requirements for patent protection are more stringent than for other forms of intellectual property, but the rewards are much greater. A successful application gives the patent owner extensive legal protection. Owners are granted exclusive rights to their invention, meaning that they have sole control over how their patent can be used in the market. The owner may choose to manufacture and market the product, or license the invention to others and collect royalties on the patent. For example, Toyota owns a number of patents related to gasoline-electric hybrid technology, but in the past couple of years they have licensed the technology to other automakers.

Most of us think that patents are only granted for advanced technology and complex applications, but this is not always the case. Patents can be decidedly low-tech. For instance, Jay Sorenson was granted a patent for inventing an interlocking cardboard sleeve. This sleeve encompasses disposable coffee cups and prevents the hot beverages from burning people's hands. Currently, most coffee shops use this patent (or some variation) to protect their customers (U.S. Patent Number: 5,425,497).[3]

Trade secrets aren't always considered a form of intellectual property, but considering that trade secrets consist of confidential information that is essential to the operation of an organization, it fits our definition of intellectual property.

Since divulging such sensitive information may harm the organization or its position in the marketplace, the law provides basic protection for trade secrets. The most famous example of a trade secret is the formula for Coca-cola. Technically, the company could apply for a patent to protect the formula, but as we've just seen, applying for a patent means disclosing information to the patent examiners. Revealing this sensitive information makes Coca-cola vulnerable to imitators; as a result, the soft drink maker is loath to register or reveal any information related to the formula to a governing body.

Defining categories of intellectual property is a good start, but it's only the beginning. The Information Age presents a whole new set of questions: Can one really "own" intangible property? If information is a commodity (section 1.2), then what are the just and fair prices for its exchange? Who owns the channels for information exchange? What are their rights?[4] Intellectual property protection and legislation have proven to be largely unenforceable, so what should we do instead? These problems require new solutions.

10.2 Real Property vs. Intellectual Property

Creators + creations + commons

The ultimate goal of intellectual property is to provide a balance between the rights of the *creator* and the rights of the *commons* (everyone else). The creator should be compensated for her intellectual output, but the commons should also benefit from access to the creator's ideas. For example, when you buy music, the musicians are compensated for their efforts (usually through royalties). They're happy because they get paid, and you're happy because you can listen to the music. This system encourages the musician to keep producing music and, by extension, society benefits.

If we give too many rights to the creator then the public doesn't benefit. For example, if musicians can't easily borrow or sample from other musicians due to high royalty fees or restrictive licensing, then the creation of new art is stunted—and the public suffers. Overcompensating the creator or intellectual property owner leads to an inefficient system.

Similarly, if we ignore the rights of the creator and give too many rights to the public, then we remove the incentive for creators to create in the first place. For example, when people stop paying for music and turn to free file-sharing services, musicians may simply stop creating. When intellectual property is unfairly distributed and artists are taken advantage of, the motivation to create disappears. Under-compensating the creator or intellectual property owner leads to an ineffective system.

In essence, intellectual property laws are designed to give creators the impetus to create by providing proper protection so that society can benefit from their creations. As such, intellectual property laws tend to reflect the laws for real property. In the pre-Internet era, these laws worked fairly well and striking an appropriate balance between creator and commons was easier to attain. However, the introduction of digital information and the development of tools for distributing that information challenge our notions of intellectual property (section 10.5). It's becoming clearer that "Law appropriate for the paper-based technology of the 18th century will not be adequate to cope with the digital technology of the 21st century.[5] Simply put, intellectual property differs from real property.

One major area of difference between intellectual property and real property is physicality. Real property is tangible (you can touch it), but intellectual property is not. Copyright, patents, and trademarks represent our attempt to protect inventions and processes, but they are not "things" in the traditional sense. At best, these forms of intellectual property signify or point to more abstract concepts. For example, suppose you write a brilliant novel. When you're finished, you will own the copyright to the expression of your ideas, but you will not own every single copy of your novel that is printed. Your "ownership" of the novel is not tied to tangible copies or physical objects, it is tied to the ideas—making your "property" much harder to quantify.

In the physical world, real property can be stolen. Your car, your laptop, or your cell phone can go missing in seconds. In the intangible world, however, intellectual property cannot be stolen. Since intellectual property doesn't exist in physical form, it is impossible to steal; instead, violations against intellectual property are classified as infringement. Let's return to your brilliant novel. If I come along and copy large portions of your work and claim them as my own, then I may be guilty of infringement. Technically, I haven't stolen anything because you still have the rights to your book, but I have disregarded your rights and asserted my own. To prove that I have violated your rights, you need to provide direct evidence of copying, or demonstrate that the similarity between my work and yours is too great to be a coincidence.[6]

Economists often consider property to be rivalrous, functioning in a zero-sum environment. For instance, if I own a piece of land, you cannot own that same piece of land. Our conflict over that one piece of land creates rivalry between us. Since I own the land, my decisions related to that land—to build a subdivision, to plant some crops, or to leave it undeveloped—exclude you from deciding what to do with that land. When we adapt this line of thinking to intellectual property, however, we encounter some difficulties. In fact, intellectual property is non-rivalrous; it does not necessarily require a zero-sum relationship.[7] In contrast to real property, intellectual property can be kept and shared at the same time. To use a simple example, a patent owner might choose to license his idea to multiple parties. In this situation, the "property" benefits everyone—a most unique arrangement.

Don't underestimate the importance of these issues. After all, our notions of property form the foundation of the modern capitalist economic system.[8] On the one hand, it makes sense to treat intellectual property like real property; we want to recognize ownership—even if that ownership points to ideas instead of things. On the other hand, defining intellectual property according to real property definitions ignores the fundamental nature of ideas. Intellectual property in the Information Age may require something more than physical-world analogies.

10.3 The Story of Copyright

Censorship + control + compensation

With increasing globalization, we face another problem when it comes to protecting intellectual property: cultural traditions. Chances are our opinions about intellectual property are heavily influenced by our culture. The West, for example, has adopted a highly individualistic approach. Intellectual property tends to be viewed as a personal right. Moreover, this right gives the creator complete control over the creation. She can transfer, exercise, or waive her right as she desires. Should she choose to transfer the rights to her ideas, those rights become property of the new owner.

In contrast, the Eastern tradition has adopted a more collective approach. In this environment, intellectual property is treated as a socially beneficial exercise. The creator is viewed as a conduit through which the creative spirit is manifested for the benefit of society. As such, the creation belongs more to the society than to the individual.[9] Even though this East-West comparison is an oversimplification, we can see the difficulty of protecting intellectual property on a global scale when we don't even share the same definition of the term.

Approaches to intellectual property also differ according to time period. While we don't have time to unpack the entire history and development of intellectual property, it might broaden our understanding if we look a little closer at the development of copyright.

In the West, most scholars suggest that copyright developed in response to one particular piece of technology—you guessed it, the printing press. While other approaches to copyright existed in ancient Greece, Rome, and China, it is Gutenberg's printing press that provides the foundation for modern copyright law. The printing press fundamentally altered information dissemination by putting the tools of production into the hands of more people (section 4.3). The political and religious establishment no longer had complete control over the ideas distributed to the people.

Obviously, the established authorities weren't willing to surrender control so easily. In 1547, for example, King Edward VI granted a monopoly over the publication of certain categories of material in an attempt to assert the power of the State (and make a little money in the process). The right to print government information (e.g. Acts of Parliament), church information (e.g. Testaments), legal information (e.g. Law books) and educational information (e.g. Latin grammars) were exclusively granted by a single printer known as the King's Printer. In essence, a single publisher printed and distributed the information that was integral to sixteenth century English society.

In the decades that followed, the Star Chamber, an English court of law, began codifying and enforcing procedures related to publishing books and pamphlets. Their procedures included four basic tenets: 1) books cannot be printed until they are properly registered; 2) books cannot be printed which contradict the Christian faith, the Church of England, or the government; 3) books must include the name of the author and the name of the printer; 4) printers must deliver a copy of every book they print to a central library.[10]

It should be noted that "the key aspects of the Star Chamber's decree were more about censorship than they were with preserving the profitability of the publishers of book, and were certainly totally unconcerned with any rights that the author of such work might have in the exploitation of that work."[11] In other words, the state attempted to control the source of the information (author and printer) *and* the information itself. Books had to be registered and attributed appropriately, so that the authors could be hanged or flogged if they published controversial material.

The Star Chamber was abolished in 1640, but the State's tendency to prefer censoring authors to compensating them continued until 1689 when the *Bill of Rights* granted increased freedoms to English citizens. Gradually, a system of copyright developed in England that granted authors and printers rights to profit from their work and protection from infringement. The only problem with this arrangement was the state only had jurisdiction over English citizens. In other words, printers from other countries like the United States could reprint the work of English authors in the New World without paying royalties or providing compensation at all.[12]

In response to these inequalities, countries started to draft bilateral and international agreements, securing mutual recognition of intellectual property law. To add an additional layer of security, agreements like the Berne Convention (1886), extended the duration of copyright protection to the life of the author plus an additional fifty years. In more recent legislation, governments have continued to extend the length of protection afforded to copyright. In some cases, copyright is protected for 95 years after the life of the author.

The Information Age, of course, adds another wrinkle. In 1998, the United States passed the Digital Millennium Copyright Act (DMCA), marking the first major attempt to adapt intellectual property legislation for the digital era. One of the most controversial aspects of this legislation is its provision for anti-circumvention measures. This law makes it illegal to circumvent or break copyright protections. It's easier to understand the significance of this law when we look at an example: DVD and Blu-Ray discs come with an encryption code designed to stop you from copying the content to your computer and distributing it online. Even though ripping a movie to your computer is a relatively simple task with free software available online, the DMCA makes such an act illegal.

Since the original motivation behind copyright legislation was to censor unpopular ideas made prevalent by the printing press, it makes sense that early legislation focused on controlling the distribution of information.[13] Even though the system evolved to protect the rights of authors, the focus on controlling the distribution of information remains the same. The DMCA, for instance, attempts to stop users from distributing content unlawfully. Of course, the act of distributing looks a lot different in the Internet era than it did in the printing press era. The Internet's decentralized design means that copyright owners no longer have control over distribution, making compensation for creators particularly difficult. Perhaps it is time for our laws to evolve again.

10.4 Digital Rights Management

The flexibility of format

In the Information Age, the digitization of intellectual property further complicates the notion of property. The inherent characteristics of the digital environment enable us to endlessly reproduce, distribute, and recycle intellectual property. Once some form of intellectual property has been encoded in digital format, the possibilities for use (and abuse) are endless. Let's take a simple example: imagine one of the president's speeches recorded in MP3 format. Technically, this speech is under copyright because it is the expression of the president's ideas; however, the fact that the speech has been recorded in a digital format makes it easy to abuse current intellectual property law:

- The digital format makes it easy to copy. Not only is it easy to copy, it is easy to copy *exactly*. When reproducing the speech there is no loss of quality. In effect, there is no perceivable difference between the original and the copies.

- The digital format makes it easy to distribute. The Internet provides a space in which information exchange can occur without the need for a physical object.[14] The speech can be shuttled to all corners of the world at virtually no cost.

- The digital format makes it easy to manipulate. With access to basic sound software, segments of the speech can be easily edited, removed, or even combined with other media. For example, a DJ could remix the president's speech into a song, or a documentarian might add images and use the speech as a voiceover.

In summary, the malleability of digital information makes it harder to restrict duplication, control distribution, prevent tampering, and prove ownership of intellectual property.[15] In this environment, then, how are we supposed to balance the rights of the creator with the rights of the commons? One proposed solution is to use technology to solve technology. Many industry insiders have developed a digital property protection scheme called Digital Rights Management (DRM). Basically, DRM uses sophisticated technology (e.g. Encryption) to enforce copyright.

Advocates of this approach claim DRM technology ensures the copyright owners will get paid what they rightfully deserve under the law. If you are not able to copy your favorite movie for your friend, then your friend might have to buy it (and the copyright holder will get the appropriate royalties). Using technology reduces the legal battles required to protect intellectual property and for users who follow the law DRM technology does not interfere with their use of content.

Big businesses support DRM because it can protect their revenue streams. Take a large multinational company like Sony, for example. Sony has a huge division devoted to creative content, producing movies, music and television. They also have a huge division devoted to computer technology, producing laptops, computers and portable media. Do you see the connection? They sell the content we want and the tools that we use to copy that content—often illegally. DRM protects both sides of their business.

Naturally, opponents of DRM point out that the technology serves the publishers (the real intellectual property owners) not the public. DRM schemes invade customer privacy by restricting freedoms, and treat everyone as criminals. Why should a big corporation get to decide how you should (or should not) listen to your music? What happens when those songs are supposed to be part of the public domain, how do you "undo" the DRM protections on your content?

In theory, DRM should help combat problems associated with the digitization of intellectual property, but in practice this hasn't proven to be the case. "Efforts to strengthen intellectual property rights (the prescription) preceded the rise of the behaviors such rights were intended to prevent (the prognosis). Much recent flouting of intellectual property occurs as a direct if inarticulate challenge to the encroachment many see of recent copyright legislation on personal liberties and well-established habits."[16] In other words, as big businesses increase pressure on governments to protect their intellectual property, the people increase their resistance to such restrictive measures. It would seem that the people are attempting to define their own balance.

10.5 The Case Against Intellectual Property

Toward a more creative commons

When you look at the history of intellectual property an interesting theme develops. Each time a threat has arisen to traditional copyright protections, the industry has suffered a little and then rebuilt itself. Here are just a few examples:

- Book publishing survived the invention of the photocopier

- Television and movie production survived the invention of video recording

- The music industry survived the invention of recordable cassettes (and will survive the invention of the MP3)

- Software companies survived illegal distribution of computer applications

These industries survived because people still saw benefit in their intellectual property. We will always want to read stories, listen to music, watch television and interact with software. The desire for content hasn't changed, just the method of its delivery.

We can even make a case against patents, the most rigid type of intellectual property. Our system requires an extensive process by which an inventor or company must prove that their invention is unique. However, the statistics show that over 95% of all patents are not commercially viable.[17] In our techno-centric world, the patent system simply cannot keep up with innovation. It's costly, slow, and resources are wasted negotiating and enforcing licenses. In the end, these intellectual property costs are simply passed on to the end consumer anyway, making products more expensive and the overall system more inefficient.[18]

Think about it for a second: if someone is infringing on your intellectual property, doesn't that mean that they're behind you? As your innovation becomes ubiquitous then you enjoy greater influence—whether you have a patent or not. For example, the browser wars between Internet Explorer (Microsoft), Firefox (Mozilla), Safari (Apple) and Chrome (Google), are an attempt to dominate the browsing experience for millions of Internet surfers. The market leader has the opportunity to set the standard—and that's more important than any patent.

Likewise, we might argue that the true secret to success is execution not protection. Studies have demonstrated companies that spend millions to protect their intellectual property do not necessarily prosper in the long run. The companies that succeed are the ones who turn their ideas into products that people actually want. Protection is defensive; execution is offensive.

Another reason that intellectual property efforts simply fall flat is that the current generation simply does not understand the need for copyright. It's not that young people are incapable of understanding the issues related to intellectual property; it's that they have grown up using the Internet to share and remix content for their own purposes. For them, the strictures of current intellectual property law seem horribly irrelevant (section 1.5).

A final challenge is that the legislation surrounding intellectual property is unenforceable. The near-anonymity provided by computer networks, the ease at which DRM technology can be cracked (section 10.4), and the global nature of the Internet, make protecting intellectual property a daunting task. For example, days after the animated movie *Shrek 2* (2004) hit theaters, pirated copies of the film could be found online. Dreamworks, the owners of the *Shrek* franchise, were not happy and sent a strongly worded letter to Pirate Bay, a popular service for pirated content, demanding they remove the links to the bootlegged version of the movie. Pirate Bay's response was less than gracious: "As you may or not be aware, Sweden is not a state in the United States of America. Sweden is a country in northern Europe [and] US law does not apply here ... It is the opinion of us and our lawyers that you are fucking morons."[19] Such are the challenges in a globally connected world.

So, should we abandon intellectual property altogether? Not yet. One innovative approach to restore the balance of copyright is the Creative Commons.

The Creative Commons does not replace existing copyright protection; it simply allows the creator more flexibility when communicating how their work can be used. If copyright law is "all rights reserved," then the Creative Commons is "some rights reserved."[20]

Under the current copyright system, for example, when a photographer snaps a picture she owns the copyright to that photograph. If I want to use that image, I need to get permission from the photographer. Intuitively, this arrangement seems fair, but it is somewhat awkward too. What happens if I can't find the photographer? Or, what happens if the photographer takes too long to grant permission? Without a clear response from the photographer, I am unable to use the image. The default setting for copyright is to lock down the rights for the original photographer—at the expense of the public.

Under the Creative Commons copyright system, when the photographer snaps a picture she can tell people how she wants the image to be used. Instead of waiting for people to ask permission, she can tell people what is permissible. The conversation has changed direction. She can indicate whether future users can use the image for commercial purposes, whether they can alter the original and create derivative works, or whether they need to share the works that they create. The goal is twofold: to encourage creators to share their work with the commons, and to encourage future creators to build on the work of others. The beauty of Creative Commons licensing is that it adheres to existing laws and updates them for the Information Age. Each license consists of three parts:

- **The Commons Deed.** This is the legal contract in plain language. It tells people how they are allowed to use the creative work. In some cases, the deed is simply represented by a series of standard icons—each of which communicates particular permissions. For example, a dollar sign with a line through it means that the work cannot be used for commercial purposes.

- **The Legal Code.** This is the full legal language behind the license. Lawyers have carefully vetted the contract to ensure that the creator's intentions are properly represented and that the code is consistent with national law. This code will vary slightly from country to country depending on existing legislation in each jurisdiction.

- **The Digital Code.** This is the most unique part of the Creative Commons license. The digital code (sometimes called metadata) is the code that gets attached to digital creative works, so that computers can also understand the rights attached to your creation. This code enables search engines to search specifically for Creative Commons work.

Creative Commons is not a perfect system—established publishers and primary copyright owners are among its main critics—but it represents a unique solution for digital works. It uses advances in technology to enhance legislation (and ensure that everyone plays fair). By providing effective tools to the creator and the commons, we can restore the intellectual property balance. Once again, we can stand on the shoulders of giants.[21]

10.6 Experiment

Patent search

It's hard to underestimate the importance of patents in the development of new technology. Giving inventors exclusive rights to profit from their ideas encourages people to invent, but it also leads to improvements in the quality of life for the rest of society. Indeed, the patent system has played a vital role in the inception and maintenance of major industries.

Although many nations have patent systems (or some equivalent), the United States Patent and Trademark Office (managed by the United States Department of Commerce) is perhaps the most well known. In fact, many foreign inventors and companies attempt to get their ideas protected in the United States to ensure access to the world's most attractive—and most competitive—market.

The first patent granted in North America was to Joseph Jenkes in 1646 for his mill that manufactured scythes (agricultural tool for harvesting crops). Over a century later (1790), President George Washington signed legislation that formally established the foundation of the modern American patent system.[22] Now, the United States Patent and Trademark Office (USPTO) receives nearly half a million patent applications each year.[23]

Each of these patent applications is made available to the public, making the Patent Office a veritable trove of historical scientific and technical information. It includes original patent applications by Thomas Edison for the electric lamp (light bulb), by Alexander Graham Bell for the telephone, and by the Wright brothers for a flying machine. Of course, the USPTO has also granted millions of patents to less successful—and sometimes downright silly—ideas.

For this experiment you will get a chance to look at some specific patent applications. Use the worksheet on the next page to get started.

Worforksheet

Name _____   Date _____

Part A

Google has created a search engine to search specifically for patent information (http://www.google.com/patents). Use this search tool to look up the following patents. Note the invention the patent number refers to in the space provided.

325316

595073

D516576

1167425

1400791

6285999

721359

2712317

2174202

D258290

Part B

Find at least five (5) objects that have U.S. patent numbers attached to them and look up each of these patents. Complete the chart below:

Object	Patent Number	Inventor	Issue Date
1			
2			
3			
4			
5			

Part C

The United States Patent and Trademark Office also provides a search interface for patent information (http://patft.uspto.gov/). You can use this search to look up specific organizations (to find out what ideas they're trying to protect). Select one of the organizations below and use the advanced search screen to search for a list of their patents. [Hint: when organizations sponsor a patent they are called the assignee, use the search tips and examples to construct your search.]

Apple   IBM

Boeing   Samsung

Cisco   Sony

Dell   Stanford

Google   Yahoo

Harvard

Hyundai

1. What was your company's most recent patent (include number and title)?

2. When was it filed? When was it granted?

Part D

If you have time, use Google of the USPTO to have a closer look at the following five patents. (Yes, these are real patents).

6681419

5109421

5076029

4834212

5885614

10.7 Reflect

Piracy

Lawrence Lessig is an outspoken critic of restrictive intellectual property legislation. He was the founder of the Creative Commons, a movement designed to give creators more legal control and flexibility over their content. In this article he defends acts of piracy and challenges the intellectual property rights of big media companies. Read his essay and respond to the questions below:

Lessig, Lawrence. "In Defense of Piracy," *Wall Street Journal* (October 11, 2008), http://online.wsj.com/article/SB122367645363324303.html

QUESTIONS

1. Lessig opens his essay with a story about Stephanie Lenz and her son, Holden. YouTube removed the video she posted of her son dancing at the request Universal Music Group because it featured a Prince song in the background. What do you think about this story? Was YouTube right to remove the video? Was Stephanie Lenz infringing on Prince's or Universal Music Group's copyright? Why or why not?

2. Lessig claims that new creative works build on old creative works: "while writers with words have had the freedom to quote since time immemorial, 'writers' with digital technology have not yet earned the right." What do you think of his statement? Is borrowing a few bars from someone else's song, the same thing as quoting a few sentences from someone else's book? Should we have different rules for these two scenarios? Why or why not?

3. At the end of his essay, Lessig lists five changes to copyright law that would make a huge difference. What do you think of his list? In your opinion, which one would have the greatest impact? Why?

10.8   Reflect

Trademark protection

David Kravets looks at the Toho Company and their aggressive trademark protection of the Godzilla franchise. Individuals and organizations that profit from unauthorized reproduction of the Japanese monster are regularly served "cease-and-desist" orders and face litigation in court. Even producing a variation on the Tokyo-destroying monster could get you in trouble. Read the article and respond to the questions below:

Kravets, David. "Think Godzilla's Scary? Meet His Lawyers." *Wired Threat Level Blog,* http://blog.wired.com/27bstroke6/2008/11/godzilla-terror.html

---

QUESTIONS

1. Kravets writes that the company's lawyers aren't necessarily suing to make money, "they're just trying to keep their flagship property from slipping into generic status." What do you think of this statement? Do you think there is a danger that too many Godzilla-like rip-offs will devalue the Godzilla brand? Why or why not?

2. Protecting trademarks can be challenging, especially when that trademark "is often regarded by the public as community property." What do you think of this statement? Does the community have a right to own popular characters like Godzilla? Or, should we grant protection to the characters' creators? Who should have more protection under the law: the creator or the community? Why?

3. Trademarked images can be easily copied and distributed, making them much harder to protect. Do you think it is a good idea for Godzilla's lawyers to protect their trademark in court? Or should they limit their litigation, and allow the proliferation of Godzilla memorabilia make the brand more popular? Should trademark owners (from all companies) aggressively protect their property in court? Why or why not?

10.9 Decide

Property + popularity

Dante and Savannah are rising stars in the independent music scene. Their band, Two-Horned Unicorns, released a short five-song album last year called *Personal Grooming* that became the surprise hit of the season. *Personal Grooming* was well received by music critics, industry insiders and fans alike. Shortly after the release, Two-Horned Unicorns was playing sold-out shows and festivals across the nation. To keep the momentum going, Dante and Savannah have been working hard to develop a full-length album.

Writing songs while on tour can be tough, but Two-Horned Unicorns believes they will have a mature release ready for next summer. Currently, the working title of their new album is *The Grass is Tastier on the Other Side.*

The major recording labels believe this new project will be a big hit, and record executives are lining up around the block to convince the band to sign a long-term recording contract with their respective companies. However, Dante and Savannah have read a lot about the state of the music industry in the digital world. They know that piracy is rampant, that the recording industry is suing customers, that new music can be easily found on peer-to-peer networks, and that video footage from concerts regularly finds its way to YouTube. Due to some of these issues, Two-Horned Unicorns is hesitant to sign with a major label.

To examine their options the band contacted Zachary, an intellectual property lawyer at the law firm of Sullivan & Peters. Like all artists, Two-Horned Unicorns wants to be fairly compensated for their creative work, but they don't want to alienate fans. They don't want to lose control over their content, but they don't want to lose their "indie cred" either.

Based on your knowledge of intellectual property, what do you think Zachary should tell Two-Horned Unicorns to do? Four options are presented on the following page.

Worksheet

Name _____ Date _____

In the space provided, discuss the advantages and disadvantages of each option and make a final recommendation.

A) The band should release their new project with a major recording label and include Digital Rights Management technology

B) The band should release their new project with a major label, but do not include Digital Rights Management technology

C) The band should release their songs independently in an unprotected format (e.g. MP3) and charge a small fee for downloading each song through an online retailer (e.g. iTunes, Rhapsody)

D) The band should adopt a Creative Commons license that allows others to build on their work creatively, but not commercially.

So, what do you think Two-Horned Unicorns should do? Why?

_____

_____

_____

_____

_____

_____

_____

Chapter 11

Accessibility

11.1 Democratization of Information

By the people, for the people

The Internet is often described as the most democratic medium ever invented and it's hard to argue with that claim. After all, the Internet is a tool for both hearing and being heard. From its very beginning, it was intended to be more than a place for information; it was designed as a place for communication and, eventually, fully interactive conversation. When the Internet burst into public consciousness in the mid-1990s, many observers immediately recognized its potential. For example, in his testimony before the United States Congress about hacking, Emmanuel Goldstein noted:

> The future holds such enormous potential. It is vital that we not succumb to our
> fears and allow our democratic ideals and privacy values to be shattered. In
> many ways, the world of cyberspace is more real than the real world itself. I say
> this because it is only within the virtual world that people are really free to be
> themselves—to speak without fear of reprisal, to be anonymous if they so
> choose, to participate in a dialogue where one is judged by the merits of their
> words, not the color of their skin or the timbre of their voice. Contrast this to
> our existing "real" world where we often have people sized up before they
> even utter a word. The Internet has evolved, on its own volition, to become a
> true bastion of worldwide democracy.[1]

Goldstein's words are strong, but he has a point: the Internet is more than a tool for communication; it is an entirely new environment. In this virtual space we are free to be our true selves—without prejudice. Goldstein also draws a clear connection between the Internet and the spread of democratic ideals. In the West, we rarely give this relationship a second thought. We assume that having access to information is consistent with our rights to freedom of speech, freedom of the press, and freedom of political expression. But, are our assumptions correct? What are the connections between the Information Age and democracy? To begin to answer these questions, we need to start with the concept of democracy.

Essentially, democracy puts the people in charge. Instead of being ruled by a few (oligarchy), or by a single person (autocracy/monarchy), or by no one at all (anarchy), democracy is the practice of ruling by the majority. Notice the utilitarian angle here (section 7.2): decisions are made to bring the greatest good to the greatest number. At the core of any democratic system are two basic principles: first, the people should have equal access to power and a voice in shaping the direction of that power (usually exercised through voting); second, citizens should be granted universal freedoms and liberties (in an unspoken social contract). Denying people either of these principles defeats the purpose of democracy.

Even though democracy and democratization (the process of adopting more democratic ideals) are usually discussed as part of political theory, these principles can be construed more broadly than that. For our purposes, we want to compare the ideas behind the democratic State to the state of the Internet.

On the surface, the Internet can certainly be described as democratic: it provides equal access to everyone and grants basic freedoms to its users. Since a central authority does not control access to the Internet, each voice can find an audience—each person can find a community. Information, therefore, is freed from the restrictive authorities and gatekeepers. Think of Wikipedia, for example: "content is influenced by individual contributors working collaboratively to achieve consensus and, when that fails, calling for a vote among interested contributors. The result can be thought of as a sort of democratized reference resource, by, of, and for the people."[2]

Wikipedia is a great example of the democratization of information, but it's not the only one. All over the Internet people are making their opinions and ideas known: we're writing book reviews on Amazon; we're voting on popular stories in Digg; we're tagging interesting photographs in Flickr; we're journaling on Blogger; and we're creating communities on Facebook and MySpace. Increasingly, we expect to contribute our ideas and opinions online.

The Internet also makes less explicit forms of opinion sharing or "voting" possible. Google's search engine, for example, includes user behavior in its algorithm. To present relevant results for each search, Google considers the contents of each web page, but it also considers the way in which those pages are linked together (section 6.3). Don't miss the significance: Google's strategy allows every web page on the Internet to cast a vote on which pages are the most interesting and most important for any given query.[3] With each click of our mouse, we vote for content that we care about. By aggregating those clicks, services like Google better meet the needs of the majority.

As you would expect, democratic systems have their critics. Some argue that democracy is inefficient because you have to consult everyone before making a decision. While this may be true in the political arena, we've just seen how technology can automate the process for the Internet environment. Valuable information, for example, rises to the top of search results because of the input of others, improving overall efficiency.

Another claim leveled against democracy is that the citizens are uninformed, uneducated, or just plain apathetic. With uninterested constituents the system is vulnerable to mob rule or tyranny by the majority. In other words, the voice of the uninformed majority could potentially overwhelm the thoughtful minority—an undesirable situation in any case. To be sure, the Internet is not immune to this criticism, but it has shown a remarkable ability to resist the force of the mob.

Democracy is also criticized for its lack of stability. Since politicians and parties in power rotate every few years, there is no consistency for the people. Moreover, the ruling parties tend to be so focused on short-term goals—in order to get re-elected—that they ignore long-term solutions. The cumulative effect is that the system never has the chance to fully stabilize. This is one area where the Internet environment differs significantly. While corporations and governments attempt to control segments of the Internet, no single organization dominates the entire network. As a result, most users enjoy a stable and consistent information experience.

Clearly, the Internet can act as a democratizing medium, and has the potential to be "a true bastion of worldwide democracy."[4] But, as we'll see in the next few sections, potential doesn't always translate into reality.

11.2 Censorship vs. Free Speech
On the offensive

As we noted in the previous section, freedom of speech is closely tied to democratic ideals. Simply put, freedom of speech is defined as the right to speak freely without fear of censorship or undue persecution. Of course, this right extends beyond mere speech to include any expression or dissemination of ideas. By necessity, freedom of speech is intertwined with freedom of expression. Together, these rights protect the message and the medium though which that message is expressed.

In the Information Age, freedom of speech extends protection even further. Citizens are also granted the right to seek ideas, the right to receive ideas, and the right to distribute those ideas.[5] Notice that the creation of ideas is protected, but so is the consumption of those ideas. For freedom of speech to be truly free, rights must encompass both the speaker and the listener.

Democratic societies need to protect freedom of speech in order to function. Without assured protection citizens will censor themselves, fearing retribution for speaking their minds. The right to freedom of speech provides an incentive for people to participate in public discourse. This has an additional advantage: when we publicly state our ideas, we submit them to the scrutiny of others. Such open discussion is one of the pillars of democracy.[6]

We want a society where speech is as free as possible, but granting freedom of speech to each person in every circumstance—to every thing said by anyone to anyone—is impossibly idealistic. What happens when someone posts indecent pictures on their Facebook profile? What happens when religious groups incite hatred toward other religious groups? What happens when a blogger in China protests government injustice? Inevitably, we are left with conflicts that must be resolved.

For many people the opposite of freedom of speech is censorship. At its broadest level, censorship refers to the suppression of ideas. These ideas are usually stifled through political, legal, religious, or other official methods. In most cases, people want to censor ideas that they find objectionable or offensive, because they believe such ideas will upset the social order.[7]

Censorship might be aimed at the information itself. For example, governments occasionally release confidential information to the public, but typically that information has been heavily edited. Censorship could also be aimed at controlling the distribution of information. For example, if an organization learns that the media is going to publish a particularly damaging story, they may attempt to block publication and stop the news from reaching the pubic.

Moreover, censorship can be reactive or proactive. Each year hundreds of challenges to controversial books and magazines happen across the United States and in Canada.[8] In some cases, the community protests are strong enough to force booksellers or libraries to react and remove the book from their shelves. In other cases, booksellers anticipate the controversy and adapt their processes, or avoid the material altogether.

Again, we see the importance of balance. If we lean too far toward protecting free speech, citizens become vulnerable to libel, abuse and exploitation, but if we lean too far toward censorship we undermine freedom entirely. The Information Age adds another consideration: the problem of enforcement. Enforcing censorship is increasingly difficult in an era without borders (section 5.5). Sometimes the purpose of censorship is to regulate group behavior. For example, countries like the United States, Germany, and Finland have experimented with banning online gambling, but with relatively simple workarounds users can still access sites for gambling. Other times, censorship is designed to protect individuals. For instance, in Canada the Young Offenders Act bars Canadian broadcast or print media companies from publishing the names of criminals under the age of 17, but organizations outside Canada's jurisdiction can easily reveal this information via the Internet.

Enforcement may be an ongoing battle, but that doesn't mean countries have stopped censoring content—the Internet simply presents new challenges.

A recent report published by Reporters Without Borders includes some of the more egregious examples:[9]

- In 2008, authorities in Iran arrested or questioned 17 bloggers for controversial political commentary and blocked over five million websites.

- In Cuba, "Internet users face up to 20 years in prison if they post an article considered to be 'counter-revolutionary' on a foreign-hosted website."

- Legislation in Burma "bans the import, possession, and use of a modem without official permission, under threat of a 15-year prison sentence."

- In China, "nearly 40,000 employees of the state and the party monitor files circulating on the Internet."

- In Saudi Arabia, social networking services like MySpace are blocked because "online exchanges are considered to be a factor in immorality."

- In Vietnam, "it is now illegal for a blogger to post articles under another identity [and] blogs can only carry strictly personal information."

After reading this list, you probably feel a little relieved—even smug—at the freedoms we enjoy in the West—but not so fast. While we may not face such overt censorship, many democratic nations still attempt to police Internet content. In Australia, for instance, authorities are permitted to intercept and inspect any suspicious email without judicial approval.[10] In the United States, many major Internet service providers have been accused of cooperating with the National Security Agency to heavily monitor the online traffic of American citizens—without warrants.[11]

This is not to suggest that censorship or controlling information is *always* wrong. After all, officials in the United States claim that monitoring Internet traffic is necessary to ensure national security—and they're probably right. But if we stop for a moment: how is this any different than Saudi Arabia wanting to protect the morality of their nation by blocking offensive content? China is not a democracy, so is it really wrong for them to suppress undesirable political commentary? The scale of censorship might be different and the practices more overt, but the goal is the same: to protect the established order from outside threats. Of course, from our perspective these nations are wrong to be so restrictive; but from their perspectives, they're perfectly justified. Censorship, you see, is more subjective than we tend to admit.

The basic concern with censorship is that the individuals, groups, or organizations responsible for censoring information are essentially imposing their views on everyone else. They're prejudging materials and making value judgments on behalf of the other people, a situation that many find untenable. Again, however, we can highlight at least a few areas where control is necessary and perfectly justified. For example, most developed nations have legislation in place to protect young children. These laws might protect children from something as simple as direct advertising, or from something as serious as sexual exploitation.

Few of us would argue against the importance of controlling the creation and distribution of child pornography; however, we need to be aware that we are positioning ourselves at the top of a slippery slope. If we can control one form of information, where do we stop? Where do we draw the line between what is acceptable and what is not? Who gets to decide?[12] In the Information Age, these questions have global implications.

11.3 The Digital Divide

Haves + have-nots

There are many inequalities in the world; that much is clear. Unequal labor conditions, unfair compensation, uneven access to healthcare, disparate opportunities for education, and the inequitable provision of basic amenities are the unfortunate byproduct of our socio-political systems. On a global scale, our distribution of resources is truly disproportionate. Due to the impact of the Information Age we can add another inequality to the list: the gap between those who have access to information and communication technologies and those who do not.

The most common term ascribed to this gap is the digital divide. At its core, the digital divide points to the fundamental problem of access. In theory, the Internet is a democratizing medium (section 11.1), where everyone has free access to information; in practice, we know this is not the case. This time lack of access to information is not due to excessive censorship (section 11.2); it is due to a host of other factors, including "linguistic, economic, educational, social and geographic reasons."[13]

The digital divide is a multidimensional problem that tends to highlight the differences among nations across the globe. As such, the inequitable access to information and technology has attracted the attention of governments and international organizations around the world. The World Economic Forum, for example, had this to say in one of their annual reports:

> There remains the stark disparity between two types of world citizens: one empowered by access to information and communication technologies (ICT) to improve their own livelihood; the other stunted and disenfranchised by the lack of access to ICT that provide critical development opportunities.[14]

Without much difficulty you can find similar statements from the United Nations, the Organisation for Economic Co-operation and Development (OECD), the World Bank, and the G8 block of countries. Why has digital inequality become such a popular topic for these organizations? Because they view information technology—the Internet in particular—as a marker of progress, leading to prosperity and potentially peace.[15] This may sound somewhat idealistic, but as we've been exploring, there can be little doubt that information technology holds the power for social, economic and political transformation.

To be clear, there has always been an inequality in information distribution. Throughout history individuals and groups regularly experienced a lack of resources or skill to satisfy their information needs. The difference in the Information Age, however, is that the entire global economy revolves around access to information. Increasingly, intellectual and intangible assets provide the foundation of value.[16] Without access to basic technology, entire nations are simply left out of the conversation.

> Indeed, those developing countries which fail to keep up with the accelerating pace of IT innovation may not have the opportunity to participate fully in the information society and economy. This is particularly so where the existing gaps in terms of basic economic and social infrastructures, such as electricity, telecommunications and education, deter the diffusion of IT.[17]

As information and technology converge, the gap between the "information poor" and the "information rich" starts to look a lot like the gap between the "technology poor" and the "technology rich." The digital divide, in other words, invites a new kind of poverty—information poverty. Traditional poverty describes the condition of having few resources (possessions, income, etc.), *and* having the inability to acquire those resources.[18] Similarly, information poverty describes a lack of information and a lack of the means to get essential information.

Upon closer inspection, information poverty touches on deficiencies in all three areas of an information system: technology, information, and people (section 3.1). Information poverty occurs when citizens do not have access to technology. The most important pieces of information are created and distributed in the digital environment. Without technology the information is inaccessible and, therefore, unknowable. Information poverty also happens when there is a lack of quality information. The technology may be in place, but the information itself is unavailable. Due to issues of affordability, availability, or sustainability, citizens remain uninformed. Lastly, information poverty occurs when the people simply do not have the ability to understand the technology or the information they encounter. The tools may be in place and the information may be available, but contextual factors (lack of experience, language barriers, literacy issues, etc.) stop them from participating.[19]

Now that we've defined information poverty, we can take a moment to identify the systemic causes of this complex phenomenon. While there are multiple dimensions to information poverty, we might imagine four basic problems:

- **The problem of property.** In the race to protect every intangible asset and piece of intellectual property, we inadvertently exacerbate the problem for the world's information poor. Proprietary information related to medical aid or economic activities, for example, is effectively unavailable to nations that cannot pay.[20] Often, the developing world simply cannot afford to participate.

- **The problem of real poverty.** Having access to information alone will not relieve information poverty because information is not an end destination; instead, people use information to learn about other essential resources (e.g. medical service). Unfortunately, when essential resources are unavailable, then the information about those services loses any meaningful context—and actually provides a disservice.[21]

- **The problem of infrastructure.** Most individuals in the developing world cannot afford personal access to information or technology, but many of these societies also lack a broader information infrastructure. They lack computing networks and Internet connectivity, but they may also lack more traditional information providers like libraries and publishers.

- **The problem of interpretation.** Accessing information is one matter, but understanding and interpreting its message is another. Many people do not possess the appropriate contextual knowledge to make sense of the information they encounter. If you don't know one of the primary languages of the Internet, your ability to communicate is limited.[22]

So far we have discussed the digital divide as it relates to nations, but there is evidence for the digital divide within nations too. Even within developed nations like Canada and the United States citizens experience different levels of access. In these cases, the divide is not as pronounced so it is more difficult to measure. Some studies use technology adoption rates, such as household Internet penetration, to gauge the digital divide, but as we've just seen, technology is not the only determining factor. We must also consider economic, racial, residential (urban, rural), and educational angles.[23]

When it comes to issues like the digital divide and information poverty, we must face an important question: do we have moral imperative to bridge the divide? Allowing information inequalities to persist means that people are excluded from the conversation. It also means that the power for ideas and technology rests in the hands of a few—not the masses. Without equal access, the digital divide permits an erosion of culture and tradition. The interests and philosophies of the developed world (the majority) overwhelm those of the developing world (the minority). Wasn't the Internet supposed to stop these sorts of things from happening?

11.4 Digital Deterioration

Preservation + obsolescence

Another consideration related to accessibility is preservation. So far we've discussed problems with accessing current information (censorship, the digital divide, etc.), but we haven't touched on the problems of accessing *historical* data or information. To ensure that information will be truly accessible in the future, we need to think about how we deal with information presently; in particular, we need to think about how we store information.

What you may not realize is that the digital media we use to store and archive information has an uncertain lifespan. Did you catch that? The compact discs (CDs), digital video discs (DVDs), magnetic tapes, flash memory, hard drives, and large databases that hold society's essential data are susceptible to deterioration. Here's the irony: the Information Age promises an unprecedented amount of information, yet our digital media may only last a matter of years. Compared to the life expectancy experienced by many artifacts from ancient civilizations, we're not doing so well.

To be clear, "no medium, whether it's marble or magnetic tape, lasts forever. But electronic media—video, audio, and digital works—are especially vulnerable."[24] For example, acid free paper is expected to last anywhere between 100 and 500 years, but magnetic tapes, which stores data from decades ago, barely last 30 years. Of course, how quickly media deteriorates depends on factors like the original quality of the media, how frequently the media is accessed, how carefully the media is handled, the storage temperature and humidity, the cleanliness of the storage environment, and the quality of devices used to write to or read the media.[25]

Perhaps it seems strange to talk about data storage in relation to characteristics of the physical environment. Why should we care about storage temperatures and humidity? Isn't that stuff best left to archivists in dusty museums? Actually, organizations care an awful lot about environmental factors. If Google stopped cooling its server farms, for example, the system would overheat and data would disappear. Similarly, if Wal-Mart didn't back-up its vast data warehouse on redundant servers, they would be one natural disaster away from a crippling data crisis.

With proper care media can outlast the equipment used to create or read the data, which, of course, leads to another problem: the data cannot be read because the devices used to read the data no longer exist. We can have all of the information we want, but if we don't have the proper technology to access the data, we are stuck in the same position.

When technology becomes outdated or falls into disuse we call it obsolescence.[26] One of the unfortunate side effects of rapidly advancing technology is the obsolescence of existing technology. As we develop more capable hardware, more flexible software, and more efficient standards, our old technology gets left behind. For example, at one time personal computers featured 3.5-inch diskettes, now they focus on optical DVD and Blu-Ray drives; in essence, if you still have data stored on diskettes, you're out of luck. In the early days of word processing, Word Perfect could not open documents created in Microsoft Word (and vice-versa). Data portability and interoperability suffered as each company fought to maintain their proprietary systems.

There are two basic strategies to combat obsolescence and keep data accessible in the Information Age: emulation and migration. Emulation imitates the obsolete systems using new technology. Nintendo's Wii game system is a perfect example of emulation. The Wii allows people to play the latest titles designed for their motion-sensitive gaming system. But the system also emulates previous Nintendo systems, so that users can play older games—without having to own the older systems.

Another approach to obsolescence is to use migration. Migration describes transferring or updating data from one generation of technology to the next. Typically, migration strategies capture the content of the data, but not necessarily the form in which it was communicated.[27] Updating old spreadsheets or word processing files to be read by the latest version of Microsoft Office is an example of migration.

Translating data from old systems to new systems sounds attractive, but there are at least two difficulties with this approach: first, accessing the information in the future depends on an unbroken chain of migrations through each generation of technology—no small feat; second, the mere act of translation means a loss of information. To make matters worse, when you migrate or translate data, the original data is discarded, making it impossible to determine whether data has been lost.[28]

Admittedly, preservation doesn't seem as controversial as some of the other issues we've tackled, but we should not ignore its importance. Because we can't see or touch digital data we think that it is immune from deterioration, when, in fact, deterioration can happen on multiple levels: "First, data resides on a physical support—a floppy disk, CD-ROM, or hard-drive, for example—and this physical container or support naturally deteriorates. Second, the data itself may decay. Third, most software is proprietary and has no long-term technical support. Finally, hardware obsolescence makes a great deal of digital media inaccessible."[29] Clearly, accessibility and preservation are two sides to the same coin.

 ## 11.5 Losing Our Legacy

Preserving history

The impact of digital deterioration and obsolescence (section 11.4) is even more significant when we think about what type of information we're losing. Most of us can see the need for organizations to maintain and preserve their data for the future—it's important for organizational memory. But what about cultural memory? How much more important is it for our cultural institutions to preserve our current cultural artifacts for posterity?

"A paradox of the digital world is that, as the ability to store bits increases, the ability to store them over time decreases."[30] Let's start with a rather simple example: the Library of Congress in the United States has tens of thousands of audio CDs in their collection. According to one extensive study, anywhere between one and ten percent of these CDs already contain serious data errors.[31] One to ten percent might not sound like a major issue, but since the Library of Congress holds some relatively unique material, even the smallest percentage is concerning.

Libraries, museums, universities and other cultural institutions do an admirable job protecting and preserving existing work, but what about the information that they don't collect? Gigabytes, terabytes and exabytes of information are being added to the Internet each year, and yet we have no coordinated attempt to archive that information. Aside from the Internet Archive project, web pages are here today and gone tomorrow. In fact, the average life span of a web page is 44 to 75 days and then it disappears forever.[32]

Most of us take the Internet for granted. We act like it will be around forever—that the information we want will always be at our fingertips, but we should be careful with such assumptions. "Think of it this way. How long will it be before the much-touted World Wide Web interface is itself a dead medium? And what will become of all those billions of thoughts, words, images and expressions poured onto the Internet?"[33]

To be sure, some of the content on the Internet isn't worth saving. Does anyone really care about preserving the pages for each and every item ever sold on eBay? Should we archive every comment on every blog post? While some information online is best described as superfluous, other online content is incredibly valuable. If the Internet is the democratizing medium that we envision, then there are thousands of pages, from various points of view that reflect the riotous diversity of the Information Age—and that certainly is worth saving. Archiving and preserving this information is essential for historians, cultural anthropologists and future generations.

The real challenge, though, is determining what to preserve and what to discard. After all, we certainly can't archive everything. "Responsible preservation of our most valued digital data requires answers to key questions: Which data should we keep and how should we keep it? How can we ensure that we can access it in five years, 100 years or 1,000 years?"[34] The accelerated development of technology has seduced us into adopting a short-term mindset, but these questions force us to think about the longevity of our information. The efficacy of the Internet caters to our need for instant gratification, but have we gone too far? In the Information Age, we should be wary of losing our culture just as fast as we're creating it.

11.6 Experiment

Web Accessibility

Accessing information on the Internet is relatively easy for most people, but not for everyone. In fact, for people with visual impairments, mobility and motor control difficulty, auditory issues, or other disabilities, the Internet can be a difficult environment to navigate. Fortunately, the flexibility of online content and the robust structure of the underlying code make the Internet a better medium for making information more accessible to people with disabilities.

Traditional newspapers, for example, were useless to people who were blind or had visual difficulty. Most newspapers did not make Braille editions or audio versions—if they existed, they were expensive. At best, blind people were dependent on friends or relatives to read them the news. In the Information Age, most newspapers publish content in a format that can be easily read by "screen readers." This technology has the ability to read the news aloud, allowing the blind person to be more independent.[35]

Screen readers are not the only kind of assistive technology. Braille terminals and screen magnification software intended to enlarge web pages for easier viewing are also available. For deaf users there is closed-captioning software designed especially for online multimedia. For those with mobility or fine motor control difficulties there is speech recognition software, which enables the user to speak rather than type or use mouse commands.

In order for these technologies to work, however, web sites need to be properly developed and accessibility needs to be a major consideration in the initial design. The World Wide Web Consortium (W3C) is one of the primary organizations behind developing interoperable technology and promoting standardization to improve accessibility. They have also developed a number of useful tools to help programmers make their content more accessible to people with disabilities.

Unfortunately, many web pages are woefully inadequate when it comes to meeting accessibility standards. For this experiment you will test some web pages against the W3C standards. Use the worksheet on the next page to get started.

Worksheet

Name _____ Date _____

Part A

1. List the URLs for five of your favorite websites.

Part B

In one browser window, open the World Wide Web Consortium (W3C) free validator tool (http://validator.w3.org/).

In a separate browser window, open up WebAIM's web accessibility evaluation tool (http://wave.webaim.org/). Test each of the sites you listed in Part A, spend a few moments comparing the reports and then reflect on the questions below.

1. Which accessibility tool did you prefer: W3C validator or the WebAIM Wave? Why?

2. Although it can be difficult to understand the errors listed in the reports, did you see any common problems among your chosen websites? Provide one or two examples.

3. Which of your chosen websites had the most accessibility errors?

4. Were any of your websites completely free of accessibility errors?

5. Why do you think websites have so many issues with accessibility?

6. Should website developers and programmers be more proactive when it comes to accessibility issues? Why or why not?

7. If you woke up tomorrow with a disability, would you be worried that you would no longer be able to access your favorite sites? Why or why not?

11.7 Reflect

Access vs. ownership

Is ownership better than access? Kevin Kelly discusses the concept of ownership in the Information Age—or, more accurately, how ownership is not as important as it used to be. Kelly claims that the Internet provides a public commons in which we can access all kinds of information, without having to worry about owning everything ourselves. Read the article and respond to the questions below:

Kelly, Kevin. "Better Than Owning." *The Technium,* January 21, 2009, http:// www.kk.org/thetechnium/archives/2009/01/better_than_own.php

---

QUESTIONS

1. Kelly argues that in the near future we won't own music or books. Instead, we will pay subscription fees to access the content we want. We "can consume a movie, music, or book without having to decide to follow up on ownership." What do you think of this statement? Do you think people will be willing to give up ownership and move to an access-based model of content consumption? Why or why not?

2. Kelly discusses the differences between renting and ownership (using high-priced handbags as his example). He claims "for short term uses sharing ownership makes sense. And for many of the things we use in the upcoming world, short term use is the norm." What do you think of this statement? Does a "short term use" world mean that ownership is less important or more important? Is the future really about the short term? Why or why not?

3. Kelly notes that physical goods have inherent rivalry (only one user can use or possess the good at a given time). However, digital products and intangible goods are non-rivalrous, meaning that many people can share them simultaneously. After reading his article, are you convinced that access is better than ownership or possession? Why or why not?

11.8 Reflect

The Great Firewall

James Fallows examines the state of Internet censorship in China. China's approach to blocking undesirable content is often called "The Great Firewall," but, in truth, the censorship strategy employs more than just erecting a barrier between the Internet and Chinese citizens. Read the article and respond to the questions below:

Fallows, James. "'The Connection Has Been Reset'," *The Atlantic* (March 2008), http://www.theatlantic.com/doc/200803/chinese-firewall

QUESTIONS

1. Fallows describes a number of strategies for circumventing the Great Firewall, but he notes that it is not the government's aim to block everything. "What the government cares about is making the quest for information just enough of a nuisance that people generally won't bother." What do you think of this statement? Imagine yourself as a Chinese citizen; do you think you would try to break through the Great Firewall? Why or why not?

2. China has recently opened its doors to large Internet companies like Google and Yahoo! In order to operate in China—and to have access to the largest market in the world—these corporations have had to bow to some of China's demands for censorship. What do you think of this situation? Google and Yahoo! were started in America, should they comply with the demands of a non-democratic regime? Is it the responsibility of these companies to spread the ideals of democracy and take a stand against China and some of its censorship policies? Why or why not?

3. China's Great Firewall and Internet censorship strategy has holes and workarounds, but it remains remarkably successful. In part, this is due to a very non-technical factor: "The presence of censorship, even if easy to evade, promotes self-censorship." Do you think this is true? Imagine yourself as a blogger in China: would you self-censor your content to avoid punishment? Would the traditional tools of social control (peer pressure, cultural accessibility, fear of retribution, etc.) stop you from speaking your mind? Why or why not?

11.9 Decide

Truth + tolerance

Three months ago, Daniel was hired as the Programming Director for the local college radio station. Daniel is an alumnus of the college's Radio and Telecommunications program and is quite familiar with the day-to-day operations of the radio station. During his tenure as a student, Daniel volunteered part time at the station and hosted two late night music shows: one for experimental jazz and the other for underground hip-hop.

When Daniel started his new position the station's broadcast was limited to a relatively short-range signal that barely covered the city limits. One of his first initiatives was to convince the board to move more content online. With broader distribution, he argued, the station could better serve the college, community and alumni. Last month, Daniel learned that the Class of '85 would provide some initial funding so that the station could deliver its programming over the Internet. Starting this Monday, the station will begin broadcasting online.

Although he is a relative newcomer to management, Daniel has quickly proven himself. In addition to improving distribution, he has done his best to align the station's programming with the college's mission to give a voice to multiple perspectives. The station's schedule includes programs on independent music, community news, and talk shows aimed at current campus issues.

At last week's programming meeting, Daniel learned that one of his most popular talk shows, *Truth and Tolerance,* was planning to feature a live interview with a prominent Holocaust denier. News of the event has spread across campus and protests have already started. Currently, the interview is scheduled for Monday at noon—the same day that the station is going live online. As the Programming Director, Daniel has the authority to stop the program, but he's unsure what he should do.

What do you think Daniel should do? Four options are presented on the following page.

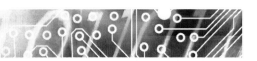

Name _____ Date _____

In the space provided, discuss the advantages and disadvantages of each option and make a final recommendation.

A) Daniel should not permit the *Truth and Tolerance* hosts to interview the Holocaust denier at all.

B) Daniel should allow the *Truth and Tolerance* hosts to interview the Holocaust denier, but not live on the air. Edited segments of the interview can be aired at a later date.

C) Daniel should allow the interview to proceed as planned.

D) Daniel should allow the interview to be broadcast over the local airwaves, but he should stop the interview from being broadcast over the Internet.

So, what do you think Daniel should do? Why?

_____

_____

_____

_____

_____

_____

Participation

12.1 The Social Web

Building an architecture of participation

For most of this book, we have treated the Internet—the primary medium of the Information Age—as if it was a static entity, but it is anything but static. Truth be told, the Internet is constantly shifting, evolving, and adapting to everything we throw at it. In fact, keen observers suggest that we are in the middle of another fundamental Internet shift—and most of us don't even realize it.

Millions of people are publishing their thoughts on blogs, anonymous contributors are building the world's largest encyclopedia one edit at a time, and people are connecting in a dizzying myriad of social network spaces. Are these examples exceptions to the rule, or are they precursors to something bigger? What is happening?

One obvious trend is that the Internet has become more than an end destination for information. In the past, we used the Internet as if it was a digital library of information. When we needed to research a topic, we would start up a search engine, type in some keywords, find some useful web pages, download relevant content, and then move on. The power of the network was that more information was available more quickly. Obviously, we still use the Internet to find information and the steps we take are remarkably similar (section 6.3), but instead of just retrieving information, the Internet now invites us to participate. The information flow has shifted from one way (downloading) to two way (downloading and uploading).

The Internet has also become more than a simple communication network. In the past, we used the Internet like the traditional telephone or postal system. When we needed to contact someone, we composed our message, located the appropriate email address or suitable web location, and sent the information. Even though information exchange was often asynchronous (not in real time), the power of the network was that it could send our messages more efficiently. Again, we still use the Internet this way (section 5.4), but instead of exchanging information with other individuals, the Internet enables us to participate in communities. The conversation has shifted from limited dialogue (between two people) to open discussion (among many people).

The current version of the Internet alters more than the ability to exchange information and communicate with others; it also changes the nature of community. In the past, we used the Internet like broadcast radio or television. When we needed to send a message to a number of people (e.g. when a business needs to advertise), we sent the same information to everyone. We left it up to each individual to decide whether or not the information was useful. The power of the network was that everyone was online—and when everyone is online, everyone is reachable. Clearly, we still use the Internet to broadcast information, but instead of treating everyone as a single mass, the Internet allows niche communities to flourish.[1] Our emphasis has shifted from homogenous community (sameness) to heterogeneous communities (diversity).

By self-selecting the communities we want to belong to we are taking advantage of the uncanny ability of the Internet to connect people. Social websites like Last.fm, Digg, Flickr, and YouTube, allow us to share opinions with other people who have similar passions for music, news, images, or video. These services do more than lead us to great content for entertainment; they introduce us to communities that have developed around the content.[2]

Web 2.0 is the catchall term used to describe some of these changes. The "2.0" is an allusion to software versioning. For example, when a software company like Adobe releases their popular Adobe Reader application, they attach a number to the end—Adobe Reader 8. Common practice dictates that when Adobe significantly updates the application, they also change the version number—Adobe Reader 8 becomes Adobe Reader 9. The only problem with applying this approach to the Internet is that Web 2.0 doesn't exactly describe a new version of the World Wide Web. Sure the current iteration of the Internet includes new code and new applications, but the basic principles, protocols, and packets of the Internet remain the same (section 5.4).

The confusion around Web 2.0 goes much beyond the version numbers discussion. The real problem with Web 2.0 is that there is no coherent definition of the concept; as a result, the term has been robbed of any consistent meaning. The controversy surrounding Web 2.0 is particularly volatile in the information technology and business communities. For some, Web 2.0 has been the victim of excessive hype. Either businesses use Web 2.0 as a marketing buzzword in an attempt to turn a quick profit on the next best thing, or web developers use Web 2.0 to attract more attention to their latest applications.

For some people, Web 1.0 was mostly about connecting computers, and Web 2.0 promises a new era of connecting people; however, this is a false dichotomy. As Sir Tim Berners-Lee, the inventor of the World Wide Web, argues, the goal of Web 1.0 was also to connect people.[3] In other words, Web 2.0 is not really something new; it's the fulfillment of the original ideals of the Internet.

Whether Web 2.0 is a trendy marketing term, a partial fulfillment of the Web's original vision, or something else altogether may ultimately be unimportant. For now, Web 2.0 is probably the best label that we have to describe the current climate of collaboration, community-building, and collective intelligence. Something is different with the Internet, and that something needs a closer look.

12.2 Production + Distribution

The motivation for making

As we noted in the previous section, the Internet frees each of us to create and distribute at will—and create we do. This new era of information production is made possible because of three basic phenomena: access to technology, access to information, and access to modes of distribution.

In the developed world, we have the tools we need to participate in information and cultural production, and those tools are almost universally distributed within society. We're able to participate in information production because we have the resources we need—or we have the means to acquire them. In addition, the "primary raw materials in the information economy, unlike the industrial economy, are public goods—existing information, knowledge, and culture."[4] New knowledge production requires that we build on the work of others. In the Information Age, we are able to participate in this process because access to information is essentially free and plentiful. Lastly, the flexibility of the Internet's architecture, organizational models and social dynamics provide a platform for modular production and widespread distribution. This sounds complicated, but this statement suggests that there is no single way of producing knowledge in the Information Age. The Internet offers a variety of ways to contribute; in fact, we're attracted to the Internet precisely *because* it provides many avenues for information production and distribution.[5]

Few would argue that the Internet changes how information is produced—in fact, it seems quite obvious. But it might be more interesting to ask: why do we create knowledge in the first place? Why do we participate in the online world so readily? What is our motivation? The typical answer to that question is people create knowledge to be compensated. In other words, the motivation behind making things (physical or virtual) is money. However, this isn't always the case in the Information Age. When we look a little closer we see that our motivations aren't necessarily tied to the market. Instead, we may participate in information production to improve our social standing, to receive recognition from the community, to participate in public discourse, or to pursue higher ideals (the good, the true, the beautiful). Motivation, for many of us, also has a social dimension.[6]

Obviously, the diversity of human motivation is not unique to the Information Age. What is different, however, is how the technology makes it possible for each of us to contribute. The liberating ethos of the Internet means "we will be able to do so for whatever reason we choose—through markets or firms to feed and clothe ourselves, or through social relations and open communication with others, to give our lives meaning and context."[7] Since we're not solely motivated by money, the production of information is not as closely bound to ownership (section 10.1) or proprietary systems. Moreover, our diverse reasons for producing information imply that an increasingly egalitarian culture is germinating online. The future, it would seem, is more about sharing than selling.[8]

12.3 The Web as Platform

Destination for doing

The Internet is still a destination for information, but this "new" version of the global network is also a destination for doing. As the Internet becomes more ingrained in our culture, we spend an increasing number of hours online. But we're not spending those additional hours researching and reading: we're playing multiplayer online role-playing games (MMORPGs) and exploring virtual worlds; we're using our browsers to edit documents and spreadsheets stored on servers miles away from us; and we're using mobile devices to send 140-character updates to friends and acquaintances around the globe. Notice the shift: the World Wide Web is now a platform—a platform on which we might attempt anything.

As we experience the full effects of a networked information economy, some interesting trends start to emerge. First, the Web provides a platform on which users can contribute content. Our contributions might be small (editing Wikipedia), significant (making research data accessible), selfless (writing code for Open Source software), or self-serving (keeping a blog). Regardless, with each contribution our information universe expands a little more.

Second, the Web provides a platform on which users can comment. In addition to contributing our own content, we can comment on the content of others. When we write a book review on Amazon, when we rank a news story for Digg, when we rate a movie on the Internet Movie Database, we are sending signals to future users. Sharing our opinions helps others select meaningful information.

Third, the Web provides a platform for organization. By bookmarking a web page with Delicious, or tagging an image on Flickr, or categorizing a podcast on PodNova, we collectively organize the content we create. These organizing schemes facilitate retrieval and connect the supply of content to the demand for content.

We've been focused on information production and distribution from the perspective of the individual, but what about the organizational perspective? This paradigm shift affects organizations too. If we view the new Web as a platform, then organizations in the Web 2.0 world need to reflect on:[9]

- **The philosophy of data.** Powerful databases form the foundation of nearly every successful online service. Google's index of websites, Amazon's collection of books, the Human Genome Project's DNA data, and the Internet Archives trove of historical web sites, all provide access to specialized data sets. In the Web 2.0 environment, owning unique data is not enough; organizations also need to add value to their data to maintain a competitive advantage.

- **The philosophy of continual improvement.** Beta is the term that software developers give to products that are in the testing phase, but are not ready for full release. In the past, developers could expect to perfect the product while it was in the beta phase and then release a polished version to the public once the bugs were worked out. In the Web 2.0 world, companies need to adopt the philosophy of perpetual beta. In this mode products are never finished—they are subject to continual evolution and improvement.

- **The philosophy of cooperation.** Traditional business practices revolve around carefully controlling product development, including aggressively protecting intellectual property. In the Web 2.0 world there is an acknowledgement that sharing is better than hoarding. Users and external experts can add value to your products if you cooperate with them. Organizations should allow and encourage people to use their products and services in new ways. In the long-term it is more rewarding to work with the community than against it.

- **The philosophy of diversity.** In the past, companies could be excused for primarily producing mainstream content, because mainstream content attracted the majority of the people. In the Web 2.0 world, the era of the blockbuster may be coming to a close.[10] To be clear, mainstream content will still prove profitable, but it's the niches that provide true opportunities for growth. As people are exposed to more diverse content, their appetite shifts away from mainstream hits to increasingly specialized products and services.

In the past, we adopted an application-based model to produce and distribute information: we created documents with word processing software, we bookmarked web pages in our browsers, and we stored photos on our own computers. The only problem with applications is that they are designed to meet the needs of individuals—not groups. As we've just seen, the platform-based model takes full advantage of the network: services improve as more people use them. By sharing a platform, individuals are free to produce and distribute, and the community can benefit. In this the new era of the Internet, "a platform beats an application every time."[11]

12.4 Wisdom of the Crowd

An exercise in groupthink

The personal computer may have introduced us to the wonders of technology, but it is the Internet that has become the hub of the Information Age. The network enables us to harness the power of the crowd.[12] When we treat the World Wide Web as a platform (section 12.3) everyone can participate. When everyone can participate, the burden for information production, distribution, and consumption becomes lighter for everyone. Working collectively, we improve the performance of the system and enrich the information universe.

Nearly every thing you do online can be recorded, measured, combined and compared with others. Each web page you visit, each piece of content you contribute, each link you create tells the information system something about you—and, by extension, something about people like you. By aggregating your behavior with the online habits of thousands of other people, we can begin to identify meaningful patterns (section 8.4). Of course, when we can identify meaningful patterns we get better at predicting behavior and anticipating users' needs.

The Internet is littered with examples of this type of collective intelligence. If you use a social bookmarking service like Delicious, for instance, you can open up your favorite pages to the public. This doesn't seem too revolutionary, until you remember that Delicious enables you to see everyone else's links too. People just like you are exploring the Internet and finding useful, interesting and poignant content—and bookmarking it for others. Delicious harnesses the power of the crowd, by acknowledging the social component of the research process. Instead of relying on the mechanics of search engine algorithms to determine relevant results, social bookmarking allows users to tell each other about relevant links. According to this mindset, research is less about you and your search engine, and more about you and your search army of like-minded web surfers.

Social music services like Last.fm uses their storehouses of user data to introduce people to new music they might enjoy. This service monitors the songs that you listen to, or that you have in your library, and compares your habits to other people who like the same bands or similar types of music. Last.fm harnesses the power of the crowd by analyzing aggregated user data and user behavior. Instead of just recommending bands within the same genre or category—which is fairly easy to do—Last.fm can identify musicians from different genres that you are likely to enjoy based on others' preferences.

Of course, recommender systems like this are not unique to music. Digg provides a recommendation engine for news stories, Amazon pioneered recommendation features for books ("People who bought this book, also bought …"), and Netflix delivers recommendation tools for movies. Social systems like these can make more intuitive recommendations because they rely on the wisdom of the crowd.

Even search engines attempt to harness the power of the crowd. Google, for example, takes the behavior of each user quite seriously. Each search query and every mouse click provide important inputs that are used to improve the relevancy algorithms. If you search for "Web 2.0" on Google and end up selecting the ninth result on the page, Google notes your behavior. If enough people searching for information on Web 2.0 do the same thing, then that ninth result will slowly rise in its ranking. Since so many people are skipping the first eight results to get to the ninth, Google assumes the page contains important information. Do you see what is happening? Collective behavior actually creates collective intelligence.

Of course, collective intelligence implies that the combined knowledge of the masses is greater than the knowledge of a few experts. If we accept this proposition, then we should also acknowledge the importance of trust as it relates to collective intelligence.[13] If you are using Wikipedia to research the War of 1812, for example, then you have to assume that each individual who contributed to that article approached the task seriously. You also have to assume that they were committed to the policies of Wikipedia, and that they had at least some knowledge of the subject matter.

For collective intelligence to work effectively, however, it takes more than trust. It takes people—and lots of them. Facebook or MySpace would be ghost towns if no one signed up to use their networks. Wikipedia would disappear if no one wrote articles. Google would become less effective if people conducted searches elsewhere. Last.fm, Digg, Amazon, Netflix, and others would be useless if people didn't participate. In some sort of strange Web 2.0 paradox, these services actually get better when more people use them.

Facebook becomes more valuable because your friends are there. Wikipedia becomes a reliable source because thousands of eyeballs monitor it constantly.[14] Last.fm provides more precise recommendations because it can analyze more music libraries. Google delivers more relevant results because more people use it. Instead of overloading under the weight of so many users, these services actually require the presence of people to succeed. Participation is the default setting for the Web 2.0 environment.

12.5 Information Personalization

It's all about you

Not everyone is convinced that this new web—this social web—is the dream it promises to be. Critics claim that Web 2.0 leaves us vulnerable to the tyranny of the majority (section 11.1). As the voices of thousands of amateurs, drown out the voices of the experts we effectively lose our way. If we're not careful, the argument goes, there will be consequences for such haphazard choices. By leveling the playing field and "democratizing" information, we degrade the notion of expertise, become incredibly narcissistic, and, ultimately, create a superficial Internet.

On the Internet, users are empowered to produce their own media. Putting tools that were once reserved for professionals (high quality cameras, photo manipulation software, web editing tools, etc.) in the hands of amateurs has led to a proliferation of information production (section 12.2). Unfortunately, professional tools do not guarantee professional work. One need only look at the hundreds of shoddy YouTube videos or thousands of incoherent blog postings to conclude that the rise of the amateur seems to directly correlate with the decline of quality content.

Sifting through gigabytes of data to find something insightful can be a time consuming chore. Senseless drivel buries quality work. When the difficulty of the search overwhelms us, we compromise our standards and simply stop looking. Ironically, the presence of more actually leads to less. The abundance of amateur content ignores the traditional gatekeepers of our culture—publishers, artists, musicians, journalists, etc.—and creates a situation of intellectual poverty.[15] As the truism goes, if everyone is a storyteller, than no one is. Web 2.0 no longer rewards the unique perspective of experts; it ignores the established approaches to information production and extends the right to produce to anyone.

Removing authority from the information production equation sounds commendable, but in reality, it destabilizes the entire process. "The great thing about the Internet is that anyone, even a lonely 16-year-old girl, can record her thoughts and draw a big following. The maddening thing about the Internet is that she might not be lonely or 16."[16] Unfortunately, when we flatten the media and open the floodgates to amateurs, we're left with chaos—even anarchy.

When everyone is a content creator, who is a content consumer? Can you see the danger? We'll be so busy trying to attract attention to ourselves, that we'll stop paying attention to those around us. In this vision, the Web serves as a personal vanity press, the medium through which we tell everyone about ourselves, and then ignore what everyone else has to say. This is "digital narcissism"[17] at its worst.

One thing is for certain: this new version of the Internet is all about you. Well, not *you* specifically—but it is all about the individual user.[18] We set up personalized information management tools to filter out the content we don't want. We subscribe to news feeds that deliver information on our schedules. We craft our online personas to achieve maximum impact. Let's face it, we like having our ego massaged, and Web 2.0 is a pretty good masseuse. Unfortunately, creating a mass customized, hyper-personalized information environment just burrows us deeper and deeper into our most comfortable niche—ourselves. If we're not careful, we'll experience the Information Age with blinders on.

Even when we do take time to listen to others, we tend to gravitate to others who say and believe similar things. If you're a conservative you converse with other conservatives (and worry about the impact of liberal policy). If you're an atheist, you gather with other atheists (and decry the evils of religion). If you're a Mac user, you hang out with other Mac users (and wonder how people tolerate PCs). Communities like these merely serve as echo chambers, reinforcing our preferences, biases, and previously held notions. In this environment the truth becomes whatever we tell each other. As long as it sounds true enough, we're satisfied. [19]

As we assemble ourselves with like-minded people we become more entrenched in our positions. Attempts at rational public discourse, quickly degrade to the lowest common denominator: juvenile insults. "Some of the comments on YouTube make you weep for the future of humanity just for the spelling alone, never mind the obscenity and the naked hatred."[20] In the process, we cheapen the democratic ideals of freedom of speech, freedom of expression, and freedom of thought:

The Web 2.0 revolution has peddled the promise of bringing more truth to more people—more depth of information, more global perspective, more unbiased opinion from dispassionate observers. But this is all a smokescreen. What the Web 2.0 revolution is really delivering is superficial observations of the world around us rather than deep analysis, shrill opinion rather than considered judgment. The information business is being transformed by the Internet into the sheer noise of a hundred million bloggers all simultaneously talking about themselves.[21]

Admittedly, some of these arguments sound elitist, but that doesn't mean they're not worth thinking about. Web 2.0 encourages people to contribute, but in some cases those contributions create cacophony: in our attempt to be heard, we've forgotten how to listen; in our attempt to be seen, we've forgotten how to watch; in our attempt to be recognized, we've forgotten how to read. We have learned a little about a lot, but we have trouble flipping that around to learn a lot about a little. How will we choose the appropriate future for the Information Age, if we don't stop long enough to reflect?

12.6 Experiment

Social bookmarking

As the amount of online information increases exponentially, we need better strategies for keeping track of the things we find. Fortunately, most browsers include a "bookmark" feature that allows us to add our favorite links to list for easy retrieval. With bookmarks we do not have to remember links, type lengthy URLs, or repeat searches. We can simply jump to the links we consult most frequently.

Browser bookmarks sound like a great solution, but they have some key drawbacks. First, all of the bookmarks are tied to a particular browser on a particular computer. If you're sitting at someone else's computer there is no easy way to access your personal bookmarks. Second, if you bookmark a lot of pages, your list becomes too cumbersome to manage easily.

Another strategy to combat some of these difficulties is to use social bookmarking. Basically, social bookmarking allows users to manage, describe (tag), and share web pages through a centralized system. By sharing links, people can help each other discover interesting, useful and relevant content.

Here's how it works: when you encounter an interesting website, you "bookmark" the link with an online service. When you submit the link you also describe the web page with a series of tags (section 6.5). These tags act as flexible folders that make your collection of links easier to sort. Using an online service makes your bookmarks accessible from anywhere. The real power of social bookmarking, however, is sharing your bookmarks with everyone else.

By making your bookmarks public, other people can find useful content by following your trail of interesting web sites. Similarly, you can find useful sites that others have bookmarked. Every link on a social bookmarking service has been selected, vetted, and edited by web users like you. This process makes the information retrieval experience much different than a traditional search engine. In essence, social bookmarking is the "word-of-mouth" approach to finding information, but the people you're sharing with are strangers.

For this experiment you will examine Delicious, one of the most popular social bookmarking services (currently owned by Yahoo!). Use the worksheet on the next page to get started.

Worksheet

Name _____ Date _____

Part A

Visit the popular tag page on Delicious (http://delicious.com/tag). Notice how the tags appear in alphabetical order, but the most popular tags appear in larger text. Scan through the list, click on one of the tags and respond to the questions below.

1. Which tag did you pick?

2. What is the first link that appears on the results page? [Just note the title]

3. How many tags are related to the tag you selected? [Hint look on the right margin]

4. Scan a couple of pages of results. What is the average number of tags associated with each Delicious link?

Part B

Return to the Delicious home page (http://delicious.com) and run a search for your favorite animal. Scroll through the results until you find a link that interests you. Once you've found a link, click on the user name who first added that link to Delicious and respond to the questions below.

1. What animal did you pick?

2. Which link did you select? [Just note the title]

3. Which user first saved that link to the Delicious platform?

4. How many total links has that user bookmarked?

5. What do the bookmarks and tags say about the user you selected? Can you tell what they are interested in? Can you determine where they live? What type of person are they? Use your imagination to connect the dots.

Part C

You can also use Delicious to see what people are saying about a particular website. Go to their URL search page (http://delicious.com/url), type the name of your academic institution (or your alma mater), and respond to the questions below.

1. List the top five tags associated with your school.

2. Do these tags surprise you? Why or why not?

3. Are there any tags associated with your school that seem out of place? If so, which ones?

Part D

Take the user name you selected in Part B and type it into the "Extisp.icio.us" tag generator (http://kevan.org/extispicious). This application will randomly scatter the tags your user has used across your screen.

1. Based on the tag explosion, list three or four tags that are most visible.

12.7 Reflect

Taste + talent + trivia

Web 2.0 has caused a lot of controversy in the technology community. In this article from *The Wall Street Journal,* two heavyweights debate the issue. Keen and Weinberger discuss talent and taste, amateurs and experts, and monkeys and cockroaches. Read the article and respond to the questions below:

Keen, Andrew and Weinberger, David. "Full-text: Keen vs. Weinberger," *Wall Street Journal,* July 18, 2007, http://online.wsj.com/article/SB118460229729 267677.html

QUESTIONS

1. Keen argues that the web is being overrun "by people who are more interested in vulgar insult than respectful intellectual intercourse." What do you think of this statement? Does the Web 2.0 crowd really suffer from the "digital narcissism" that Keen describes? Does the snarky tone of many contributors indicate a loss of taste and critical judgment online? Why or why not?

2. Keen says that talent in a Web 2.0 world is scarce; Weinberger claims that talent is much more widespread—distributed in a much smoother curve. In the Information Age, which approach do you think is closer to the truth? Will the proliferation of amateur voices on the Internet drown out true talent? Should we be worried that professional writers, musicians, and other creative artists will be unable to "monetize their expertise"? Will we lose talent in the Web 2.0 world? Why or why not?

3. Toward the end of the article, Keen compares the top six books on the New York Times bestseller list to the top six blogs on Technorati. He concludes, "Web 2.0 is a miasma of trivia and irrelevance." What do you think of this comparison? Is it fair or accurate? Should we be concerned that web users don't seem interested in intellectual pursuits? Why or why not?

12.8 Reflect

Bits + books

Kevin Kelly (section 11.7 and section 4.8) discusses the future of books in a digital world. Compared to other Information Age technology, books seem arcane—almost quaint; however, books still play a primary role in how we come to know things. Read the article and reflect on the questions below.

Kelly, Kevin. "Scan This Book!" *New York Times Magazine,* May 14, 2006, http://www.nytimes.com/2006/05/14/magazine/14publishing.html

---

QUESTIONS

1. Kelly argues "once digitized, books can be unraveled into single pages or be reduced further, into snippets of a page." What do you think of this statement? Do you foresee any difficulties with separating the content of a book from its pages? Does the "liquidity" of digitized books sound promising? Why or why not?

2. Kelly contends, "The universal library of all books will cultivate a new sense of authority." What do you think he means by this claim? Will access to this universal library of information clear up our collective ignorance? Or, will the universal library simply be too overwhelming to use?

3. Toward the end of his article, Kelly argues that the previous publishing model was based on cheap mass-produced copies of books. Since digital copies are essentially free, the old economic model is likely to collapse. "Value has shifted away from a copy toward the many ways to recall, annotate, personalize, edit, authenticate, display, mark, transfer and engage a work." What do you think of this statement? Can authors and artists make money in the era of the "free copy?" Why or why not?

12.9 Decide

Corporate blogging

Dominic was recently appointed Chief Executive Officer of Acorn Financial Management, a mid-sized financial services company. Acorn offers a range of personal financial management services, including mortgages, debt consolidation, refinancing, and investment opportunities. In particular, the company specializes in serving young professionals who are planning for the future.

From the head office, Dominic and his team of senior officers oversee the operation of 34 branch locations. A handful of these branches are exceeding last year's performance, but most of Acorn's branches are struggling to meet their targets. The financial management sector can be challenging in the best of times, but given the plunging economic climate, Acorn needs to find an edge.

Last month, Dominic asked his senior management team to brainstorm ways in which the company might increase brand awareness, attract more customers, and improve internal workflows. The team identified some predictable solutions—deliver targeted advertising, streamline the approval process, make application forms accessible online, etc.—but most members felt that Acorn needed something more. To truly dig out of its current hole, the company wants to implement a bold new strategy.

The Public Relations expert on the team, Nicole, argued for implementing a series of corporate blogs. She suggested that each Acorn branch start its own blog to improve the lines of communication with current and potential customers. Instead of consulting the standard Acorn website for information, customers would have the option to read about their particular Acorn branch— from the perspective of branch employees. Nicole argued that this would give the company a more local feel and make financial management services less intimidating for their target market—young professionals. Besides, if the blogs were successful, the company could further expand their use of Web 2.0 technology to include wikis, podcasts and even videos.

Most of the team members felt that Nicole's suggestion had the most potential, but it also had the most risk. William, Acorn's Manager of Information Systems for the past 18 years, expressed his concern that these blogs would lead to potential violations of client confidentiality, would increase the vulnerability of the company's information systems, and ultimately distract employees from doing their jobs.

Nicole's solution was certainly provocative. It represented a departure from the traditional method of doing business within the industry, but that didn't mean it was wrong. Ultimately, the responsibility for this decision rests with Dominic.

What do you think Dominic should do? Four options are presented on the following page.

Worksheet

Name _____ Date _____

In the space provided, discuss the advantages and disadvantages of each option and make a final recommendation.

A) Dominic should proceed with Nicole's suggestion and implement blogs at each branch.

B) Dominic should implement blogs at each branch, but Acorn's Public Relations department should moderate every blog post before it is published online.

C) Dominic should implement a single corporate blog from Acorn's headquarters.

D) Dominic should pay attention to William and avoid implementing blogs altogether.

So, what do you think Dominic should do? Why?

_____

_____

_____

_____

_____

_____

_____

Potential Future(s)

Imagining the future of the Information Age is a challenging proposition. The development of technology will continue to make things possible that we once thought were impossible. The production of information will repeatedly outpace our capacity for consumption. And the number of people participating online will lend a multiplicity of voices to the Information Age. One thing is for certain: our future will have more—more information, more technology, and more people.

We will solve previously inscrutable problems with more information. By collecting more data we'll do things like: map deep space, model disease outbreaks, measure demand for commodities, and monitor the energy grid.[1] Clearly, information will become a tool in and of itself:

> This is a world where massive amounts of data and applied mathematics replace every other tool that might be brought to bear ... Who knows why people do what they do? The point is they do it, and we can track and measure it with unprecedented fidelity.[2]

Did you catch that? Data combined with processing power and mathematical prowess become the blunt force that can be applied to every imaginable problem. It's like the old adage: To a man with a hammer everything looks like a nail. But the Information Age requires a remix: "To a man with a computer, everything looks like data."[3] The true source of power in the Information Age is information itself.

There can be little doubt that the future will also have more technology. What remains unclear is what type of technology we will have. In the short term, we may have a better version of what already exists. For instance, the Semantic Web will make it easier for machines to read and manage our contextual information on our behalf. Sir Tim Berners-Lee is currently working on improving the capabilities of his original invention, the World Wide Web. To hear him tell it:

> I have a dream for the Web [in which computers] become capable of analyzing all the data on the Web—the content, links, and transactions between people and computers. A 'Semantic Web', which should make this possible, has yet to emerge, but when it does, the day-to-day mechanisms of trade, bureaucracy and our daily lives will be handled by machines talking to machines. The 'intelligent agents' people have touted for ages will finally materialize.[4]

By structuring web content and integrating web data, we can teach our machines to identify meaning—we can teach them to be more like us.[5]

We may prefer to go even further than intelligent software agents. We may choose to develop a future full of physical information appliances that can talk to each other. All gadgets—from refrigerators to radiators—will be classified "smart" and have the capacity to communicate without our input. Forget the Internet of Information, this vision promises the Internet of Things. By implementing Radio Frequency Identification and other technologies we'll have intelligent clothing, seamlessly merging the analog life with the digital one.[6] We may even wear personal "life recorder" devices that record every word we utter, every thing we see, and every experience we have. In the future, even our memories will be outsourced to the machine.[7]

As the world's population grows and information technology becomes more accessible, the future will most certainly have more people. The demographics of the Information Age will change drastically as entire populations in China, India and parts of the developing world come online. English may not be the lingua franca of the Internet forever. The true force of diversity will be felt online as millions of new voices join the crowd and clamor to be heard.

The most striking thing about the future is that we'll have more convergence. Throughout this book, we've discussed all three components of an information system: information, technology, and people. Currently, it is still fairly easy to distinguish between these three components; however, in the future it may be difficult to separate information from technology, technology from people, and people from information. Indeed, some of the boldest predictions about the future feature a convergence of all three elements:

> With tomorrow's technology, [the world's knowledge] will all fit onto your iPod. When that happens, the library of all libraries will ride in your purse or

wallet—if it doesn't plug directly into your brain with thin white cords. Some people alive today are surely hoping that they die before such things happen, and others, mostly the young, want to know what's taking so long.[8]

Yes, you read that right. The future may include fusing our minds directly to the information environment via technical implants. This vision of convergence is more than simply doing everything online; it's being online—it's being *one* with the online world. "In a ubiquitous computing environment the new intelligence is extelligence."[9] In other words, we will increasingly rely on external technology to augment our personal abilities. Essentially, the Internet acts as one central computer. Once we're jacked in *Matrix*-style, we can harness that computer to do our bidding.

In the future, we'll be squeezing more meaning from machines. If you think this is futuristic hyperbole, then consider what Larry Page and Sergey Brin, the founders of Google, had to say in an interview with *Playboy* magazine. The interviewer asked, "Is your goal to have the entire world's knowledge connected directly to our minds?" Brin's response is telling:

> It's credible to imagine a leap as great as that from hunting through library stacks to a Google session, when we leap from today's search engines to having the entirety of the world's information as just one of our thoughts.[10]

It would appear that Google's ultimate aim is to have all of the world's knowledge—current and historical—connected to and accessible by the human mind. This is not science fiction; this is the cyborg future. This is the pinnacle of convergence.

Before we get too carried away with these lofty ideas we must consider some obvious difficulties. First, machines and man do not share the same fundamental language. Binary code is either/or, on/off, one/zero, or black/white, but human language resists such mechanical expression. Second, technology changes the manner in which we experience our world: "New technologies alter the structure of our interests: the things we think *about*. They alter the character of our symbols: the things we think *with*. And they alter the nature of community: the area in which thoughts develop."[11] By turning everything we touch into bits and bytes, we fundamentally alter the future we choose for ourselves. Now might be the time to ask: is this the future we want?

Here be monsters (still)

The problem with writing about issues in the Information Age is deciding where to stop: there are always new edges to explore. We opened this book with a look at the sixteenth century explorers and their attempts to map the seas in their quest for the New World. Let's return there for a moment.

These early adventurers made their maps through trial and error—not unlike our approach to understanding the Information Age. Hopefully, this book has provided some insight and helped you fill in the details of your map a little more. But before we leave this exploration analogy behind, we might take a moment to look at the peculiar nature of maps. By definition, maps are scaled-down, simplified versions of the world. You see, maps aren't just useful for what they include; they're just as important for what they leave out.

Obviously, having a map is better than not having one. But looking at a map doesn't really tell you everything you want to know. It might help you get to places, but it won't tell you what's happening in those places. Similarly, this book will help you learn about the Information Age, but it won't tell you what to think as you explore.

Perhaps when you read this book you felt that some issues were oversimplified. For you, I treated these issues like the nondescript blue lakes on a map: you can see the shoreline, but it's impossible to gauge the depth of the water or the direction of the current. Maybe you felt that some of the issues were given more prominence than they deserved. From your perspective, these issues seemed like the quirky tourist attractions on a map: you know where they are, but you have no interest in visiting. You might have even felt that I missed some important issues altogether. My ignorance of these issues makes you wonder if we're reading the same map at all: you know there must be new developments, but you just can't find any evidence on the map.

By the time you read this book, the seas of change may have carried us in entirely new directions—such is the anxiety and anticipation of living in our techno-centric world. As a result, it should not surprise you to learn that this book was designed to be incomplete. It's coherent, but not comprehensive. All

I've done is highlight some themes, introduce some issues, and raise some questions. Ultimately, it is your responsibility to decide what to do with them. It is your turn to go out and start charting the edges of the Information Age. Good luck.

Acknowledgements

First and foremost I need to thank my wife, Jen. Writing a book is primarily a solo activity, being part of a family is not. Without her support this book would have never been written.

I also want to acknowledge Paulette Padanyi and Melanie Lang in the Marketing & Consumer Studies department at the University of Guelph. Paulette and Melanie had the foresight—or foolishness—to believe that a librarian like me could make a unique contribution to their program. They gave me the opportunity to teach and now there is no turning back—for that, I am forever grateful.

I also need to thank some of the professionals at the McLaughlin Library. In particular, I wish to thank Mike Ridley, Helen Salmon and Catherine Steeves for providing an environment where librarians are encouraged to take risks. I am also indebted to Doug Horne for his insight (and his willingness to discuss technology of all shapes and sizes); to Robin Bergart for her encouragement (and for picking up some of my slack these last few months); and to Randy Oldham for his knowledge of web security and accessibility (and his ridiculously prompt replies to my email queries).

I first encountered a number of the issues presented in this book when I was a library school student at Dalhousie University. I can still remember sitting in Dr. Bertrum MacDonald's "Information in Society" class wondering why we were spending so much time talking about information. I guess that thought really came back to bite me. Dr. MacDonald and Dr. Fiona Black at Dalhousie remain two of my staunchest supporters and I am a better librarian because of them.

I need to thank the fine people at Kendall Hunt publishing too. From Alexis Sciuk who first convinced me that I had something worthwhile to say (hopefully, she was right), to Ronda Swolley who caught more typos than I care to admit, to Ryan Schrodt and Jay Hays who carried this project through to completion. Obviously, I couldn't have done it without you.

Like most writing projects, the ideas presented in these pages are based on the great work of people who have come before me. Here are just a few names that come to mind: Russell Ackoff, Chris Anderson, John Perry Barlow, John Seely Brown, Nicholas Carr, Thomas Davenport, Peter Drucker, Malcolm Gladwell, Jane Jacobs, Andrew Keen, Kevin Kelly, Farhad Manjoo, Michael Porter, Neil Postman, Bruce Schneier, Clay Shirky, David Weinberger, and Alex Wright. Even though I have not met these people, their words have started conversations in my mind.

Thank you to all. The students who take my course and the people who read this book are better off because of you.

M.J. D'Elia
April 2, 2009

Notes

Chapter 1 Notes

1. David Turnbull, "Cartography and Science in Early Modern Europe: Mapping the Construction of Knowledge Spaces," *Imago Mundi* 48 (1996): 5-24. Turnbull includes a much more academic discussion of the connection between map-making, imperial politics, and scientific knowledge spaces. Suffice it to say that geographic information was increasingly important—and, like most important information, increasingly difficult to keep secret.

2. F. Grenacher, "The Basle Proofs of Seven Printed Ptolemaic Maps," *Imago Mundi* 13 (1956): 166-171; Margaret Small, "From Jellied Seas to Open Waterways: Redefining the Northern Limit of the Knowable World," *Renaissance Studies* 21, no. 3 (2007): 315-339. Grenacher reproduces a number of sixteenth century Ptolemaic maps. In these maps, the sea serpents do not include the inscription "Here be monsters." But in at least one case, a monster is eating a capsized ship—sending essentially the same message. Small's discussion of early maps is focused on the Northern region of the world (Nordic countries, and the Arctic circle). This area was considered uninhabitable and was largely ignored by early explorers (and ancient philosophers). Not surprisingly, it was also deemed to be full of monsters.

3. Peter D. Jeans, *Seafaring Lore & Legend: A Miscellany of Maritime Myth, Superstition, Fable, and Fact* (New York: McGraw-Hill, 2004), 3.

4. Muriel Barnett, "Here be Monsters," *Contemporary Review* 255, no. 1485 (1989): 206.

5. Steve Gorman, "Text messaging figures in L.A. train wreck probe," *New York Times,* December 8, 2008.

6. Sarah Boesveld, "No online sex please, we're British," *Globe and Mail,* November 14, 2008, http://www.theglobeandmail.com/servlet/story/RTGAM.20081114.waffair1114/BNStory/International/home (accessed February 2, 2009).

7. K.C. Jones, "Florida Teen's Suicide Streamed Live on Internet," *InformationWeek,* November 21, 2008, http://www.informationweek.com/news/internet/social_network/showArticle.jhtml?articleID=212101445 (accessed January 13, 2009).

8. Micheline Maynard, "United Airlines shares fall on false report of bankruptcy," *International Herald Tribune,* September 9, 2008, http://www.iht.com/articles/2008/09/09/business/AIR.php (accessed January 13, 2009).

9. At best, the Information Economy can be described as an economy based upon the exchange of information and information services (as opposed to physical goods and services). Since information is notoriously difficult to measure or evaluate, the term may be falling out of favor. Certainly there are other descriptions, which provide different nuances—see the Digital Economy, the Knowledge Economy, the Post-industrial Economy, or the Information Society. For the purposes of this discussion, Information Economy is the most succinct term, and the most appropriate for introducing the commodity characteristics of information.

10. George Macgregor, "The nature of information in the twenty-first century: Conundrums for the informatics community?" *Library Review* 54, no. 1 (2005): 11.

11. Rick Whiting, "Who's Buying and Selling Your Data? Everybody," *InformationWeek,* no. 1097 (2006): 30. Ironically, one of ChoicePoint's largest customers in the United States is the federal government—maybe governments don't know as much about its citizens as we like to believe.

12. Audrey Fenner, "Placing Value on Information," *Library Philosophy and Practice* 4, no. 2 (2000), http://libr.unl.edu:2000/LPP/fenner.html (accessed January 13, 2009).

13. John Perry Barlow, "The Economy of Ideas," *Wired* 2, no. 3 (1994), http://www.wired.com/wired/archive/2.03/economy.ideas.html (accessed January 14, 2009); Hal Varian, "How much will two bits be worth in the digital marketplace?" *Educom Review* 31, no. 1 (1995): 44-46, http://net.educause.edu/apps/er/review/reviewArticles/31144.html (January 13, 2009).

14. *Oxford English Dictionary Online,* s.v. "Commodity," http://dictionary.oed.com/ (accessed December 28, 2008).

15. Jesse Alpert and Nissan Hajaj, "We knew the web was big ..." *Google Blog,* (July 25, 2008), http://googleblog.blogspot.com/2008/07/we-knew-web-was-big.html (accessed February 2, 2009). To give a sense of scale, the original Google index from 1996 included a mere 26 million pages.

16. Alvin Toffler is usually credited with coining the term information overload in his book *Future Shock* (1970). Toffler suggested the impact of accelerated technological change would leave us disconnected, disoriented and "future-shocked."

17. Angela Edmunds and Anne Morris, "The problem of information overload in business organizations: A Review of the Literature," *International Journal of Information Management* 20, no. 1 (2000): 17-28; Martin J. Eppler and Jeanne Mengis, "The Concept of Information Overload: A Review of Literature from Organization Science, Accounting, Marketing, MIS, and Related Disciplines," *Information Society* 20, no. 5 (2004): 325-344; Claudia Klausegger, Rudolf R. Sinkovics and Huan "Joy" Zou, "Information Overload: A Cross-national investigation of influence factors and effects," *Marketing Intelligence & Planning* 25, no. 7 (2007): 691-718. Other examples from these literature reviews include: communication overload, information flood, information deluge, information avalanche, data trash, information burden, and overchoice.

18. *Oxford English Dictionary Online,* s.v. "Information overload," http://dictionary.oed.com/ (accessed December 30, 2008).

19. Daniel Rosenberg, "Early Modern Information Overload," *Journal of the History of Ideas* 4, no. 1 (2003): 1-9. Rosenberg provides a coherent overview of the concept of information overload in the age of the printing press and subsequent centuries.

20. Eppler and Mengis, "Concept of Information Overload," 333.

21. Thomas H. Davenport and John C. Beck, "The Strategy and Structure of Firms in the Attention Economy," *Ivey Business Journal* 66, no. 4 (2002): 49. I've borrowed Davenport's mention of "human bandwidth" because it fits nicely with the technology construct of this book. Davenport suggests that in addition to information overload, the increasing speed and complexity of the business environment contributes to our attention deficit.

22. Michael Goldhaber, "Attention shoppers!" *Wired* 5, no. 12 (1997), http://www.wired.com/wired/archive/5.12/es_attention.html (accessed January 4, 2009).

23. Thomas H. Davenport and John C. Beck, *The Attention Economy: Understanding the New Currency of Business* (Boston, MA: Harvard Business School Press, 2001): 20.

24. Jeff De Cagna, "Your Attention Please: A Conversation with Tom Davenport," *Information Outlook* 5, no. 9 (2001): 31.

25. Goldhaber, "Attention shoppers!"

26. Po Bronson, "HotMale," *Wired* 6, no. 12 (1998), http://www.wired.com/archive/6.12/hotmale.html (accessed January 7, 2009).

27. John Cloud, "The Gurus of YouTube," *Time* (December 16, 2006), http://www.time.com/time/magazine/article/0,9171,1570721-1,00.html (accessed January 6, 2009).

28. Facebook, "Facebook Statistics," (2009), http://www.facebook.com/press/info.php?statistics (accessed January 13, 2009).

29. Marc Prensky, "Digital Natives, Digital Immigrants Part 1," *On the Horizon* 9, no. 5 (2001): 1, 3-6. Prensky details the characteristics of digital natives from a pedagogical perspective. He claims, for example, these new students expect more than the traditional methods of education, which are taught by "digital immigrants" (to use Prensky's corollary). But the digital native-digital immigrant divide is increasingly important in other organizational contexts as well.

30. Marc Prensky, "Digital Natives, Digital Immigrants Part 2: Do They Really Think Differently?" *On the Horizon* 9, no. 6 (2001): 4.

31. Jerome Buvat, Priya Mehra and Benjamin Braunschvig, "Digital Natives: How Is the Younger Generation Reshaping the Telecom and Media Landscape?" Capgemini Consulting, Telecom & Media Insights, no. 16 (April 2007): 9, http://www.de.capgemini.com/m/de/tl/Digital_Natives.pdf (accessed January 21, 2009).

32. Prensky, "Digital Natives, Digital Immigrants Part 1," 3.

33. Richard Naish, "The digital ages of man," *e.Learning Age* (June 2008): 10.

34. William Boddie, Jeanne Contardo and Robert Childs, "The Future Workforce: Here They Come," *Public Manager* 36, no. 4 (Winter 2007/2008): 25-28.

35. David Weinberger, "Digital Natives, Immigrants and Others," *KM World* 17, no. 1 (2008): 24.

36. L. Gordon Crovitz, "The Information Age: Unloading Information Overload," *Wall Street Journal*, July 7, 2008.

37. I was reading the Twentieth Anniversary Edition of *Amusing Ourselves to Death* by Neil Postman (Penguin 1985, 2005). In the introduction Andrew Postman discusses a professor who makes her students do an "e-media fast" (xii) and write a reflection paper. I'm assuming that this assignment is designed to give the students a break from media messages, but I thought the experiment could be easily adapted to a broader break from information and communication technology—and it could potentially provide some interesting observations.

Chapter 2 Notes

1. Marc Uri Porat, *The Information Economy: Definition and Measurement* (Washington, DC: U.S. Department of Commerce, Office of Telecommunications, 1977): 2.

2. June Lester and Wallace C Koehler, Jr., *Fundamentals of Information Studies: Understanding Information and Its Environment* (New York: Neal-Schuman, 2003): 14.

3. Helmut Theiss, "On terminology," in *Information Science in Action: System Design,* ed. Anthony Debons and Arvid G. Larson, (The Hague: Martinus Nijhoff, 1983), 1: 88.

4. William Paisley, "Information and Work," in *Progress in Communications Sciences,* ed. Brenda Dervin, Melvin J. Voigt, (Norwood, NJ: Ablex, 1980), 2: 118.

5. Lester and Koehler, Jr., *Fundamentals of Information Studies,* 13.

6. A.S. Madden, "A Definition of Information," *Aslib Proceedings* 52, no. 9 (2000): 348.

7. Ibid., 344.

8. Richard L. Derr, "The Concept of Information in Ordinary Discourse," *Information Processing and Management* 21, no. 6 (1985): 498. Derr reviews the concept of information from an information science perspective and concludes that there is no widely accepted definition. He ends his article with the claim that information "is concerned with the resolution of uncertainty,

in the sense that it is a record of resolved uncertainty." I like the simplicity of the definition, so I borrowed it for the section subtitle.

9. Russell L. Ackoff, "From Data to Wisdom: Presidential Address to ISGSR, June 1988," *Journal of Applied Systems Analysis* 16 (1988): 3.

10. Syed Ahsan and Abad Shah, "Data, Information, Knowledge, Wisdom: A Doubly Linked Chain?" (2006), http://ww1.ucmss.com/books/LFS/CSREA2006/IKE4628 (accessed August 15, 2007).

11. Ackoff, "From Data to Wisdom," 4.

12. Gene Bellinger, Durval Castro and Anthony Mills, "Data, Information, Knowledge, and Wisdom," (2004), http://www.systems-thinking.org/dikw/dikw.html (accessed August 15, 2007).

13. Ahsan and Shah, "Data, Information, Knowledge, Wisdom," 2006.

14. Bellinger, Castro and Mills, "Data, Information, Knowledge and Wisdom," 2004.

15. Ibid.

16. This list consists of some of the most popular YouTube videos (most have been viewed over a million times). These videos have become so popular, that they are often referred to as Internet memes.

17. Brian Vickery and Alina Vickery, *Information Science in Theory and Practice* (London: Butterworths, 1987): 41-43.

18. Lester and Koehler, Jr., *Fundamentals of Information Studies*, 19-20. Lester and Koehler provide more detail on the semantic, technical and pragmatic approaches to changing messages.

19. Mitsubishi Motors. "Facts & Figures," http://www.mitsubishi-motors.com/corporate/ir/share/pdf/e/fact2005.pdf (accessed January 19, 2009).

20. Chameleon Translations, "Further information on the Mitsubishi Pajero SUV," http://chameleon-translations.com/Index-Companies-pajero.shtml (accessed January 19, 2009).

Chapter 3 Notes

1. *Oxford English Dictionary Online,* s.v. "Technology," http://dictionary.oed.com/ (accessed January 6, 2009).

2. Ibid.

3. *Wikipedia,* s.v. "Papermaking," http://en.wikipedia.org/wiki/Papermaking (accessed January 12, 2009).

4. Paige Baltzan, Amy Phillips and Brian Detlor, *Business Driven Information Systems,* 1st Canadian ed. (Toronto: McGraw-Hill Ryerson, 2008): 34.

5. Philip Elmer-Dewitt, "Battle for the Soul of the Internet, *Time* 144, no. 4 (July 25, 1994), http://www.time.com/time/magazine/article/0,9171,981132,00.html (accessed January 15, 2009).

6. Clifford Stoll, "The Internet? Bah! Hype Alert: Why Cyberspace isn't, and will never be, nirvana," *Newsweek* (February 27, 1995), http://www.newsweek.com/id/106554 (accessed January 15, 2009).

7. *Wikipedia,* s.v. "Archie search engine," http://en.wikipedia.org/wiki/Archie_search_engine (accessed February 2, 2009).

8. John C. Dvorak, "The Myth of Disruptive Technology," *PC Magazine* 23, no. 14 (2004): 55, http://www.pcmag.com/article2/0,2817,1628049,00.asp (accessed January 15, 2009). Dvorak takes issue with the whole disruptive technology thesis, claiming, "There is no such thing as a disruptive technology." He is particularly critical of Clayton Christensen's argument from *The Innovator's Dilemma* (Boston, MA: Harvard Business School Press, 1997).

9. Rosalind Williams, "The Political and Feminist Dimensions of Technological Determinism," in *Does Technology Drive History? The Dilemma of Technological Determinism,* ed. Merritt Roe Smith and Leo Marx (Cambridge, MA: MIT Press, 1994): 218.

10. Stacey Schiff, "Know it All," *New Yorker* 82, no. 23, http://www.newyorker.com/archive/2006/07/31/060731fa_fact (accessed

February 2, 2009). Interestingly, the original version of Wikipedia (called Nupedia) involved a much more laborious process for the contributors and was largely unsuccessful.

11. "Hawaiian words; Hawaiian to English," http://www.mauimapp.com/moolelo/hwnwdshw.htm (accessed February 2, 2009).

12. Kenneth C. Laudon and Jane P. Laudon, *Management Information Systems: Managing the Digital Firm,* 3rd Canadian ed. Adapted by Mary Elizabeth Brabston (Toronto: Pearson-Prentice Hall, 2007): 13-15.

13. Peter F. Drucker, "What Executives Should Remember," *Harvard Business Review* 84, no. 2 (February 2006): 147.

14. Ibid.

15. Michael E. Porter and Victor E. Millar, "How information gives you competitive advantage," *Harvard Business Review* 63, no. 4 (1985): 150. Porter more fully develops the value chain approach in his book *Competitive Advantage* (New York: Free Press, 1985).

16. Ibid., 152.

17. Peter F. Drucker, "Beyond the Information Revolution," *Atlantic Monthly* 284, no. 4 (1999): 47-57, http://www.theatlantic.com/doc/199910/information-revoution (accessed January 13, 2009).

18. Nicholas Carr, "IT Doesn't Matter," *Harvard Business Review* 81, no. 5 (2003): 42. This article was a flashpoint in the IT industry; in response, Carr published a more comprehensive argument in a book provocatively titled, *Does IT Matter? Information Technology and the Corrosion of Competitive Advantage* (Boston, MA: Harvard Business School Press, 2004).

19. Ibid., 43.

20. Ibid., 44.

21. Nicholas Carr, "The End of Corporate Computing," *MIT Sloan Management Review* 46, no. 3 (Spring 2005), http://sloanreview.mit.edu/the-magazine/articles/2005/spring/46313/the-end-of-corporate-computing/ (accessed February 2, 2009).

22. John Seely Brown and John Hagel III, "Does IT Matter?" *Harvard Business Review* 81, no. 7 (2003): 109.

23. Hal Varian, "Does IT Matter?" *Harvard Business Review* 81, no. 7 (2003): 112.

24. James Champy, "Technology Doesn't Matter—but Only at Harvard," *Fast Company* 77 (December 2003): 119; Scott Leibs, "The tract of matter," *CFO* 20, no. 8 (Summer 2004): 50-51.

25. Carr, "The End of Corporate Computing." Again, Carr develops a much more comprehensive argument of technology as a utility in his book *The Big Switch: Rewiring the World, from Edison to Google* (New York: Norton, 2008).

26. Carr, "IT Doesn't Matter," 48.

Chapter 4 Notes

1. American Library Association, Association of College and Research Libraries (ACRL), "Information Literacy Competency Standards for Higher Education," http://www.ala.org/ala/mgrps/divs/acrl/standards/informationliteracy-competency.cfm (accessed February 8, 2009).

2. American Library Association. "Presidential Committee on Information Literacy: Final Report," http://www.ala.org/ala/mgrps/divs/acrl/publications/whitepapers/presidential.cfm (accessed January 30, 2009).

3. John Seely Brown, "Growing Up Digital," *Change* (March/April 2000): 12.

4. Kevin Kelly, "Becoming Screen Literate," *New York Times Magazine* (November 21, 2008), http://www.nytimes.com/2008/11/23/magazine/23wwln-future-t.html (accessed January 30, 2009).

5. Farhad Manjoo, *True Enough* (Hoboken, NJ: John Wiley & Sons, 2008). Manjoo doesn't look at producer/consumer roles *per se,* but he does examine the effects of a fragmented media (where the traditional authorities aren't the only sources of knowledge). His book presents a fascinating (and frightening) look at the "post-fact society."

6. ACRL, "Information Literacy Competency Standards for Higher Education." This paragraph is loosely based on ACRL's five

core competencies for Information Literacy, but I've construed them a little more broadly.

7. Brown, "Growing Up Digital," 14.

8. Chris Anderson, *The Long Tail* (New York: Hyperion, 2006): 54.

9. Ibid., 55.

10. Ikujiro Nonaka, "The Knowledge-Creating Company," *Harvard Business Review* 85, no. 7 (July/August 2007): 164.

11. Ibid., 165.

12. Brown, "Growing Up Digital," 15.

13. Peter Klein, "What's so Great about Tacit Knowledge?" Organizations and Markets blog, October 26, 2006, http://organization-sandmarkets.com/2006/10/26/whats-so-great-about-tacit-knowledge/ (accessed January 26, 2009); Nicolai Foss, "What's so Great about Tacit Knowledge? Cont'd," Organizations and Markets blog, October 27, 2006, http://organizationsandmarkets.com/2006/10/27/whats-so-great-about-tacit-knowledge-contd/ (accessed January 26, 2009).

14. Nonaka, "The Knowledge-Creating Company," 164.

15. Ibid., 165-166.

16. Ibid., 166.

17. Clay Shirky, *Here Comes Everybody* (New York: Penguin Press, 2008). Our discussion was focused on knowledge creation in organizations, but Shirky's book includes many examples of knowledge creation without organizations. In fact, the subtitle of his book is "The power of organizing without organizations." The use of social software and new information technology enables us to produce knowledge even in a disorganized environment—Wikipedia being a prime example.

18. Alireza Noruzi, "Application of Ranganathan's Laws to the Web," *Webology* 1, no. 2 (December 2004), http://www.webology.ir/2004/v1n2/a8.html (accessed January 22, 2009). While there have been many riffs on Shiyali Ramamrita Ranganathan's famous *Five Laws of Library Science* (1931), Noruzi provides a good description for the web environment.

19. George Macgregor, "The nature of information in the twenty-first century: Conundrums for the informatics community?" *Library Review* 54, no. 1 (2005): 15.

20. *Wikipedia,* s.v. "Neutral point of view," http://en.wikipedia.org/wiki/Wikipedia:NPOV (accessed February 9, 2009).

21. Alexa Web Information Company, "Top sites in United States," http://www.alexa.com/site/ds/top_sites?cc=US&ts_mode=country&lang=none (accessed February 23, 2009).

Chapter 5 Notes

1. Michael B. Arthur, Robert J. Defillippi, and Valerie J. Lindsay, "On Being a Knowledge Worker," *Organizational Dynamics* 37, no. 4 (2008): 365. Peter Drucker is usually credited with coining the term "knowledge work" back in 1959, but more recently people like Tom Davenport have updated the discussion.

2. While not everyone likes the term "knowledge worker," a number of researchers have pointed to the significant shift in how we work. For example, Richard Florida developed the notion of the "creative class" suggesting that more people rely on their minds (creativity) for their livelihood than in previous generations. Daniel Pink also articulated the changing nature of work in his book, *A Whole New Mind* (New York: Riverhead Books, 2005).

3. Arthur, Defillippi, and Lindsay, "On Being a Knowledge Worker," 365.

4. Jeff De Cagna, "Your Attention Please: A Conversation with Tom Davenport," *Information Outlook* 5, no. 9 (2001): 34.

5. Frederick A. Hayek, "The Use of Knowledge in Society," *The American Economic Review* 15, no. 4 (September 1945): 519.

6. Arthur, Defillippi, and Lindsay, "On Being a Knowledge Worker," 367-368. These three ways of knowing are loosely based on the model presented by Arthur et al. However, their paper primarily focuses on the identity of the knowledge worker, not on knowledge itself. As a result, I've substituted

"knowing-what" for their concept of "knowing-why," because it connects this section with the previous section on explicit and tacit knowledge.

7. *Oxford English Dictionary Online,* s.v. "Collaboration," http://dictionary.oed.com/ (accessed February 6, 2009).

8. This subtitle is borrowed from *The Colbert Report* and his satirical segment on "Wikiality"—a word invented to mean "truth by consensus" (first broadcast on July 31, 2006). It is also a play on the title of Joe Trippi's book, *The Revolution will not be Televised* (New York: Harper, 2005).

9. Reima Suomi, "Management of Infrastructures: What Can the Internet Developers Learn from the History of Railways?" *Management Decision* 45, no. 5/6 (2005): 897.

10. Ibid., 898.

11. Ibid., 897. Suomi's article is a provocative comparison of the Internet and railways. I've summarized his discussion somewhat. He also includes: the digital divide, regional effects of networks, and the professional staff associated with each industry.

12. Peter F. Drucker, "Beyond the Information Revolution," *Atlantic Monthly* 284, no. 4 (1999): 47-57, http://www.theatlantic. com/doc/199910/information-revoution (accessed January 13, 2009).

13. Ibid.

14. Peter F. Drucker, "The Next Information Revolution," *Forbes* (August 24, 1998: Supplement): 46-53.

15. Vannevar Bush, "As We May Think," *The Atlantic,* (1945), http://www.theatlantic.com/ doc/194507/bush (accessed February 4, 2009).

16. Ibid.

17. Ibid.

18. Ibid.

19. Kevin Kelly, "We Are the Web," *Wired* 13, no. 8 (August 2005), http://www.wired.com/ wired/archive/13.08/tech.html (accessed February 4, 2009).

20. "The Race to Come," *Time* 70, no. 17 (October 21, 1957), http://www.time.com/ time/magazine/article/0,9171,937918,00. html (accessed February 9, 2009); "The Beeper's Message," *Time* 70, no. 17 (October 21, 1957), http://www.time.com/time/ magazine/article/0,9171,937932-2,00.html (accessed February 9, 2009).

21. Jane Abbate, "Government, Business, and the Making of the Internet," *Business History Review* 75, no. 1 (Spring 2001): 150.

22. Ibid., 151.

23. Ibid., 172.

24. Robert Zakon, "Hobbes' Internet Timeline v. 8.2," http://www.zakon.org/robert/internet/ timeline/ (accessed February 4, 2009).

25. Kelly, "We are the Web."

26. Abbate, "Government, Business, and the Making of the Internet," 150-151.

27. "Brief History of the Domain Name System," http://cyber.law.harvard.edu/icann/ pressingissues2000/briefingbook/ dnshistory.html (accessed February 4, 2009).

28. Kenneth Neil Cukier, "Who Will Control the Internet? Washington Battles the World," *Foreign Affairs* 84, no 6 (2005): 7-13. I've borrowed my subtitle from Cukier's article on Internet governance. The original quotation reads like this: "the open network is like the open society—crime thrives, but so does creativity."

29. David Talbot, "The Internet is Broken," *Technology Review* 108, no. 11 (December 2005/January 2006), http://www. technologyreview.com/InfoTech/ wtr_16051,258,p1.html (accessed February 4, 2009).

30. Ibid.

31. Joshua Davis, "Secret Geek A-Team Hacks Back, Defends the Worldwide Web," Wired 16, no. 12 (December 2008), http://www. wired.com/techbiz/people/magazine/ 16-12/ff_kaminsky (accessed February 9, 2009). Davis details Dan Kaminsky's discovery of a key flaw in the Domain Name System and how security experts patched the flaw.

32. Cukier, "Who Will Control the Internet? Washington Battles the World"
33. Ibid. To expand a little further: the Internet Corporation of Assigned Names and Numbers (ICANN) is the body that registers unique identifiers (domain names and IP addresses) and has been accused of protecting American interests. In fact, in the early stages of the Internet many developing nations couldn't understand why "the Internet was essentially run by a nonprofit corporation whose 15-person board of directors was accountable to the attorney general of the State of California and under the authority of the U.S. government." As further evidence of American interests, some people point to the fact that ten of the 13 root servers still reside in the United States. As more nations and international bodies clamor to participate in Internet governance, the United States is increasingly hesitant to relinquish its role—understandably so.
34. Jeff Johnson, "The Information Highway: A Worst-Case Scenario," *Communications of the ACM* 39, no. 2 (1996); Andrew Shapiro, "Street Corners in Cyberspace," *The Nation* (July 3, 1995).
35. Kelly, "We Are the Web."
36. James Gleick "The Information Future: Out of Control, for good," In *What Just Happened: A Chronicle of the Information Frontier* (New York: Pantheon Books, 2001): 69.
37. Michael R. Nelson, "Let the Internet Be the Internet," Issues in Science and Technology 22, no. 3 (Spring 2006), http://www.issues.org/22.3/p_nelson.html (accessed February 9, 2009).

Chapter 6 Notes

1. Jonathan B. Spira, "In Praise of Knowledge Workers," *KMWorld* 14, no. 2 (February 2005): 26.
2. *WordNet: A lexical database for the English language (Princeton)*, s.v. "Ontology," http://wordnetweb.princeton.edu/perl/webwn?s=ontology

3. *University of California Museum of Paleontology (UCMP)*, s.v. "Carl Linnaeus," http://www.ucmp.berkeley.edu/history/linnaeus.html (accessed February 13, 2009).
4. University Library, University of Illinois at Urbana-Champaign, "Dewey Decimal in the UIUC Bookstacks." http://www.library.uiuc.edu/circ/tutorial/dewey-schedule-numerical.html (accessed June 2, 2009).
5. U.S. Census Bureau, "North American Industry Classification System," http://www.census.gov/eos/www/naics/ (accessed February 13, 2009); Statistics Canada, "Standard Industry Classification," http://www.statcan.gc.ca/concepts/industry-industrie-eng.htm (accessed February 13, 2009).
6. *WordNet: A lexical database for the English language (Princeton)*, s.v. "Taxonomy," http://wordnetweb.princeton.edu/perl/webwn?s=taxonomy
7. Richard Veryard, "Abstraction," http://www.users.globalnet.co.uk/~rxv/infomgt/abstraction.htm (accessed February 13, 2009).
8. David Weinberger, *Everything is Miscellaneous: The power of the digital disorder* (New York: Times Books, 2007). Weinberger includes an insightful chapter that sums up the entire act of categorization as two basic processes: lumping and splitting. I borrowed those concepts for the subtitle of this section.
9. Stephen Jay Gould, *Wonderful Life: The Burgess Shale and the Nature of History* (New York: W.W. Norton & Company, 1990): 98.
10. This subtitle is a play on the phrase: "information wants to be free." While this phrase has been adopted (unofficially) by the free content movement, the original statement comes from Stewart Brand, who was speaking at the first Hackers' conference in 1984. Brand was talking about how the cost of distributing information was falling rapidly due to information technology—now the challenge is to actually find that information.

11. "IMDb statistics," http://www.imdb.com/database_statistics (accessed February 19, 2009).

12. Curt Franklin, "How Internet Search Engines Work," http://computer.howstuffworks.com/search-engine.htm (accessed February 16, 2009).

13. John Battelle, *The Search: How Google and Its Rivals Rewrote the Rules of Business and Transformed our Culture* (New York: Portfolio Books, 2004). Battelle provides a much more comprehensive look at Google and the impact of search engines on the Information Age.

14. Net Applications. Market Share, "Top Search Engine Share Trend," (March 2008 - January 2009), http://marketshare.hitslink.com/search-engine-market-share.aspx?qprid=5 (accessed February, 18, 2009).

15. In their original paper, Google's founders cite Eugene Garfield and his pioneering work in the 1950s as developing the field of citation analysis.

16. iProspect, "Search Engine User Behavior Study," (April 2006), www.iprospect.com/premiumPDFs/WhitePaper_2006_SearchEngineUserBehavior.pdf (accessed February 18, 2009).

17. Nicholas Carroll, "Search Engine Optimization and User Behavior," Hastings Research, Inc. Technical Paper, (November 1, 2008), http://www.hastingsresearch.com/net/09-SEO-ELIS-encyclopedia-article.html (accessed February 18, 200).

18. "The Ultimate Guide to the Invisible Web," Online Education Database, http://oedb.org/library/college-basics/invisible-web (accessed February 19, 2009). This article provides an adequate primer and more information on the types of information that cannot be found via standard search engines.

19. Jaime Teevan, Christine Alvarado, Mark S. Ackerman, and David R. Karger, "The Perfect Search Engine is Not Enough: A Study of Orienteering Behavior in Directed Search," *Proceedings of the SIGCHI Conference on Human factors in computing systems* (2004): 415-422.

20. Nathan Eagle, "Can Serendipity Be Planned?" *MIT Sloan Management Review* 46, no. 1 (Fall 2004): 10-14.

21. Clay Shirky, "Ontology is Overrated: Categories, Links and Tags," http://www.shirky.com/writings/ontology_overrated.html (accessed March 9, 2009).

22. Bruce Sterling, "Order Out of Chaos," *Wired* 13, no. 4 (April 2005), http://www.wired.com/wired/archive/13.04/view.html?pg=4 (accessed March 9, 2009).

23. Shirky, "Ontology is Overrated: Categories, Links and Tags."

24. Ernst-Jan Pfauth, "Why you should tag your Flickr pictures," The Next Web, http://thenextweb.com/2008/04/25/why-you-should-tag-your-flickr-pictures/ (accessed March 9, 2009).

25. Sterling, "Order Out of Chaos."

Chapter 7 Notes

1. Thomas White, "Why Do the Right Thing?" http://cba.lmu.edu/Assets/Colleges+$!2b+Schools/CBA/CEB/Essays/Why+Do+the+Right+Thing$!3f.pdf?method=1 (accessed March 1, 2009).

2. Martha M. Eining and Grace M. Lee, "Information Ethics: An Exploratory Study From an International Perspective," *Journal of Information Systems* 11, no. 1 (Spring 1997): 8. Eining and Lee used four ethical scenarios to compare ethical reasoning among Chinese and American business students. The results suggest that the hope for a "global ethic" related to information technology, may not be as close as we would like to believe.

3. Krystyna Gorniak-Kocikowska, "The Computer Revolution and the Problem of Global Ethics," http://www.southernct.edu/organizations/rccs/resources/research/global_info/gorniak/comp_rev_intro.html (accessed February 25, 2009).

4. James H. Moor, "What is Computer Ethics?" *Metaphilosophy* 16, no. 4 (October 1985): 266.

5. Ibid., 267.

6. Gorniak-Kocikowska, "The Computer Revolution and the Problem of Global Ethics."

7. Moor, 269. Moor calls this revolutionary quality of computers "logical malleability." While Moor applies the term to computers, the concepts are relevant to more recent developments in information technology (cell phones, Internet, etc.).

8. Neil Postman, *Technopoly: The Surrender of Culture to Technology* (New York: Vintage, 1993). Postman provides a stunning treatise on how technology has weaved its way into our culture, without us noticing. Although his observations and examples are slightly dated, his arguments remain relevant to the Information Age.

9. Gorniak-Kocikowska, "The Computer Revolution and the Problem of Global Ethics."

10. *The Internet Encyclopedia of Philosophy,* s.v. "Jeremy Bentham," http://www.iep.utm.edu/b/bentham.htm (accessed March 2, 2009).

11. James H. Moor, "Is Ethics Computable?" *Metaphilosophy* 26, no. 1&2 (January/April 1995): 3. More of Bentham's moral philosophy can be found in his *Introduction to the Principles of Morals and Legislation* (1789).

12. Ibid., 4-5.

13. Thomas White, "Ethics Toolbox: Philosophical Ethics," Center for Ethics and Business at Loyola Marymount University, http://www.ethicsandbusiness.org/toolbox/philoethics.htm (accessed March 2, 2009).

14. *The Internet Encyclopedia of Philosophy,* s.v. "Immanuel Kant," http://www.iep.utm.edu/k/kantmeta.htm (accessed March 2, 2009).

15. Thomas White, "Ethics Toolbox: Philosophical Ethics."

16. Ibid.

17. These themes are taken from the codes of conduct of two associations of information professionals (accessed March 2009): The Association of Independent Information Professionals, (http://www.aiip.org/Default.aspx?pageId=88881) and The Association of Information Technology Professionals, (http://www.aitp.org/organization/about/ethics/ethics.jsp).

18. Chris MacDonald, "A Guide to Moral Decision Making," Ethics Web, http://www.ethicsweb.ca/guide/ (accessed March 2, 2009); Thomas I. White, "Resolving an Ethical Dilemma," Center for Business Ethics, Loyola Marymount University, http://www.ethicsandbusiness.org/pdf/strategy.pdf (accessed March 2, 2009). I've combined ethical reasoning approaches proposed by MacDonald and White to create a hybrid more inline with the discussion on information technology ethics.

19. Roberta Brody, "Information Ethics in the Business Research Environment," *Online* 30, no. 1 (Jan/Feb 2006): 39; John C. Maxwell, *There is No Such thing as "Business Ethics"* (New York: Warner Books, 2003): 5-9. Maxwell suggests that we cannot separate business ethics from regular ethics. We need to use a consistent ethical approach whether we're at home or at work. Maxwell argues that the Golden Rule provides sufficient guidance, but Brody counters with the claim that this alone is too simplistic for sound ethical reasoning.

20. Amar Bhide and Howard H. Stevenson, "Why Be Honest if Honesty Doesn't Pay," *Harvard Business Review* 68, no. 5 (September-October 1990): 121-129.

21. Moor, "Is Ethics Computable?"

Chapter 8 Notes

1. Gary Marx, "What's in a Name? Some Reflections on the Sociology of Anonymity," *The Information Society* 15, no. 2 (1999): 100-102.

2. *Oxford English Dictionary Online,* s.v. "Privacy," http://dictionary.oed.com/ (accessed March 18, 2009).

3. Cathy Goodwin, "Privacy: Recognition of a Consumer Right," *Journal of Public Policy and Marketing* 10, no. 1, (1991): 150-151.

4. Peter Wayner, "Technology for Anonymity: Names by Other Nyms," *The Information Society* 15, no. 2 (1999): 91-92.
5. Marx, "What's in a Name? Some Reflections on the Sociology of Anonymity," 109.
6. Helen Nissenbaum, "The Meaning of Anonymity in an Information Age," *The Information Society* 15, no. 2 (1999): 141.
7. Robert Kling, Ya-ching Lee, Al Teich and Mark S. Frankel, "Assessing Anonymous Communication on the Internet: Policy Deliberations," *The Information Society* 15, no. 2 (1999): 87.
8. Al Teich, Mark S. Frankel, Rob Kling and Ya-ching Lee, "Anonymous Communication Policies for the Internet: Results and Recommendations of the AAAS Conference," *The Information Society* 15, no. 2 (1999): 71.
9. European Commission, "Data Protection," http://ec.europa.eu/justice_home/fsj/privacy/index_en.htm (accessed March 23, 2009).
10. Jeff Langenderfer and Dan Lloyd Cook, "Oh, what a tangled web we weave: The state of privacy protection in the information economy and recommendations for governance," *Journal of Business Research* 57, no. 7 (2004): 736.
11. Government of Canada, "Personal Information and Protection of Electronic Documents Act: Bill C-6," http://www2.parl.gc.ca/HousePublications/Publication.aspx?pub=bill&doc=C-6&parl=36&ses=2&language=E (accessed March 23, 2009).
12. Sheila Taylor, "Protecting Privacy in Canada's Private Sector," *Information Management Journal* 37, no. 4 (July/August 2003): 4.
13. Erica L. Wagner and Olga Kupriyanova, "Data-driven Ethics: Exploring Customer Privacy in the Information Era," *Cornell Hospitality Report* 7, no. 10 (June 2007): 9.
14. Mike Whitehorn, "The Parable of Beer and Diapers," *The Register,* August 15, 2006, http://www.theregister.co.uk/2006/08/15/beer_diapers/ (accessed March 10, 2009). The common pairing of beer and diapers is a well-known example used to illustrate the

benefits of identifying seemingly unrelated products. Unfortunately, it's an urban legend.
15. Nissenbaum, "The Meaning of Anonymity in an Information Age," 142.
16. Kling et al., "Assessing Anonymous Communication on the Internet: Policy Deliberations," 86-87.
17. Ibid., 86.
18. Charles Piller, "Zero Privacy? Zero Knowledge May Have A Way Around That," *Los Angeles Times,* February 8, 1999, http://articles.latimes.com/1999/feb/08/business/fi-6013 (accessed March 11, 2009).
19. James Gleick, "The Telephone Transformed into almost everything," *New York Times,* May 16, 1993, http://query.nytimes.com/gst/fullpage.html?res=9F0CE7DD143FF935A25756C0A965958260 (accessed March 12, 2009).
20. Samuel J. Best, Brian S. Kreugar and Jeffrey Ladewig, "Privacy in the Information Age," *Public Opinion Quarterly* 70, no. 3 (Fall 2006): 375-401.
21. Nissenbaum, "The Meaning of Anonymity in an Information Age," 141.
22. Wayner, "Technology for Anonymity: Names by Other Nyms," 91-92.
23. Andrew Keen, *Cult of the Amateur* (New York: Broadway Business, 2007): 175.
24. Harriet Barovick, "When Confession Happens Online," *Time,* October 23, 2008, http://www.time.com/time/magazine/article/0,9171,1853325,00.html (accessed March 23, 2009).

Chapter 9 Notes

1. Bruce Schneier, "Security vs. Privacy," http://www.schneier.com/blog/archives/2008/01/security_vs_pri.html (accessed March 9, 2009).
2. "Britain is 'surveillance society,'" *BBC News,* November 2, 2006, http://news.bbc.co.uk/2/hi/uk_news/6108496.stm (accessed March 9, 2009).

3. David Murakami Wood, ed., "A Report on the Surveillance Society," (September 2006), http://www.ico.gov.uk/upload/documents/library/data_protection/practical_application/surveillance_society_full_report_2006.pdf (accessed March 9, 2009).

4. "How we are being watched," *BBC News,* November 3, 2006, http://news.bbc.co.uk/2/hi/uk_news/6110866.stm (accessed March 9, 2009).

5. Although dataveillance is a somewhat awkward combination of data and surveillance, the term accurately describes how people are tracked by their trails of data. It was originally coined by Roger Clarke (http://www.rogerclarke.com/DV/) and has been adopted by many in the privacy industry.

6. G. Daryl Nord, Tipton F. McCubbins, and Jeretta Horn Nord, "E-Monitoring in the workplace: Privacy, Legislation, and Surveillance Software," *Communications of the ACM* 49, no. 8 (August 2006): 73-77.

7. Bruce Schneier, "The Tech Lab: Bruce Schneier," *BBC News,* February 26, 2009, http://news.bbc.co.uk/2/hi/technology/7897892.stm (accessed March 11, 2009).

8. Using surveillance activities to monitor authorities is sometimes called inverse surveillance or to borrow from the French: "sousveillance" (surveillance from below).

9. Robert Trigaux, "We Are Hackers," *St. Petersburg Times,* June 14, 1998, http://www.sptimes.com/Hackers/history.hacking.html (accessed March 11, 2009).

10. Ibid.

11. Steven Levy, *Hackers: Heroes of the Information Revolution* (New York: Anchor Press/Doubleday, 1984): 26-36 [Chapter 2]. I've combined his last three points into one.

12. Ibid., 27.

13. Steven Mizrach, "Is there a Hacker Ethic for 90s Hackers?" http://www.fiu.edu/~mizrachs/hackethic.html (accessed March 14, 2009).

14. Levy, *Hackers: Heroes of the Information Revolution,* 28.

15. Mizrach, "Is there a Hacker Ethic for the 90s Hackers?"

16. Ibid.

17. Ibid.

18. Marshall Brain, "How Computer Viruses Work," http://www.howstuffworks.com/virus.htm (accessed March 15, 2009).

19. Wikipedia, s.v. "Computer Virus," http://en.wikipedia.org/wiki/Computer_virus (accessed March 14, 2009).

20. Paul Boutin, "Slammed!" *Wired* 11, no. 7 (July 2003), http://www.wired.com/wired/archive/11.07/slammer.html (accessed March 14, 2009). Although there are more recent worms, Boutin's article provides a better play-by-play example of the Slammer worm in action.

21. Brain, "How Computer Viruses Work."

22. Mizrach, "Is there a Hacker Ethic for the 90s Hacker?"

23. Wikipedia, s.v. "Denial-of-service attack," http://en.wikipedia.org/wiki/Denial-of-service_attack (accessed March 14, 2009).

24. Secure Computing, Inc., "Zombie Stats," http://research.ciphertrust.com/statistics.php (accessed March 23, 2009).

25. CIA World Factbook, "Estonia," March 19, 2009, https://www.cia.gov/library/publications/the-world-factbook/geos/en.html (accessed March 23, 2009).

26. "World War 2.0" *PBS & Wired Science,* http://www.pbs.org/kcet/wiredscience/story/9-world_war_2_0.html (accessed March 15, 2009). This web content features a series of videos on botnets and cybercrime. In particular, there are some useful segments animating the timeline of the attacks on Estonia.

27. Joshua Davis, "Hackers Take Down the Most Wired Nation in Europe," *Wired* 15, no. 9 (September 2007), http://www.wired.com/politics/security/magazine/15-09/ff_estonia (accessed March 15, 2009). Davis provides a fascinating overview of the events in Estonia, including perspectives of the Internet Security experts from around the world.

28. Paige Baltzan, Amy Phillips and Brian Detlor, *Business Driven Information Systems,* 1st Canadian ed. (Toronto: McGraw-Hill Ryerson, 2008): 279-284.

Chapter 10 Notes

1. Ian G. DiBernardo and William D. Latza, "Copyrights and Trademarks and Patents! Oh, My!" *Best's Review* 107, no. 4 (August 2006): 78-80. There are many sources for intellectual property information, but DiBernardo and Latza have written a very concise overview. With the exception of the information on trade secrets, my discussion of intellectual property follows their lead.
2. Ibid., 79.
3. "Inventor: Jay Sorenson," Respect Rights, http://www.respectrights.org/inventions_marketplace/index.htm (accessed March 27, 2009).
4. Richard O. Mason, "Four Ethical Issues of the Information Age," *Management Information Systems Quarterly* 10, no. 1 (March 1986), http://www.misq.org/archivist/vol/no10/issue1/vol10no1mason.html (accessed March 18, 2009). Mason's classic article provides a number of intriguing questions related to the problem of treating ideas as property.
5. Hal Varian, "How much will two bits be worth in the digital marketplace?" *Scientific American* (September 1995), http://people.ischool.berkeley.edu/~hal/pages/sciam.html (accessed March 20, 2009).
6. DiBernardo and Latza, "Copyrights and Trademarks and Patents! Oh, My!" 78.
7. Mark A. Lemley, "Property, Intellectual Property and Free-Riding [DRAFT]," *Texas Law Review* 83 (2005), http://papers.ssrn.com/sol3/papers.cfm?abstract_id=582602 (accessed March 20, 2009); Audrey Fenner, "Placing Value on Information," *Library Philosophy and Practice* 4, no. 2 (Spring 2002), http://www.webpages.uidaho.edu/~mbolin/fenner.pdf (accessed March 20, 2009).

8. Roger A. McCain, "Information as Property and Public Good: Perspectives from the Economic Theory of Property Rights," *Library Quarterly* 58, no. 3 (1988): 265.
9. Martha M. Eining & Grace M. Lee, "Information Ethics: An Exploratory Study From an International Perspective," *Journal of Information Systems* 11, no. 1 (Spring 1997): 1-17. Although this study is over a decade old, it provides some reliable evidence for differences between traditions in the East and the West on information issues.
10. Brendan Scott, "Copyright in a Frictionless World: Toward a Rhetoric of Responsibility," *First Monday* 6, no. 9 (September 2001), http://firstmonday.org/htbin/cgiwrap/bin/ojs/index.php/fm/article/view/887/796 (accessed March 20, 2009).
11. Ibid.
12. Ibid.
13. Ibid.
14. David Beer, "Sooner or later we will melt together: framing the digital in the everyday," *First Monday* 10, no. 8 (August 2005), http://firstmonday.org/htbin/cgiwrap/bin/ojs/index.php/fm/article/view/1268/1188 (accessed March 20, 2009).
15. John Perry Barlow, "The Economy of Ideas," *Wired* 2, no. 3 (March 1994) http://www.wired.com/wired/archive/2.03/economy.ideas_pr.html (accessed March 20, 2009).
16. Siva Vaidhyanathan, "Celestial Jukebox," *The American Scholar* 74, no. 2 (Spring 2005).
17. David H. Freedman, "Relax. Let your guard down. Why patents, trademarks, and other intellectual property are bad—that's right, *bad*—for business," *Inc. Magazine* 28, no. 8 (August 2006): 110.
18. McCain, 270-271.
19. Clive Thompson, "The BitTorrent Effect," *Wired* 13, no. 1 (January 2005), http://www.wired.com/wired/archive/13.01/bittorrent.html (accessed March 20, 2009).
20. Creative Commons, "About the Creative Commons," http://creativecommons.org/ (accessed March 23, 2009).

21. Isaac Newton, the seventeenth century scientist, used "to stand on the shoulders of giants" most famously, but the origins of this phrase pre-date Newton (http://en.wikipedia.org/wiki/Standing_on_the_shoulders_of_giants). In contemporary usage, to "stand on the shoulders of giants" means to build on the intellectual property and ideas of those who have come before. Naturally, Google has adopted the phrase for their Google Scholar search engine (http://scholar.google.com/).
22. Mary Bellis, "Patent, Trademark, and Copyright Primer for Students," http://inventors.about.com/cs/lessonplans/a/student_primer.htm (accessed March 23, 2009).
23. U.S. Patent and Trademark Office, "U.S. Patent Statistics Chart: Calendar Years 1963-2007," http://www.uspto.gov/go/taf/us_stat.htm (accessed March 23, 2009).

Chapter 11 Notes

1. Off the Hook, "Emmanuel Testifies Before Congress," (June 1993), http://www.2600.com/offthehook/1993/0693.html (accessed March 29, 2009). Eric Corley, the founder of *2600: The Hacker Quarterly* (http://www.2600.com/), used Emmanuel Goldstein as his pen name and pseudonym. Emmanuel Goldstein was the name of the unseen leader behind "The Brotherhood" in George Orwell's *Nineteen Eighty-Four*. Goldstein was dedicated to taking down "The Party" and the totalitarian state; as such, it seems like an appropriate pseudonym for a hacker.
2. Danny P. Wallace and Connie Van Fleet, "The Democratization of Information? Wikipedia as a Reference Resource," *Reference & User Services Quarterly* 45, no. 2 (Winter 2005): 100.
3. Leo Dirac, "Democratization of Information," Embracing Chaos blog, http://www.embracingchaos.com/2006/10/democratization.html (accessed March 27, 2009).
4. Off the Hook, 1993.

5. Andrew Puddephatt, *Freedom of Expression: The Essentials of Human Rights* (London, UK: Hodder Arnold, 2005): 128, quoted in *Wikipedia*, s.v. "Freedom of Speech," http://en.wikipedia.org/wiki/Freedom_of_speech (accessed March 26, 2009).
6. Jan Narveson, "The meaning and extent of freedom of speech," *Western Standard,* February 21, 2008, http://www.westernstandard.ca/website/article.php?id=2732 (accessed March 28, 2009).
7. Culture Shock, "Definitions of censorship," http://www.pbs.org/wgbh/cultureshock/whodecides/definitions.html (accessed March 29, 2009). This page of definitions provides a nice overview of the different nuances when it comes to defining censorship.
8. Freedom to Read, "Challenged Books and Magazines," http://www.freedomtoread.ca/censorship_in_canada/challenged_books.asp (accessed March 28, 2009); American Library Association, "The most frequently challenged books of 1990-2000," http://www.ala.org/ala/aboutala/offices/oif/bannedbooksweek/bbwlinks/100mostfrequently.cfm (accessed March 28, 2009).
9. Reporters Without Borders, "Internet Enemies," http://www.rsf.org/IMG/pdf/Internet_enemies_2009_2_.pdf (accessed March 28, 2009). The information about Iran, Cuba, Burma, China, Saudi Arabia and Vietnam are gleaned from this extensive report.
10. Ibid.
11. Ryan Singel, "AT&T Sued over NSA Eavesdropping," *Wired: Science News,* http://www.wired.com/science/discoveries/news/2006/01/70126 (accessed March 29, 2009); David Kravets, "Top Internet Threats: Censorship to Warrantless Surveillance," *Wired: Threat Level Blog,* http://blog.wired.com/27bstroke6/2009/03/wireds-top-inte.html (accessed March 29, 2009).
12. Culture Shock, "Who Decides? How and why?" http://www.pbs.org/wgbh/cultureshock/whodecides/index.html (accessed March 29, 2009). This project

produced by WGBH Boston for PBS Online provides a number of interesting examples and thought provoking questions related to censorship.

13. Parliament of Victoria, Scrutiny of Acts and Regulations Committee, "Victorian Electronic Democracy, Final Report, May 2005," http://www.parliament.vic.gov.au/SARC/ E-Democracy/Final_Report/Glossary.htm (accessed March 29, 2009).

14. World Economic Forum, "Annual Report of the Global Digital Divide Initiative" (Geneva: World Economic Forum, 2002).

15. Brendan Luyt, "Who benefits from the digital divide?" *First Monday* 9, no. 8 (August 2004), http://firstmonday.org/htbin/cgiwrap/bin/ojs/ index.php/fm/article/view/1166/1086 (accessed March 28, 2009).

16. Johannes J. Britz, "To know or not to know: a moral reflection on information poverty," *Journal of Information Science* 30, no. 3 (2004): 192.

17. Digital Opportunities Taskforce (dotforce). "Okinawa Charter on the Global Information Society," Japan, Ministry of Foreign Affairs, http://www.mofa.go.jp/POLICY/economy/ summit/2000/charter.html (accessed March 28, 2009).

18. *Oxford English Dictionary Online,* s.v. "Poverty," http://dictionary.oed.com/ (accessed March 26, 2009).

19. Britz, "To know or not to know: a moral reflection on information poverty," 193-195.

20. Ibid., 196.

21. Ibid., 195.

22. Ibid., 196-197.

23. George Sciadas, "The Digital Divide in Canada," Statistics Canada Catalogue no. 56F0009XIE, 2001, http://dsp-psd.tpsgc.gc. ca/Collection/Statcan/56F0009X/ 56F0009XIE2002001.pdf (accessed March 29, 2009); Norris Dickard and Diana Schneider, "The Digital Divide: Where We Are Today," *Edutopia,* July 1, 2002, http:// www.edutopia.org/digital-divide-where- we-are-today (accessed March 29, 2009).

24. Independent Media Arts Preservation (IMAP), "Preservation 101," http://www. imappreserve.org/pres_101/index.html (accessed March 30, 2009).

25. Michael, W. Gilbert, "Digital Media Life Expectancy and Care," http://www.softpres. org/cache/DigitalMediaLifeExpectancyAnd Care.html (accessed March 30, 2009).

26. *Oxford English Dictionary Online,* s.v. "Obsolescence," http://dictionary.oed.com/ (accessed March 26, 2009).

27. Suzanne Keene, "Technical obsolescence," http://www.suzannekeene.info/conserve/ digipres/index.htm (accessed March 30, 2009).

28. Jeff Rothenberg, "Ensuring the Longevity of Digital Information," February 22, 1999, http://www.clir.org/pubs/archives/ensuring.pdf (accessed March 30, 2009).

29. Independent Media Arts Preservation.

30. Matthew Broersma, "It's the end of your data as you know it," *ZDNet* (UK), April 23, 2007, http://resources.zdnet.co.uk/articles/ features/0,1000002000,39286796,00.htm (accessed March 30, 3009).

31. Chandru J. Shahani, Basil Manns, and Michele Youket, "Longevity of CD Media: Research at the Library of Congress," http:// www.loc.gov/preserv/studyofCDlongevity.pdf (accessed March 30, 2009).

32. Jim Barksdale and Francine Berman, "Saving Our Digital Heritage," *Washington Post,* May 16, 2007, http://www.washingtonpost. com/wp-dyn/content/article/2007/05/15/ AR2007051501873.html (accessed May 30, 2009).

33. Bruce Sterling, "Dead Media Manifesto," http://www.deadmedia.org/modest- proposal.html (accessed March 30, 3009).

34. Barksdale and Berman, "Saving our Digital Heritage."

35. Web Accessibility in Mind (WebAIM), "Introduction to Web Accessibility," http:// www.webaim.org/intro/ (accessed March 30, 2009).

Chapter 12 Notes

1. Chris Anderson, *The Long Tail* (New York: Hyperion, 2006). Chris Anderson has called this trend the "Long Tail." I've detailed some of the forces behind the Long Tail in section 4.3. Admittedly, Anderson's argument is an economic argument, but his statements about niche markets fit well here too.

2. Creative Commons, "A Shared Culture," (Online video), http://creativecommons.org/videos/a-shared-culture (accessed April 3, 2009).

3. Nate Anderson, "Tim Berners-Lee on Web 2.0: 'nobody even knows what it means,'" *Ars Technica,* September 1, 2006, http://arstechnica.com/business/news/2006/09/7650.ars (accessed April 1, 2009).

4. Yochai Benkler, *The Wealth of Networks: How Social Production Transforms Markets and Freedom* (New Haven, CT: Yale University Press, 2007): 105.

5. Benkler, *The Wealth of Networks,* 105-106; Nicholas Carr, *The Big Switch* (New York: W. W. Norton, 2009): 140.

6. Benkler, 96.

7. Ibid., 106.

8. Carr, *The Big Switch,* 141.

9. Tim O'Reilly, "What is Web 2.0?" September 30, 2005, http://www.oreillynet.com/pub/a/oreilly/tim/news/2005/09/30/what-is-web-20.html (accessed April 3, 2009).

10. Chris Anderson, "The Long Tail," *Wired* 12, no. 10, (October 2004), http://www.wired.com/wired/archive/12.10/tail.html (accessed April 5, 2009).

11. O'Reilly, "What is Web 2.0?"

12. James Surowiecki, *The Wisdom of the Crowds* (New York: Anchor, 2005). Surowiecki uses numerous examples to demonstrate the power of the majority. Not all of the examples are web-related, but it isn't hard to see how technology contributes to the phenomenon.

13. When it comes to social media, the term "trust" isn't strong enough for many observers. After all, social media requires you to trust people you've never met and probably never will meet; therefore, some observers prefer to use the term "radical trust" when discussing collective intelligence in the online world.

14. This concept is reminscient of Eric S. Raymond's "with enough eyeballs all bugs are shallow." Raymond used this phrase to refer to the Open Source software movement, where thousands of programmers work collaboratively to improve code (and catch errors). Similarly, Wikipedians take care to monitor their pages for errors and vandals.

15. Andrew Keen and David Weinberger, "Full text: Keen vs. Weinberger," *Wall Street Journal,* July 18, 2007, http://online.wsj.com/article/SB118460229729267677.html (accessed April 2, 2009).

16. Howard Kurtz, "As seen on YouTube, Lonelygirl dumps Middleman," *Washington Post,* September 18, 2006, http://www.washingtonpost.com/wp-dyn/content/article/2006/09/17/AR2006091700789.html (accessed April 5, 2009).

17. Keen and Weinberger, "Full text: Keen vs. Weinberger."

18. Lev Grossman, "Time's Person of the Year: You" *Time,* December 13, 2006 http://www.time.com/time/magazine/article/0,9171,1569514,00.html (accessed April 3, 2009). In 2006, *Time* magazine named "You" as their Person of the Year. With the ability to control and contribute to the Web 2.0 world, each of us suddenly became the center of the online world.

19. Farhad Manjoo, *True Enough: Learning to Live in a Post-Fact Society* (New York: Wiley, 2008). Manjoo examines the dangers of living in a world of fragmented media and information. His book is insightful and scary at the same time.

20. Grossman, "Time's Person of the Year: You."

21. Andrew Keen, *The Cult of the Amateur: How blogs, MySpace, YouTube, and the rest of today's user-generated media are destroying our economy, our culture, and our values* (New York: Broadway Business, 2008): 16.

End Matter Notes

1. "The Petabyte Age: Because More Isn't Just More—More is Different," *Wired* 16, no. 7 (July 2008), http://www.wired.com/science/discoveries/magazine/16-07/pb_intro (accessed April 2, 2009).
2. Chris Anderson, "The End of Theory: The Data Deluge Makes the Scientific Method Obsolete," *Wired* 16, no. 7 (July 2008) http://www.wired.com/science/discoveries/magazine/16-07/pb_theory (accessed April 2, 2009).
3. Neil Postman, *Technopoly* (New York: Vintage, 1993): 14.
4. Tim Berners-Lee, *Weaving the Web,* (New York: HarperCollins, 2000): Chapter 12.
5. Mark Frauenfelder, "Sir Tim Berners-Lee," *Technology Review* 107, no. 8 (2004): 40-45.
6. Rob van Kranenburg, *The Internet of Things: A critique of ambient technology and the all-seeing network of RFID* (Amsterdam: Institute of Network Cultures, 2007): 15, http://www.networkcultures.org/_uploads/notebook2_theinternetofthings.pdf (accessed April 4, 2009).
7. Schneier, Bruce. "The Tech Lab: Bruce Schneier" BBC News, http://news.bbc.co.uk/2/hi/technology/7897892.stm (accessed April 2, 2009); van Kranenburg, *The Internet of Things: A critique of ambient technology and the all-seeing network of RFID:* 13.
8. Kevin Kelly, "Scan This Book!" *New York Times Magazine,* http://www.nytimes.com/2006/05/14/magazine/14publishing.html (accessed June 2, 2009).
9. van Kranenburg, *The Internet of Things: A critique of ambient technology and the all-seeing network of RFID:* 19.
10. David Sheff, "Google Guys," *Playboy,* (September 2004). A portion of the interview also appears in Amendment No. 7 to Google's S-1 filing with the Securities and Exchanges Commission, August 13, 2004, http://www.sec.gov/Archives/edgar/data/1288776/000119312504139655/ds1a.htm (accessed April 5, 2005).
11. Postman, *Technopoly:* 20.